400
Questions & Answers
ABOUT THE LIFE AND TIMES OF
JESUS CHRIST

400
Questions & Answers
ABOUT THE LIFE AND TIMES OF
JESUS CHRIST

SUSAN EASTON BLACK

Covenant Communications Inc

Cover image *Transfiguration of Christ* by Carl Heinrich Bloch, courtesy of Det Nationalhistoriske Museum på Frederiksborg, Hillerød.

Cover design copyrighted 2010 by Covenant Communications, Inc.

Published by Covenant Communications, Inc.
American Fork, Utah

Printed in China
First Printing: September 2010

15 14 13 12 11 10   10 9 8 7 6 5 4 3 2 1

ISBN 978-1-60861-061-7

Introduction

A student asked, "Can it be said with confidence, knowing that there are two Bethlehems in Palestine, that Joseph and Mary journeyed to Bethlehem of Judea?" Another questioned whether Capernaum was on the international trade route between Egypt and Syria and whether the Mount of Olives was a series of mountains. Yet another asked, "Why were the Pharisees so determined to destroy Jesus when he said to the man with the withered hand, 'Stretch forth thine hand. And he stretched it forth; and it was restored whole, like as the other?'" To these students and hundreds of others, a feeble answer would not suffice. They wanted to know details about the life and ministry of Jesus Christ, and as their professor, I felt the burden of searching for answers to their questions. Students wanted more than a broad brushstroke that affirmed their testimony of Jesus. They wanted and deserved to know the historic background of his life and to see that background through the lens of the Restoration.

In hopes of answering their questions, I read dozens of Bible commentaries, dictionaries, narratives, gazetteers, and social histories about Jesus Christ. I visited theological schools and purchased bookshelves filled with insights about the Savior. I spent anxious days waiting for interlibrary loans from Harvard, Yale, Berkeley, and other great institutions of higher learning in hopes of gleaning just one more insight about our Lord. And I traveled again and again to the Holy Land to study.

In this immersion of studying, more questions were raised and additional answers received. The process began as a personal study to help students at Brigham Young University but has now moved beyond the classroom. I make this move knowing that few have done justice to the life and ministry of Jesus in print form. After all, he is the Son of God, the King of Kings. Writers, poets, researchers, and theologians have tried to express his greatness, but all seem to come short. Artists, composers, and sculptors express what words alone cannot convey but they, too, fail to capture the greatness of my Savior.

Knowing in advance my own limitations, I approached several colleagues in religious education seeking advice. I wish to thank Richard Draper, professor of ancient scripture and former faculty director of publications in the Religious Studies Center at Brigham Young University, for reading the manuscript and making valuable historical suggestions. I am grateful to my friend and mentor Robert J. Matthews, a former dean of religious education at Brigham Young University, for his scriptural insights that has given greater depth to the text. I express appreciation to Frank Judd, an emerging New Testament scholar, whose exactness for detail has strengthened the manuscript. And I thank D. Kelly Ogden and Andrew Skinner for their untiring efforts to present the life of Jesus.

To my readers, I present *400 Questions & Answers about the Life and Times of Jesus.* I am accountable for any limitations or errors within its pages. It is my hope that they are few and forgivable and that the reader will know of my love and testimony of Jesus Christ.

A Child Is Born

"Behold, a virgin shall conceive, and bear a son," prophesied Isaiah (Isa. 7:14). Yet hundreds of years had passed without his prophecy being fulfilled. Only a few young Jewish maidens still dreamed of becoming the promised virgin, and yet fewer old men dared imagine the birth of the Chosen Son. The despair stemmed from centuries of foreign servitude, as it had been nearly one thousand years since one of their own—King David—had ruled over Judea. Since then, Babylon, Egypt, Greece, and Rome had subjected the Jewish population to the atrocities of war and bondage. As our story begins, Rome ruled Judea with an iron hand.

Was Judea an imperial province of the Roman Empire?

Under Roman rule, there were two types of imperial provinces. Larger provinces were governed by men from the senatorial or higher order of Roman society. These rulers served as the military governor and chief magistrate or legate. Smaller provinces were governed by a prefect (also known as a governor) appointed by the Roman emperor and responsible to him.

Pontius Pilate

The prefect had absolute power to govern the affairs of people residing within his jurisdiction.

The governor of a minor province, like Judea, was regularly drawn from the "equestrian order," meaning the second order of Roman society, and not from the first, or senatorial order. The second order of Roman society is often compared to medieval knights.

Pontius Pilate, the prefect of Judea, was from the second order of Roman society. As such, soldiers under his command were "auxiliary cohorts, not legionnaires." His soldiers were recruited from the indigenous population of gentiles like the Syrians. In case of emergency, Pilate could request additional soldiers from the Syrian legate, who had thousands of soldiers at his command. Soldiers were not normally recruited from among the Jewish population, since they were exempt from military service.[1]

Why was Herod, the Roman appointed ruler of Judea, referred to as "king of Judea" (Luke 1:5)?

Although Herod was called king, he was not an independent sovereign. Beginning around 63 BC, Syria, which included Judea at the time, became a Roman province—one of thirty such provinces that stretched from Britain to the Red Sea and covered about 200 million square miles. Herod's territory stretched from Mount Hermon on the north to the Dead Sea on the south. That geographical area was relatively small when compared to the land ruled by Rome at the time of Jesus, but the area was one of the most strategic locales in the Roman world.

Herod, who was appointed to be client-king of Palestine, ruled from 37 to 4 BC. Herod's reign over Palestine was oppressive to those who longed for a messiah to deliver them from foreign rule. Even though Jews under Herod's reign were permitted to traffic in merchandise, administer land holdings, and conduct business affairs on farms and waterways without government interference, many sought occasion to take offense and murmur against his rule. Nowhere in Judea were complaints louder than in Jerusalem, the city named for peace and built on the sacred site of ancient Salem—a city of holiness. Complaints centered on what inhabitants perceivead as Herod's purposeful defilement of

Herod

lowers among some groups of Jews.[2]

Why did Rome appoint Herod the Great to be a client-king?

Herod, although a man of questionable moral character and despised by many Jews, befriended various Roman rulers in his quest for power. They recognized in Herod an ally of Rome, "an able general, shrewd politician, [and] excellent administrator" and strongly endorsed his appointment before the Roman emperor.

After being appointed a client-king, Herod continued to court the goodwill of Rome. His hospitality to soldiers and politicians alike was so lavish and his building efforts within the province so splendid, the Roman emperor was pleased with his choice despite Herod's personal shortcomings. Herod rebuilt the Hasmonean fortress and named it the Antonia Fortress in honor of Mark Antony. He also constructed an amphitheater, palace, stadium, and other grand facilities, the most elegant being the temple complex at Jerusalem.[3]

the Holy City. His ordering of Roman soldiers into the city and destroying genealogical registers of the Holy Temple angered worshipers of Jehovah. These two acts, spoken of in byways and on corners throughout Jerusalem, were despised by local Jews who longed for the coming of the Messiah to relieve them from foreign oppression.

Dislike of Herod reached such a feverish pitch that when he died, a Jewish feast was declared, and there was widespread celebration and even revolt among many of his Jewish subjects. It must be noted, however, that Herod did have loyal fol-

Was Herod the Great a believing Jew?

Caesar Augustus believed Herod to be a Jew and said of him, "It is better to be Herod's pig than his son." Augustus's statement referred to the fact that Herod executed his own sons and recognized that, as a Jew, Herod would not kill and eat a pig. Caesar rationalized that it was safer to be a pig in Herod's domain than to be a son, whom he would and did kill.

Outwardly, Herod professed to be an adherent of Judaism and a worshiper of Jehovah. However, by birth he was an Idumaean, born in the province of Idumaea (Edom), located south of Judea. Traditionally inhabitants of Idumaea were understood to be Edomites, meaning from the "posterity of Esau." Knowledge of Herod's nativity and ancestry caused many conservative followers of Jehovah to look upon his observance of Judaism with suspicion. By tradition, if not cultural understanding, Pharisees and Essenes would not have recognized an Idumaean like Herod as king of the Jews.[4]

Is it true that Herod the Great rebuilt the Holy Temple in Jerusalem?

The temple on Mount Moriah, the mount where Abraham was willing to offer Isaac as a sacrifice and

Tomb of Herod's son

where Solomon built a temple, was rebuilt by Herod the Great, who wanted to provide more space for worshipers or pilgrims coming to the Temple Mount for festivals and high holy days. Reconstruction of the temple complex technically took more than eighty years to complete, from approximately 19 BC to AD 63. However, Josephus, a Jewish historian from the first century AD, said the temple proper was finished in only a year and a half, and the courtyards and porticoes were under construction for eight years.

Herod hired approximately ten thousand laborers and trained a thousand Levites as masons and carpenters to work on the elaborate complex. A precise description of the reconstructed temple does not exist. Illustrative details are speculative, but most suggest that the temple was magnificent. Josephus reported that the temple stood about 150 feet in height and was "topped by golden spikes to prevent birds from resting on the roof and fouling it." The Talmud reported that the temple was beautiful.

It is important to note that the reconstructed temple was almost as important to the Jewish people as was their worship of Jehovah.[5]

During Herod's reign over Judea, the story of Zacharias in the temple is told. Zacharias was from the priesthood course of Abia. What is meant by "the course of Abia" (Luke 1:5)?

King David, living a thousand years before Zacharias, separated the priests of Levi into twenty-four "courses"—divisions or orders. Only four of the courses returned from Babylonian exile (538 BC) to Judea—Jedaiah, Immer, Pashur, and Harim. To restore the original number of courses to twenty-four, each of the returning courses was subdivided; the new courses then equaled twenty-four. The newly numbered courses—of which Abia (Abijah) was the eighth—bore the ancient names of the original courses. Zacharias, meaning "Jehovah has remembered," belonged to the course of Abia.

Members of this course, like members of the other reconstituted courses, resided near Jerusalem and journeyed to the Holy City twice a year to officiate in priestly duties at the temple. Priests from the course of Abia journeyed from their village in the hill country of Judea (believed to be Hebron, the locale where Abraham and Sarah had lived) to the Holy Temple in Jerusalem to serve for a week. In the temple, they performed sacred rites and ordinances, such as burning incense.[6]

> **While in service on the Temple Mount, the lot fell upon Zacharias "to burn incense" (Luke 1:9). What did the burning of incense entail?**

Lots were cast to determine which member of a particular priestly course had the privilege of entering the temple sanctuary and burning incense. Before casting lots, it is supposed that the priests of Abia assembled in the Hall of Polished Stones to offer prescribed prayers to Jehovah, such as, "With great love hast Thou loved us, O Lord our God, and with much overflowing pity hast Thou pitied us. . . . Blessed be the Lord, who in love chose His people Israel." After prayers, the assembled priests repeated the Shema, the Hebrew creed or belief. (See Deut. 6:4–9; 11:13–21; Num. 15:37–41.) Then followed the casting of lots to determine which priest would burn incense on the temple altar.

According to the Gospel of Luke, the lot fell upon Zachari- as. Although elderly, he was not disqualified by age or infirmity from the honor. According to tradition, Zacharias would have chosen two assistants to prepare the sacred rite of incense burning. The duties of the assistants were to remove debris from the altar and spread live coals from the burnt offering on the altar. When the assistants' duties were completed, they were to worship before the altar and then retire.

When everything was thus prepared, tradition suggests that Zacharias would have walked up the temple steps alone and entered the sanctuary to offer incense. Zacharias would likely have repeated this ritual each morning and evening during the week that he was performing his priestly duties on the Temple Mount. (See Ps. 141:2.)[7]

> **What was Zacharias doing in the Holy Temple before the angel appeared to him?**

Zacharias would have entered into the Holy Place of the Temple sanctuary by parting an embroidered veil that concealed the golden altar of incense, a seven-branched candelabrum, and a table on which lay twelve loaves of shewbread. Behind another curtain that he did not enter lay the Holy of Holies. Only on the Day of Atonement did a high priest enter the Holy of Holies, symbolic of entering into the presence of God to offer a sacrifice.

Zacharias would have stood alone in the temple between the curtains, facing the golden altar to his west. To his north would have been the table of shewbread and to his south the golden candelabrum. There he would have waited until a signal marked that "the time of incense had come." The signal also alerted priests in the temple to leave the inner court and prostrate themselves in silent worship.

After hearing the signal, Zacharias would have spread incense on the altar near the curtain that concealed the Holy of Holies. When he saw the incense kindling on the coals, he would have bowed down in worship and withdrawn from the holy area. Seeing the angel arrested his steps.[8]

Were there angelic appearances in the Holy Temple other than the appearance of the angel Gabriel to Zacharias?

Gabriel's appearance to Zacharias is the first and only recorded angelic manifestation in the temple at Jerusalem. Gabriel, meaning "Man of God," is the name given to one of the seven archangels (see Dan. 8:16; 9:21). Jewish rabbis taught that the names of angels

East wall of the Temple Mount

represented their divine assignments.[9]

> "And in the sixth month the angel Gabriel was sent from God unto a city of Galilee, named Nazareth" (Luke 1:26). Does the village of Nazareth still exist? If so, where is it located?

Nazareth today is located thirty miles from the Mediterranean Sea and fifteen miles west of the Sea of Galilee near the international caravan route to Egypt. The community is built on the foothills of lower Galilee on the ancient land of Zebulun. At the time of angel Gabriel's appearance to Mary, there were fewer than four hundred people living in approximately seventy-five residential homes in the community.

The name Nazareth is derived from a Hebrew word meaning "guard place" or "watch tower," suggesting that the village was once an outpost of a nearby town. The village of Nazareth is not mentioned in the Talmud, the Old Testament, or by the Jewish historian Josephus. Today the village is known as En-Nazirah, or Flower of Galilee.[10]

> Gospel writers tell of Joseph and Mary living in Nazareth. What is the meaning of the names Joseph and Mary?

The name Joseph means "He will add." Mary means "rebellion" or "bitterness." The name Mary is equivalent to Mara, the name used by Naomi to describe her perceived misfortunes (see Ruth 1:20). It should be noted that both Joseph and Mary were common names at that time in Palestine.[11]

> Gospel writers also tell of Joseph and Mary being espoused. What was the Jewish espousal ceremony?

Marriage customs at the time of Jesus were dictated by Mosaic law. As such, the law regarded a betrothal (also known as an espousal) as a solemn agreement, a covenant between a devoted man and woman. Jewish men were typically betrothed at age twenty. Jewish women were betrothed at a younger age, usually fifteen. It can be assumed that both Joseph and Mary were betrothed at these ages, even though apocryphal accounts depict Joseph as an elderly widower.

Traditionally, a formal betrothal ceremony was attended by witnesses who attested that the young woman was promised to her future husband. The ceremony frequently occurred in the house of the betrothed-to-be. There a tent or booth, in which the ceremony would take place, was raised before the formal ceremony began. The sacred portion of the ceremony occurred when the woman was promised to the man. Witnesses watched as the man gave the woman a piece of money or its equivalent, and said, "Lo, thou art betrothed unto me." A written document bearing his words and the woman's name was proof of the betrothal.

After the formal ceremony, the woman was known as the wife and wore a veil when venturing out-of-doors. The man was known as the husband. Even though the wife lived with her family or friends and communication between her and her husband was done only through family members or friends, she became a widow if her husband died during the espousal period. Any unfaithfulness during the period by either the man or woman was denounced as adultery, and the penalty for adultery was death (see Deut. 22:23–24).

During the espousal period, the husband prepared a home for his wife and the wife prepared her wedding clothes.[12]

What were the central messages of the angelic annunciation to Mary?

The angel Gabriel began his greeting with "Hail Mary." According to the Latin Vulgate Version of the Bible, hail translates as "Ave," which forms the phrase Ave Maria.

There are four central messages in the angelic annunciation. First, the phrase "highly favoured"

Annunciation

means imbued or endowed with grace from God (Luke 1:28). Mary's reaction to the high praise is recorded in the Gospel of Luke as fear (see Luke 1:30). Another way to translate her reaction is awe, revealing Mary's innate humility and limited understanding of why she was chosen to be the prophesied virgin (see Luke 1:28–30).

Second, the child to be conceived in Mary's womb was to be begotten of the Eternal Father, "not in violation of natural law but in accordance with a higher manifestation." This most sacred event is berated by unbelieving scholars as an imitation of Greek and Roman mythology that depicts gods "consorting with mortal women" and siring children. The sacred angelic pronouncement was not an imitation of mythology, but the basis for the belief that Jesus is the Son of God.

Third, the name Jesus is the Hebrew equivalent of Yehoshua or Jeshua, meaning "Jehovah is salvation." The Hebrew/Aramaic term for Messiah is "anointed one," whereas the corresponding word in Greek is "Christ." The phrase Jesus the Christ results from a combination of the Hebrew name with the Greek title.

Fourth, Mary's reply to the annunciation "Be it unto me according to thy word" bespeaks her willingness to be obedient to the will of God and become a handmaiden, meaning "servant of the Lord" (Luke 1:38). Her response does not mirror the Arabic greeting of bowing with hand against breast as a symbolic promise to obey another's command.[13]

> The angel Gabriel told Mary that Elisabeth was with child. After the angelic visitation, Mary journeyed to see Elisabeth. Did she journey alone? Was Elisabeth a close cousin to Mary?

Although artists and storytellers would have us believe that Mary traveled alone to the hill country of Judah (nearly a hundred miles) to visit Elisabeth, such would not have occurred. It was dangerous for any Jewish woman, let alone a veiled betrothed woman, to journey alone from one community to another during the Roman occupation of Judea.

If Mary had journeyed alone, she might have fallen prey to soldiers, transients, and robbers on the road between Nazareth and Judea. It is very likely that she

Mary and Elisabeth

> The words that Mary spoke to Elisabeth—"My soul doth magnify the Lord"—are often referred to as "the Magnificat" (Luke 1:46). What does that mean?

As Mary spoke to Elisabeth, her words echoed the sayings of prophets and the Song of Hannah, mother of the prophet Samuel. (See 1 Sam. 2:1–10.) Hannah's plea for a son was answered by Jehovah. In her gratitude and praise of Jehovah, Hannah's song depicted God as the savior of the poor.

Mary's repetitive phrases containing Hannah's words reveal her knowledge of holy writ and anticipated joy at bearing the promised Messiah. Praising God, Mary declared, "My soul doth magnify the Lord" (Luke 1:46). The Latin Vulgate translation of "magnifies" or "glorifies" is *magnificat*.[15]

> After Mary stayed with Elisabeth for about three months, she returned to Nazareth. It was then that Joseph the carpenter desired to end their betrothal. Did Joseph have legal grounds for ending the betrothal?

was accompanied by family or friends as she journeyed.

We don't know the exact nature of the kinship bond between Mary and Elisabeth. In the King James Version, Elisabeth is referred to as "thy cousin" (Luke 1:36). It was John Wycliffe, the father of the English Bible, who suggested a cousin relationship between the two women. The Greek translation suggests only a familial relationship. The precise relationship between Mary and Elisabeth remains obscure.[14]

The betrothal ceremony was religiously and legally binding, and legal action was needed to end a betrothal (see Deut. 24:1). The pregnancy of Mary would have been considered legal grounds for divorce among conservative Jews. According to Jewish law, if a betrothed wife was discovered to be unfaithful to her husband, she was to be put to death unless she had been forcibly raped (see Deut. 22:23–27).

Joseph's choice to annul the betrothal was two-fold. First, a public trial could be held, testimonies openly expressed, and a judgment rendered. This would have resulted in public humiliation even if Mary were found innocent. Second, a private agreement could be reached in the presence of two witnesses. This agreement would be in the form of a written document known as a bill of divorce or certificate of dismissal, signed by witnesses (see Matt. 1:19). The witnesses could be family members, and the reasons for divorce could be kept from civil authorities (see Deut. 24:1).

Although an espoused husband could divorce his betrothed wife for many reasons, there was no provision in the law of Moses for a wife to divorce her husband. Later Jewish tradition stipulated that if the husband were employed in an odiferous trade, such as tanning hides or collecting dung, the wife could seek a divorce. A divorce was granted if the wife claimed that the stench and impurity of the husband's employment was worse than she had expected.[16]

> Joseph the carpenter had an inspired dream in which an "angel of the Lord appeared unto him" and told him to "take unto thee Mary thy wife" (Matt. 1:20). Did Joseph respond quickly to the angelic directive?

It is not known how quickly Joseph responded to the angelic directive. However, it is known that he pondered and prayed before he received an answer in a dream. The Gospel writer Matthew mentions Joseph's dreams five times. Tradition holds that a good dream was regarded by Jewish men as a sign of God's favor. According to tradition, it would have been unwise to unduly postpone obedience to an inspired dream. To thwart or put off the Lord's favor was to reap his wrath.[17]

Near the time that Joseph took Mary as "thy wife," a decree was issued by Caesar Augustus "that all the world should be taxed" (Matt. 1:20; Luke 2:1). At the time of the decree, was Augustus recognized as a god throughout the Roman Empire?

Caesar Augustus was recognized as a god by pagan worshipers in the communities and villages of Palestine. Augustus, meaning "worthy of reverence," was an honorific title given to Roman rulers who attained the pagan status of godhood. Caesar was a title for an emperor. Octavian, the son of Gaius Octavius and Atia and the great-nephew of Julius, begrudgingly accepted the title of Augustus, but did not claim personal divinity or savior-like qualities even though he was worshiped as a god at pagan temples in Caesarea, Sebaste, and possibly other Hellenized towns within Palestine.

Caesar Augustus is remembered as an energetic ruler of the Roman empire from 27 BC to 14 AD. His reign marked an era of order, lawfulness, and honesty in the Roman bureaucracy. He is credited with reorganizing provincial governments and establishing a fiscal reform policy that included taxation of all provinces within his empire. He died in AD 14 at Nola in Campania.[18]

What was the Roman taxation process that Caesar Augustus implemented?

Under the reign of Augustus, a number of enrollments for taxation of Roman citizens were conducted in Italy and in other provinces. There were three censuses undertaken during the reign of Augustus: 28 BC, 8 BC, and AD 14. He also required a yearly tax on personal wealth or possessions beginning about 9 BC.

The purpose of the enrollment tax was to determine population,

Caesar

citizenship, and property holdings in a given Roman province. This fact may suggest that Joseph the carpenter had land in the area of Bethlehem. Although the taxation process can be compared to a census, Roman taxation was more than a registering of males. The process determined how much tax each province was to pay to the emperor. It is important to note that individual men did not pay tax directly to Rome. Instead, the individual paid an assessment to tax collectors. The King James Version calls tax collectors "publicans."[19]

Was it typical for Roman taxation to be administered in lands of nativity and ancestry within each Roman province?

The decree required conquered provinces to tax or register males in the residential towns or cities in which they resided. Those residing on farms or in hillside villages were to register at the town nearest their place of birth.

Although most Roman provinces likely followed the above pattern, later traditions claim that modifications were made in Palestine by a Jewish council. According to the tradition, Jewish males were required to register in ancestral or family lands. Most Jews, like Joseph the carpenter, registered in family lands. It is suggested that Joseph and Mary traveled ninety miles—a four- to five-day journey—from Nazareth to Bethlehem, the family land of the house of David. They either took a direct route through Samaria or through Jericho and the Judean desert to reach Bethlehem.[20]

Were Joseph and Mary formally wed before they undertook their journey to Bethlehem?

According to Jewish custom, an espoused wife could not journey unaccompanied with her husband. Therefore, it is plausible that Joseph and Mary were wed before their journey began.

The day of the week Joseph and Mary were wed is not known. Traditionally Jewish couples began their wedding festivities on the third day of the week, Tuesday. Basis for that tradition is the use of the word *good*. *Good* is recorded "twice for the third day of creation" (see Gen. 1:9–13). The double usage of the word *good* held great significance to some Jewish families, who believed that to be married on the third day was to receive a double blessing from God on the marriage.[21]

Can it be said with confidence, knowing that there are two Bethlehems in Palestine, that Joseph and Mary journeyed to Bethlehem of Judea?

Bethlehem of Judea is the proper name of the town near Jerusalem. This name distinguishes it from Bethlehem of Galilee, which is located near the Sea of Galilee in the territory of Zebulun (see Josh. 19:10). The word *Bethlehem* means "place of food" or "house of bread." The name has led some historians to conclude that the trade of baker was a common occupation in both communities.

Bethlehem of Judea was first mentioned in Genesis: "And Rachel died, and was buried in the way to Ephrath, which is Bethlehem" (Gen. 35:19). In the fields east of Bethlehem, Ruth met Boaz, and from their union came Jesse, father of King David. Isaiah tells of the Messiah being born in the homeland of David, meaning Bethlehem of Judea—and, like his ancestors, becoming a shepherd (see Isa. 9:1, 6–7; 11:1, 10).

The Judean community is situated about five miles south of Jerusalem on a terraced countryside near a wilderness, where predators—including bears, leopards, jackals, and hyenas—were known to roam.[22]

When Joseph and Mary arrived in Bethlehem, they found that there was no room in the inn. Was the inn in Bethlehem a caravansary?

The Greek word for inn means "guest chamber" or "room for rent in a private house." The word does not mean a caravansary, which was built near the town of Bethlehem to accommodate travelers traversing the route between Jerusalem and Egypt.

A field outside Bethlehem

The caravansary near Bethlehem was purported to be built of stone or sun-dried brick and to be rectangular in shape. According to tradition, rooms, storage chambers, and stalls in the caravansary surrounded a central courtyard. Inside the courtyard was a well used by travelers to fill water bags.

If travelers reached the caravansary early in the day, they were welcomed. If they reached the structure in the evening, travelers found the door closed. They were encouraged by shouts from those inside to move along.

It is not likely that Joseph the carpenter sought shelter for Mary in a public, noisy caravansary. It is more probable that he looked for a private room to rent in Bethlehem. Failing to find such a room, Joseph and Mary possibly lodged in a nearby limestone cave. Several caves on the hillside of Bethlehem were artificially enlarged, creating an upper chamber used as a dwelling place and a lower chamber intended for animals. It is possible that Joseph found shelter for Mary in a lower chamber in which there was a manger or feeding trough intended for animals.[23]

On the hillside of Bethlehem, "the days were accomplished that she should be delivered. And she brought forth her firstborn son" (Luke 2:6–7). What year was Jesus born?

The modern Western system for designating years—before Christ, BC, and after Christ, AD—did not begin until the sixth century AD and was first developed by Dionysius Exiguus, Abbot of Rome. The large gap of hundreds of years between when this calendar system was implemented and when the events in the Savior's life took place has resulted in errors and discrepancies that place the birth of Jesus as early as 7 BC and as late as AD 1.[24]

Can a better approximation of the year of Jesus' birth be determined using the Jewish system for reckoning time?

The Jewish year is based on a lunar calendar. The year consists of twelve to thirteen lunar months, each having twenty-nine to thirty days. Anciently, the Jewish new year was celebrated on or near the autumnal equinox. After the Babylonian exile, it was celebrated in spring. The issue of uneven months and days and variable seasons using the Jewish system leads to even greater difficulty in calculating the year of Jesus' birth than using another calendar system.[25]

Since the year of the Lord's birth is questioned, can it also be questioned that Jesus was born of Davidic lineage?

At the time of Jesus, it was important to authenticate ancestry, which enabled a person's credibility and even legitimacy to be established. In spite of other discrepancies, such as the year of His birth, genealogical recitations in the Gospels of Matthew and Luke agree that Jesus was of the tribe of Judah and descended from David. However, it should be noted that Matthew and Luke record differing pedigrees. The reason for the

Nativity

difference is that Matthew traces Joseph's royal lineage or legal descent of Jesus from Abraham to King David, while Luke reveals a personal pedigree or the parentage descent, citing descendancy from David without preference to kingly succession. (See Ps. 132:11; Isa. 11:1; Jer. 23:5.)

Matthew divides the pedigree of Jesus into three sections of fourteen names each—Abraham to David, David to the Babylonian captivity, and captivity to the birth of Jesus. It may not be coincidental that fourteen is the numerical value of the three Hebrew consonants in the name David (D V D = 4+6+4). This may be one way that Matthew testifies to his Jewish audience that Jesus was truly the son of David. When reviewing this pedigree, remember that Rome ruled Judea at the birth of Jesus and the Davidic monarchy ended centuries earlier.[26]

After the birth of Jesus, his mother "wrapped him in swaddling clothes, and laid him in a manger" (Luke 2:7). What are swaddling clothes?

Before being wrapped in swaddling clothes (a banding process), a newborn baby was washed and rubbed with salt. Jewish mothers believed the skin of their babies would be preserved if salted immediately after birth. The baby was then placed on a square cloth and the swaddling began. Four-inch-wide strips, five to six yards long, were wrapped tightly around the infant.

For the first six months of life, Jewish babies were confined in long linen strips called in the King James Version "swaddling clothes." Swaddling restrained movement of the arms and legs. Jewish mothers believed that the infant's limbs would "grow straight and strong" if kept in swaddling clothes.[27]

The Child Jesus

On that night of nights, the angelic promise to "bring forth a son" was fulfilled (Luke 1:31). Mary tenderly held her newborn infant.

News of the birth of Jesus was first announced by an angel of the Lord to shepherds "abiding in the field" (Luke 2:8). Why were these shepherds so privileged?

Jewish tradition purports that the Messiah will be revealed from Migdal Eder, meaning the "tower of the flock," located near Bethlehem on the road between Jerusalem and the city of David. According to the Mishnah, shepherds who watch their flocks atop the Migdal Eder guard sheep destined for sacrifice at the great altar of the Holy Temple. They will be the first to hear of the birth of the Christ Child.

In support of this tradition, shepherds who saw the angel heralded the good news, meaning "good tidings" and "God's story." They went to the temple courts on Mount Moriah and told others of the birth of Jesus: "And all they that heard it wondered at those things which were told them" (Luke 2:18).[28]

Angel of the Lord visits the shepherds

The angelic declaration is similar to an ancient Bedouin custom in which women who attend a mother in travail announce a successful birth by exclaiming, "We bring you good news of a great joy, for to you is born this day" (see Luke 2:10–11). However, there are significant differences between the Bedouin custom and the angelic announcement.

First, the "glory of the Lord," which is the ancient glory—the Shekinah that was seen in the Holy of Holies—"shone round about" the shepherds (Luke 2:9). Second, the greeting, "Glory to God in the highest, and on earth peace, good will toward men," is not a Bedouin greeting and becomes clearer when it reads "on earth peace among men of good will" (see Luke 2:14). Third, the announced child was not just another baby born to a wandering people. He was the Son of God.[29]

Was Jesus circumcised when he was eight days old?

It is probable that the Child Jesus was circumcised. Circumcision was the ancient sign of the Abrahamic covenant, showing "descendants of the great patriarch are to be separate and apart from the world, cut off from the world, dedicated to God."

The ritual of circumcision was performed eight days after the birth of a Jewish son even when the eighth day fell on the Sabbath. Rabbi Yohanan explained, "It is like a king who entered a province and issued a decree, saying, 'Let no visitors that are here see my face until they have first seen the face of my lady'"—meaning Sabbath. According to later Jewish rabbis, the newborn male was to experience the covenant of Sabbath before the covenant of circumcision.

During the circumcision ritual, the words "Blessed be the Lord our God, who hath sanctified us by his precepts and hath given us the law of circumcision" were uttered. The father of the newborn son added, "Who hath sanctified us by his precepts and hath commanded us to enter the child into the covenant of Abraham our father."

It is likely that Jesus was circumcised in Bethlehem on the

eighth day after his birth, for Luke records, "And when eight days were accomplished for the circumcising of the child" (Luke 2:21). His circumcision shows the conformity or obedience of Mary and Joseph to the Hebrew law and the covenant that God made with Abraham. (See Ex. 12:48–49.)[30]

Does an infant son receive his name during the circumcision ceremony?

Yes. It was the Jewish custom to name the firstborn son after his grandfather. This may explain why some expressed displeasure with Elisabeth, mother of John the Baptist, when she wanted to name her newborn son John. "And they said unto her, There is none of thy kindred that is called by this name" (Luke 1:61).[31] Joseph had been instructed to name God's son Yeshua, meaning "savior" or "salvation."

Luke records, "And when the days of her purification according to the law of Moses were accomplished, they brought [Jesus] to Jerusalem, to present him to the Lord" (Luke 2:22). Of the purification rites that existed at that time, which rite did Mary participate in when she took the Baby Jesus to the Temple Mount?

For forty days after the birth of a son and eighty days after the birth of a daughter, Jewish mothers were to remain in isolation or seclusion, "which meant that [they were] not allowed to leave the house or to touch any holy object." (See Lev. 12:2–8.) At the end of this period, Jewish mothers were to journey to the temple in Jerusalem and offer a sacrifice for the ceremonial redemption of their firstborn son. During the redemption ceremony, the mother was immersed and pronounced ritually clean by a priest.[32]

Was Joseph required to pay temple dues for Baby Jesus?

Jewish fathers were not relieved from the financial obligation to help maintain the temple during the Roman rule of Palestine. For a population of more than one million Jews in Palestine, the temple revenue in silver alone was estimated at 14.5 tons each year. It is likely that when Joseph entered the Temple Mount, he had five shekels, about four-tenths of an ounce of silver, the exact amount of temple dues required to redeem a firstborn son. His offering would have been carried in his hands, indicating that the shekels were for an immediate, holy purpose.

As he entered the Temple Mount, Joseph would not have carried a staff, because a staff would appear that the giver was on business or on pleasure instead of a sacred journey. He would not have worn shoes, because shoes were not allowed on the mount; only sandals could be worn. He would not have had dust on his feet or scrip in a purse, as such were also unacceptable in the temple courts.[33]

Why did Mary offer turtledoves for her purification sacrifice instead of a lamb?

When the purification period ended, Jewish women "brought to a priest a lamb for a burnt offering and either a young pigeon or a turtledove for a sin offering. If she could not afford both the lamb and the bird, then she was permitted to bring two pigeons or two turtle doves." (See Lev. 12:8.) Typically, a poor woman offered a pair of turtledoves and a rich woman offered an additional lamb.

In the case of the firstborn male child, these sacrifices became part of the redemption ceremony that exempted the newborn male from later Levitical ministerial service. The meager financial circumstances of Mary is apparent in her sacrificial offering.[34]

Did Mary purchase turtledoves in the Holy Temple? (See Luke 2:24.)

Only priests were allowed to enter the temple sanctuary. Women were restricted as to where they could walk on the Temple Mount. In the colonnade portico around the Court of the Gentiles, it is likely that Mary purchased the turtledoves with Tyrian shekels. (See Lev. 1:14; 5:7; 12:8.) Men, known as money changers, traded "foreign and local currency into Tyrian shekels, the only acceptable coins for Temple offerings."[35]

Did Mary literally offer turtledoves as her purification sacrifice, or did she give the equivalency of the turtledoves in money?

This question begs for an answer. Located in the Court of the

Turtledove

Women on the Temple Mount was a treasury building. Inside the treasury were thirteen chests shaped like trumpets—nine trumpets were receptacles for shekels legally due from Jewish males, and four held voluntary contributions. Women deposited the required money to purchase turtledoves as part of their purification offering into the third trumpet. Money was taken from the third trumpet and the corresponding number of turtledoves were sacrificed on the Temple Mount each day. This practice spared temple priests from the additional labor involved in separate daily sacrifices and allowed women to make an almost anonymous purification offering.[36]

Was the purification offering of Mary the only type of sacrifice offered at the temple during the days of Jesus?

There were different kinds of offerings, including non-blood and blood sacrifices. Non-blood sacrifices included drink offerings, the first sheaf at Passover, two loaves at Pentecost, and shewbread. Blood sacrifices involved animals such as sheep, goats, oxen, turtledoves, and pigeons. Priests were commanded to salt all sacrifices—"every oblation of thy meat offering shalt thou season with salt; neither shalt thou suffer the salt of the covenant of thy God to be lacking from thy meat offering" (Lev. 2:13).[37]

Were turtledoves offered as a burnt offering?

According to the law of Moses, turtledoves were an acceptable burnt offering (see Lev. 1:14–17). Burnt offerings were completely consumed on the altar, symbolizing "the entire surrender unto God, whether of the individual or of the congregation, and His acceptance thereof."

During the days of Jesus, turtledoves were sacrificed during the morning and evening services in the temple with additional sacrifices offered on Sabbaths, new moons, and festivals.[38]

Was there symbolism in offering turtledoves as a sacrifice?

Symbolism is suggested in the form of a dove. The Hebrew word for dove is *yonah,* meaning "moaning sound." From its predictable migratory habits—first appearing in Palestine in March of each year and leaving for southern climes as winter approaches—the dove symbolized to the Jewish people their years of wandering in the wilderness. Additional symbolisms can be gleaned from the dove's pattern of pairing for life, fidelity to mate, and gentle nature.

Rock, ring, and palm doves were not acceptable burnt sacrifices at the Temple Mount. Priests accepted only full-grown turtledoves and young domestic pigeons as sacrificial offerings. These birds were given as a sin offering and substitute offering for the purification of women after childbirth.[39]

Did Simeon, a man who knew "that he should not see death, before he had seen the Lord's Christ," quote prophecy when he took the Babe Jesus in his arms (see Luke 2:26)?

Simeon took Jesus in his arms and praised God. He uttered prophecies that drew on the four Servant Songs found in the later chapters of Isaiah (see Isa. 60–66). These songs depict an unnamed servant bringing justice to the nations, giving sight to the blind, and freeing imprisoned captives. Yet, the servant was tortured and

The Infant Jesus in the temple with Simeon

killed by his enemies. The songs conclude happily with the servant being blessed by God.[40]

> **At the Temple Mount, Anna, a prophetess, "gave thanks unto the Lord" for the Christ child (Luke 2:38). Why is she called a prophetess?**

The term *prophetess* does not refer to a priesthood office. In the Old Testament, there are five women who were given the title prophetess: Miriam (see Ex. 15:20), Deborah (see Judges 4:4), Huldah (see 2 Kgs. 22:14), Noadiah (see Neh. 6:14), and Isaiah's wife (see Isa. 8:3). The most common explanation given is that a prophetess is a woman who has received a witness that Jesus is the Christ. The word prophetess, when applied to Anna, is also used as an epithet due an elderly woman who has lived a devout and faithful life.[41] On the Temple Mount that day, Anna bore her witness that Jesus is the Christ.

Associating the birth of a great man or a great event with the "appearance of stars was a common feature in the ancient world." For example, ancient authors associated the appearance of a new star with the fall of Troy and the birth of Alexander the Great. The appearance of a new star leading wise men to the Child Jesus is the best-known example to Western Christians.

Some associate the star seen by the wise men with the prophecy, "There shall come a Star out of Jacob, and a Sceptre shall rise out of Israel" (Num. 24:17). A few contend that the star was no more than Halley's Comet, a supernova seen by Chinese astronomers at the time. Others suggest that "the rising of his star" should be understood as the future greatness of Jesus and not a literal star. In so doing, both negate the Greek translation of Matthew, "the star at his rising."[42]

The interpretation given of the King James Version is that the wise men followed "the direction of the star."[43] The word *east* in the phrase is translated as "orient." East was often the direction used by ancient Israelites to get their bearing, just as north is the direction used by modern Westerners to get their bearing. All directions given in ancient scripture are as if facing east.[44]

At this point, all that is known is that the wise men came from the east. Lands east of Judea included the Arabian Desert and Mesopotamia. Christian tradition depicts the wise men as kings. Matthew calls them *magi,* a Persian word suggesting the men came from a portion of the Babylonian Empire that was conquered by the Persians. The word *magi* usually refers to men of the sacerdotal or priestly class from the nations east of Palestine. According to Herodotus, magi were from the tribes of Media and had a strong influence on government authorities after the Persian invasion.

Traditionally, magi were astrologers noted for their studies of the "secrets of nature, divination, astrology, and medicine." Ancient sources report that magi were skilled in interpreting dreams and understanding religious mysteries.

The wise men who worshiped Jesus knew of an ancient prophecy foretelling of a rising star at the birth of a Jewish king. Their words before Herod could imply that he also knew of a new star appearing at the birth of a king.[45]

Herod was troubled at the sayings of the wise men. Was Herod angry when the wise men failed to present him with a gift?

There is no record that the wise men presented gifts to Herod or his sons even though it was customary to approach monarchs and princes with gifts. It is possible that the bringing of costly gifts for an unknown king sparked jealousy in Herod and was perceived as a direct threat to his reign. For Herod, retaining power over Palestine required delicate diplomacy with politicians of Rome, revolutionaries in Judea, and enemies within his own household.[46]

Why did Herod ask scribes for details about the birth of the prophesied king?

Jewish scribes were highly respected for their years of study. Some of them later bore the honorary title of rabbi. They were schooled in the Torah and the prophets and knew that the prophecy foretelling the Messiah's birth was found in the writings of Micah. (See Micah 5:2.)

A scribe should not be confused with a public writer, a common

Wise men follow the star

trade in the East. Among the tasks assigned to a public writer was the marking of lines on material for the scribes. On the material, scribes often copied words of the Torah. According to later rabbinic law, it was forbidden to write any words of the Torah on unlined material.[47]

The wise men departed from Herod and went to Bethlehem seeking the newborn king. Were there three wise men seeking the newborn king?

Later traditions portray the number of wise men being anywhere from three to twelve. It is the number of gifts given the Christ child—three—that led to the Christian tradition that the number of wise men was three.

If the wise men were not Jews, their adoration symbolized the relevance of the birth of Jesus to the Gentiles. The magi would be the first Gentiles to worship Jesus, just as the shepherds were the first Jews to do so. Because the wise men knew that the promised Messiah had been born, whether Jew or Gentile, it is probable that they were divinely inspired much like Simeon, Anna, and the shepherds.[48]

Where was Jesus living when the wise men found him?

When the wise men found Jesus, there is no mention of a manger. They found him in a house in Bethlehem. At that time, Jesus was referred to as a "young child," not a babe (Matt. 2:11). [49]

Is there symbolism in the gifts of the wise men to the Child Jesus—gold, frankincense, and myrrh?

The precious gifts—gold, frankincense, and myrrh—dramatically contrasted with the simple domestic surroundings of the Child Jesus in Bethlehem.

The gifts of the wise men have symbolic meaning in Christian tradition. The gift of gold symbolically recognizes Jesus as King of Kings. Gold was a precious metal not found in the Jerusalem area during the time of Jesus.

Frankincense symbolizes the priestly role of Jesus as the High

Gold

Frankincense

Priest of High Priests. Incense is a resin derived from boswellia and balsam trees growing in South Arabia, East Africa, and India. It is obtained by notching tree bark and gathering the hardened substance that drips from the notches. The resin was used in Palestine as a perfume for the wealthy and as an incense for sacrificial purposes in the Holy Temple (see Ex. 30:34–36). Priests stored incense in the temple treasury.

Myrrh symbolizes the death and burial of Jesus and was used to prepare the body of Jesus for burial (see Matt. 27:57–61). Myrrh was extracted from shrubs growing in southern Arabia and eastern Africa. It was used as a painkiller for the sick and an embalming ingredient for the dead. It was also used in consecrated oils at temple altars and in sacred vessels.[50]

When Herod "saw that he was mocked of the wise men," he ordered soldiers to kill children in Bethlehem (Matt. 2:16). How many infants in the area of Bethlehem were slaughtered by Herod's soldiers?

The number of babies slaughtered in Bethlehem may have been small, possibly fewer than twenty. Although the number may have been small, the magnitude of Herod's atrocity is not lessened. The slaughtered infants are remembered as the "'proto-martyrs,' the first witnesses, of Christ."

It is curious, and perhaps noteworthy, that Bethlehem was prominent in Gospel accounts before the slaying of the babies. Afterward Bethlehem and communities south of Jerusalem were never mentioned again by Gospel writers.[51]

Myrrh

How did John, the son of Zacharias, and Jesus, the Son of God, escape death at the hands of the soldiers?

Tradition has it that Zacharias, knowing of Herod's evil verdict, encouraged Elisabeth to take their young son John into the mountains. When Zacharias refused to reveal the whereabouts of his wife and son, he was slain by Herod's soldiers between the porch and the altar in the Holy Temple at Jerusalem. Zacharias gave his own life to save the life of his promised son.

As for Jesus, "the angel of the Lord appeareth to Joseph in a dream, saying, Arise, and take the young child and his mother, and flee into Egypt" (Matt. 2:12–13). Joseph heeded the angelic directive. His actions led the Gospel writer Matthew to see a fulfillment of Hosea's prophecy—"called my son out of Egypt"—in the flight of the Holy Family from Judea to Egypt (Hosea 11:1).

Joseph, Mary, and the Child Jesus journeyed across the sands of the Negev and Sinai deserts to reach Egypt. They were not the first Israelites to flee from Judea to Egypt. Patriarchs Abraham and Jacob sought refuge in Egypt. Prophets Joseph and Moses played a significant role in the political structure of that land. Jeremiah was forced into Egypt, and Jeroboam fled into Egypt to escape political dangers.[52]

Who ruled Egypt at the time the Holy Family entered that land?

Egypt was governed by Ptolemaic rulers from 332 to 30 BC. One of the more famous Greek rulers was Cleopatra, who reigned from 51 BC to 30 BC. Following her reign, Egypt was ruled by the Roman Empire. During Roman

Holy family's flight into Egypt

rule, the province was recognized by the Jews as a place of refuge. Several Jewish communities emerged in the province at that time, the largest being Alexandria.

By the time the Holy Family arrived in Egypt, nearly a million Jews resided in that Roman province. Most of them lived in the commercial city of Alexandria, although a few settled in smaller communities. Jews successfully participated in the economic life of Egypt despite heavy taxation.[53]

Did the Holy Family reside in Alexandria, Egypt?

Alexandria, named for Alexander the Great, was a commercial center located on the Mediterranean Sea at the western edge of the Nile Delta, approximately 130 miles from Cairo. By AD 1 Alexandria was dubbed "Little Jerusalem" due to its dominant Jewish population.

However, Alexandria is not purported to be the residence of the Holy Family. Christian tradition suggests that the Holy Family lived along the Nile River, possibly in a community where Joseph the carpenter could practice his trade.

That tradition suggests that they lived in Heliopolis, a city north of Cairo.[54]

The Holy Family did not leave Egypt until after the death of Herod the Great. Was there pomp and ceremony in Judea when Herod died?

The Jewish historian Josephus wrote that when Herod died in Jericho, his son "Archelaus saw to it that his father's burial should be most splendid, and he brought out all his ornaments to accompany the procession for the deceased. Herod was borne upon a golden bier studded with precious stones . . . and with a cover of purple over it. The dead man too was wrapped in purple robes and wore a diadem." In addition, according to Josephus, Archelaus employed pipers and professional mourners to join in the funeral procession and follow the remains of Herod to the burial site.

Relatives, bodyguards, Thracians, Germans, and Gauls moved toward the burial site "all equipped for battle. Right behind them came the whole army as if marching to war . . . followed by five hundred servants carrying spices." The traditional site of Herod's burial is the Hero-dium.[55]

Who governed the Roman province of Palestine after the death of Herod the Great?

A few days before his death, Herod changed his will and divided his domain between three of his sons—Herod Archelaus, Herod Antipas, and Herod Philip. Archelaus, according to the wishes of his father, was appointed ruler over Judea, Samaria, and Idumea. His reign was as oppressive as that of his father. After ten years of being ruled by Archelaus (4 BC to AD 6), Jews and Samaritans sent a delegation to Rome complaining of his tyrannical rule. Caesar Augustus listened to their complaints and deposed Archelaus, banishing him to Gaul. Judea was then attached to Syria and placed under the rule of the Roman Governor Coponius (AD 6–9), who was eventually succeeded by Pontius Pilate (AD 26–36).

Herod's son Antipas, initially named as the successor of Herod's domain, was appointed tetrarch of Galilee and Perea (4 BC to AD 39). Gospel writers referred to Antipas by his family name, Herod. Although Herod Antipas held the title of tetrarch, his supporters called him king (see Mark 6:14, 22–27). Herod the Great's son Philip was appointed tetrarch or ruler over a part of the territory northeast of the Sea of Galilee, which occupied a portion of the modern Golan Heights. He ruled from 4 BC to AD 34.

Herod made the divisions of rule among his three sons "dependent on the approval" of Caesar Augustus. Caesar accepted the divisions with the exception of the small principality of Abilene.[56]

3

The Child Grew and Waxed Strong in Spirit

An angel appeared to Joseph in a dream, saying, "Arise, and take the young child and his mother, and go into the land of Israel: for they are dead which sought the young child's life" (Matt. 2:20). Joseph took Mary and the Child Jesus across the Negev and Sinai deserts toward their homeland.

Can it be determined when the Holy Family returned to Judea?

It is probable that the Holy Family returned to Palestine sometime before AD 6 during the reign of Herod Archelaus (see Matt. 2:21–22). Joseph was warned in a dream not to return to the land ruled by Herod Archelaus, however.

In compliance with the warning, Joseph took Mary and the Child Jesus to Nazareth in Galilee—or, as Luke said, "their own city Nazareth" (Luke 2:39).57

The Holy Family "turned aside into the parts of Galilee" (Matt. 2:22). Why was Galilee referred to as the "Galilee of the gentiles" at this time?

In the days of Jesus, Galilee was a Roman province ruled by Herod Antipas. The province included the ancient lands of four Israelite tribes—Issachar, Zebulun, Naphtali, and Asher.

The history of Galilee contains many examples of Gentile occupation. King Solomon gave the region to Hiram, a gentile who was King of Tyre, as payment for transporting timber from Lebanon to Jerusalem. Isaiah noted the number of non-Israelites in the region and referred to it as the "Galilee of the nations" (Isa. 9:1; see also Judg. 1:30–33). The Hebrew word for gentiles is translated in the King James Version as "the nations." Jerusalem Jews called the region "Galilee of the gentiles" because of intermarriage of Jews with foreigners in that area (see Matt. 4:15). Northeastern or upper Galilee was inhabited by Jews who had intermarried with non-Israelites—Phoenicians, Syrians, Arabs, and Greeks.

Judean religious leaders often distrusted Galilean Jews, believing them to be casual in their observance of the Mosaic law and influenced by foreign culture. After all, more than one million Jews living in more than two hundred communities in Galilee had been exposed to Greek influence. In spite of this influence, Galilean Jews viewed themselves as observant Jews.[58]

What was the dominant language spoken by the Galileans at that time?

Galileans spoke "an Aramaic dialect that sounded crude and uncultured" to Judean Jews. The Aramaic language had three dialects—northern, southern, and western. Northern or Galilean

Sunset on the Sea of Galilee

Aramaic was spoken by Jews and Syrians living near the Sea of Galilee. Southern or Chaldean Aramaic was spoken by Judean Jews. Western Aramaic, known as Aramean, was spoken by northern Syrians. The major differences between the three dialects were pronunciation and colloquialisms. When the various dialects were spoken outside their accepted locations, the individual speaking the dialect was subject to ridicule.[59]

Most of the Galileans lived near the Sea of Galilee. Is the Sea of Galilee the lowest freshwater lake in the world?

The Sea of Galilee is 686 feet below sea level, making it the lowest freshwater lake in the world. Although fewer than eight miles wide and only about twenty miles long, this body of water is referred to as a sea. The confusion over lake and sea stems from the Hebrew word *yam,* which is translated as either word.

The sea has been known by different names through the centuries. Gospel writers referred to it as both the Sea of Galilee and Gennesaret (see Luke 5:1). When Herod Antipas built the capital city of Tiberias

near the shore of the sea, he called the sea Tiberias. The modern name for the sea is Kinneret, meaning "harp." The modern name reflects the harp-like shoreline along that body of water.[60]

Out of the nearly two hundred villages that bordered the Sea of Galilee, Gospel writers feature only a few villages. None is more prominent to these writers than Nazareth during the youth of Jesus. Is there an ancient prophesy that tells of the Son of God growing to maturity in Nazareth?

The prophecy that was fulfilled when Jesus grew to maturity in Nazareth is not found in the Old Testament or in other Jewish literature (see Matt. 2:23). In fact, the town of Nazareth is not mentioned in the Old Testament. When the Jewish historian Josephus listed forty-five villages and towns in Galilee, he did not mention Nazareth. Likewise, of the sixty-three Galilean communities referred to in the Talmud, there is no mention of Nazareth.[61]

Does the term *Nazarene* have greater meaning than simply a resident of Nazareth?

"There is similarity in sound and possibly in meaning between the Aramaic word for Nazareth and the Hebrew word translated branch." Isaiah refers to the future deliverer as a branch (see Isa. 11:1). The reference to Jesus as a Nazarene may be a misunderstanding of Isaiah's prophesy. Traditionally, the term Nazarene was used in derision, possibly referring to the lowly status of the small village.[62]

Why is the title Jesus of Nazareth used by Gospel writers instead of Jesus of Bethlehem or Jesus, the Son of God?

It is likely that when the Child Jesus resided in Nazareth, His true paternity was known only to a few. Because of Herod's edict, which ordered the death of male babies in Bethlehem, it was safer for the growing child to be called Jesus of Nazareth, a title that appears seventeen times in the Gospels and Acts, instead of Jesus of Bethlehem. It is evident that as He grew to manhood in Nazareth, villagers knew Him as the son of Joseph, not the Son of God (see Luke 4:22).

It was a common practice among the Jews to call an individual after the community of his youth to distinguish that individual from others with the same first name. Thus, Jesus was called Jesus of Nazareth. [63]

The scriptures are very vague about the childhood of Jesus: "And the child grew, and waxed strong in spirit, filled with wisdom: and the grace of God was upon him" (Luke 2:40). Is there a believable record of the childhood experiences of Jesus beyond that written in the scriptures?

The childhood and youth of Jesus is known as the silent period of His life. The silence stretches from His childhood in Nazareth to the beginning of His ministry in Cana. Isaiah provides a credible insight into these years: "For he shall grow up before him as a tender plant, and as a root out of a dry ground: he hath no form nor comeliness; and when we shall see him, there is no beauty that we should desire him" (Isa. 53:2). Martin Luther adds, "Christ in his childhood and youth looked and acted like other children, yet without sin; in fashion like a man."[64]

Should credence be given to apocryphal accounts of the childhood of Jesus?

Apocryphal accounts describe the childhood of Jesus in fanciful stories. They place Him in the village of Nazareth overlooking the Jezreel Valley and the international route between Palestine and Egypt. Jesus is also found in the crowded marketplace and in fields and vineyards on the outskirts of Nazareth. These fictional stories are told with descriptive narratives.

The benevolent stories portray Jesus carrying spilt liquid in his cloak, lengthening a short board by pulling on it, and clapping His hands to give life to clay sparrows. Vengeful stories are of His silencing those who attempt to teach Him, rebuking Joseph the carpenter, turning playmates into goats, and striking dead obnoxious neighborhood boys. The vengeful tales evoke anger and retaliation against the 150 villagers of Nazareth and trepidation and wonder in Mary, His mother. These apocryphal accounts and hundreds of others "mar rather than embellish the childhood and youth of Jesus."[65]

What symbols of faith were found in Jewish homes during the childhood of Jesus?

The most obvious Jewish symbol was a folded piece of parchment located on the doorpost of the house. The scriptural words on the parchment read, "Hear, O Israel: The Lord our God is one Lord: And thou shalt love the Lord thy God with all thine heart, and with all thy soul, and with all thy might" (Deut. 6:4–5). These verses are known as the Shema, meaning a reminder to those who enter the house to hear and listen to the word of God. As members of a Jewish household entered or left the house, they touched the Shema with a finger and then touched their lips with the same finger as a symbolic remembrance and prayer to God.

Less obvious Jewish symbols of home worship were lullabies based on the book of Psalms and selected teachings from the writings of ancient prophets. Mothers sang lullabies while fathers taught scriptural passages, prayers, and wise sayings to their children. It can be assumed that the parchment, lullabies, and scriptural teachings were an important part of the childhood of Jesus.[66]

Can it be assumed that Jesus attended a synagogue in his youth?

Before the age of six or seven, Jewish sons were taught by their fathers the Shema, some passages from the book of Proverbs, and verses from the book of Psalms. After reaching the age of six or seven, Jewish sons received further education at a local synagogue. Education offered at village synagogues included reading, writing, and arithmetic. The principal topic of study, however, was the law or legal observance of Judaism.

Once the boys were conversant with the law and had reached the age of thirteen, they were invited to pray and speak in the synagogue. To the rabbis, who taught male children at the synagogue, "The knowledge of God was everything; and to prepare for or impart that knowledge was the sum total, the sole object of his education."

Although all sons of Judah were invited to learn in local synagogues, those identified as bright students or those whose fathers would pay for additional education became scribes or doctors of the law.

It is assumed that the formal education of Jesus was limited to his youthful studies at the local Nazareth synagogue and did not include additional schooling needed to become a scribe or doctor of the law.[67]

The only recorded event in the youth of Jesus was when the Holy Family went to Jerusalem to observe Passover festivities. What time of year was Passover held?

The date of Passover varied slightly from year to year, as did the date on which Joseph and Mary began their journey from Nazareth to Jerusalem (see Luke 2:41). Passover was celebrated each year in Jerusalem at the end of winter. The exact date of Passover varied, but the time period corresponded to the last week of March and the first week of April in the modern calendar (see Ex. 12:18.) The date varied because of the problematic Hebraic calendar, which was based on the phases of the moon and consisted of 354 days in a year. The days in each month varied from twenty-nine to thirty and depended on the appearance of a new moon.

Jesus with the doctors, listening and asking questions

The first sighting of a new moon was attested by credible witnesses before the Sanhedrin in Jerusalem. If the new moon was seen at the beginning of the thirtieth day, days being calculated from evening to evening, the Sanhedrin declared the previous month to be twenty-nine days long, or imperfect. They then announced the beginning of a new month and sent men to a signal station on the Mount of Olives to light beacon fires, wave torches, and blow horns until a flame was seen or a sound heard from a distant hill.

By using horns and fire as signals, the announcement of a new moon was carried from hill to hill to distant borders throughout Palestine and as far away as Mesopotamia.[68]

What was the Feast of the Passover?

Anciently, Passover was known as Pesach and was a nature festival held to celebrate the outward signs of the coming of spring. At the time of Jesus, the Feast of the Passover was a commemoration of the deliverance of Israel from oppressive Egyptian servitude, or "Jehovah's passing over (hence 'Passover') the homes of the children of Israel in Egypt when he smote the first-born of the land of Egypt and delivered the covenant community from Egyptian bondage" (see Ex. 12:3–11; 13:8–9). As Jewish scholar Hayyim Schauss wrote, "The Jews spoke of Egypt but they meant Rome. They spoke of the discomfiture of Pharaoh and the Egyptians, hoping at the same time for the identical plagues to be visited upon the Roman emperor, his governors, and his soldiers."

Passover was the greatest of the three annual Jewish festivals at which "all males of the covenant were to appear before the Lord at the place of his choosing" (see Ex. 23:14–17; Deut. 16:16.)

The "place of his choosing" at the time of Jesus was the Holy Temple Mount.[69]

Were all Jewish males required to attend Passover? Was attendance still required if they lived a great distance from the Holy Temple?

Mosaic law required Jews living in or near Jerusalem to go to the Temple Mount three times a year and to participate in the major festivals. Those living great distances from Jerusalem were expected to be on the mount only once a year. The law required all Jewish males to present themselves at the Passover feast. Jewish women were asked to attend Passover "if not lawfully detained."[70]

Why was the journey to Jerusalem referred to as a "pilgrimage" during the Passover festivities?

To journey to Jerusalem for the Passover festivities was a pilgrimage if accompanied by others of the same faith—family, kinsfolk, or villagers. The distinction between a journey and a pilgrimage was that a pilgrimage could not be undertaken alone, whereas a journey could be taken alone. Those who resided great distances from Jerusalem and desired to return to their spiritual roots made a pilgrimage.

Before a pilgrimage could begin, a man was elected leader of a caravan of pilgrims. Once elected, the leader said, "Arise ye, and let us go up to Zion, to the House of our God." As he began moving in the direction of Jerusalem, members of his caravan followed. The rich drove chariots, the afflicted rode beasts of burden, but most journeyed on foot. It was considered "more meritorious to make the pilgrimage that way." As they journeyed, the pilgrims sang from the book of Psalms.

At the time of Jesus, great multitudes of Jews, estimated at nearly one hundred thousand, made the pilgrimage in caravans to Jerusalem for the Passover festivities.[71]

Was Herod Archelaus still ruling Judea when Jesus "went up to Jerusalem after the custom of the feast" (Luke 2:42)?

Archelaus, son of Herod the Great, ruled Judea from 4 BC to

AD 6. He was succeeded by the Roman procurator Coponius. Coponius ruled Judea when youthful Jesus made his pilgrimage to Jerusalem for the Passover festivities.[72]

Was it customary for twelve-year-old males to attend Passover festivities?

Jewish law required every twelve-year-old male be formally tested by doctors of the law at the Temple Mount before "taking upon himself the yoke of the law" or becoming a Son of the Law. *Son of the Law* meant that the young male could hold a position in a local synagogue congregation, be recognized as a member of his home community, choose a vocation, enter into advanced studies, and no longer be sold as a bond servant by his parents. It was expected that after becoming a Son of the Law, the young male would dine with Abraham, Isaac, and Jacob and other noble patriarchs at a future messianic feast.[73]

Jesus "tarried behind in Jerusalem" after the Passover festivities. Mary and Joseph, "supposing him to have been in the company, went a day's journey" before realizing Jesus was not among the pilgrims (Luke 2:43–44). Where were Joseph and Mary when they realized that Jesus was not among the pilgrims?

There are conflicting notions as to the route that Joseph and Mary took as they began their return to Nazareth. The traditional route places the first stop of their journey at Beeroth, a Hebrew word meaning "wells," located eight miles north of Jerusalem near the town of Ramallah. Beeroth is identified as the traditional Christian site where Mary and Joseph first missed Jesus.

Credence is given to this site because of the scriptural saying that Joseph and Mary went "a day's journey" before realizing that Jesus was not with them (Luke 2:44). Beeroth was a day's journey from Jerusalem.

From the account in Luke, we learn that Mary and Joseph discovered that Jesus was missing on the first day. The second day they returned to Jerusalem seeking him. The third day, they searched for him on the Temple Mount.[74]

After three days, Mary found Jesus "sitting in the midst of the doctors, both hearing them, and asking them questions" (Luke 2:46). Is there any record of doctors asking questions of or learning from Jesus?

It was not unusual for learned doctors and scribes to answer questions posed by twelve-year-old males on the Temple Mount. Ancient Jewish records reveal sporadic instances of precocious and education-ally advanced young men conversing with and learning from rabbis, scribes, and doctors near the Holy Temple. However, historical records of learned men being taught by a youthful sage are nonexistent.

The Joseph Smith Translation (JST) of the Gospel of Luke conveys the notion that Jesus taught the doctors. It states, "and they [the doctors] were hearing him, and asking him questions" (JST Luke 2:46).[75]

Christ in the temple with the doctors

In what area of the Temple Mount did Jesus converse with doctors of the law?

It is probable that Jesus conversed with learned doctors, noted for their interpretive commentary and narratives of the law—halakah, the "legal commentary," and haggadah, the "traditional commentary"—in the Court of the Women, which had a "fortified inner wall with towers and gates" and occupied nearly 40,000 square feet. Jewish tradition purports that since the days of Babylonian captivity and the rebuilding of the temple at Jerusalem, learned doctors sat in the northeast corner of the Court of the Women. It has been speculated that they sat in this area because the Ark of the Covenant was buried beneath the "north-eastern angle of the Court of the Women."[76]

How did the Court of the Women obtain its name? Was there a specific purpose for this court?

It was not named Court of the Women because only women could enter the area. It was named Court of the Women be-cause women were not allowed to proceed beyond the area. In each corner of the court were chambers that allowed for specific functions. For example, in the eastern chamber, Nazarites made vows and prepared their sacrifices. In the western chamber, olive oil was stored and purification baths were prepared for lepers.[77]

Gospel writers tell of Jesus returning with Joseph and Mary to Nazareth and being "subject unto them" (Luke 2:51). Was it in Nazareth that Jesus learned the carpenter's trade?

It is probable that Jesus was an apprentice to Joseph the carpenter in Nazareth. According to the Talmud, "a father is obliged not only to support his son but also to teach him a trade." Rabbis taught, "It is incumbent on the father to circumcise his son, to redeem him, to teach him the Law, and to teach him some occupation." Rabbis often remarked, "He who does not teach his son a trade brings him up to be a robber."

Proficiency in manual labor was respected by the ancient Jews. The question would be better posed if worded, "Can we assume that Joseph the carpenter taught Jesus to be a worker of wood?" The Greek word for carpenter is *tekton,* meaning "artificer" or "craftsman." It is not clear from the Greek translation whether Jesus learned the trade of a wood worker or a smith.

There is little indication from the Gospel writers that Joseph and Jesus were workers of wood. Matthew and Luke record only one reference to the manual process of carpentry: "Why beholdest thou the mote [speck or splinter] that is in thy brother's eye, but considerest not the beam [wooden beam used in constructing houses] that is in thine own eye?" (Matt. 7:3; Luke 6:41). However, contemporary writers and artists depict Joseph and Jesus working together as master carpenters making ploughs, yokes, and other wooden tools for the residents of Nazareth. Such may not be the case.

Before the influence of western civilization reached the Middle East, wood carpentry was an insignificant trade. The woodworking craft was mostly practiced by men on their own house and property. Only in times of prosperity was carpentry a public trade.

The idea that Joseph and Jesus were artificers or craftsmen of stone should not be discounted. Limestone in Judea and black basalt in the Galilee region were more abundant than wood in Palestine and more frequently used in the building trades. Stone cutters, masons, and sculptors were among the proudest Jewish professions. It is of interest that much of the imagery in the teachings of Jesus is of stone and rock.[78]

Why did so many Jews at the time of Jesus choose to be tradesmen instead of government officials?

If Palestine had been independent of foreign rule, a tradesman may have been a man of inferior social status or a man with a "voluntary or necessary preoccupation

Growing in wisdom

with the things of this world that perish with the using." Since Palestine had been ruled by foreigners for centuries, being a tradesman was extolled in Jewish communities and may have been a means of displaying manly independence.

Most trades in Nazareth and throughout Palestine were family enterprises that had passed from father to son for generations. Members of competing or similar trades did business in the same geographic areas of the Jewish society much like their fathers before them. For example, in Jerusalem there was a street occupied by butchers, one by bakers, and another by iron smiths.

Craftsmen often wore a sign of their trade in the marketplace. It was not unusual to see a dyer wearing a brightly colored cloth, a tailor with a large bone needle in his cloak, or a public writer with a wooden ruler behind his ear.[79]

Was Joseph the carpenter alive during the youthful years of Jesus?

Joseph is never mentioned by name in the Gospels after the Passover Feast that occurred when Jesus was age twelve. Tradition suggests that he died.[80]

Did Joseph the carpenter die from old age?

Traditional stories purport that Joseph the carpenter was much older than Mary and had a previous marriage, in which he fathered six children. Although the traditional accounts of Joseph, depicted as an elderly widower, have been accepted by certain Christians for centuries, the accounts lose validity by asking simple questions. If Joseph had older sons, how could Jesus be the heir apparent to David's throne? What became of the six children when Joseph and Mary went to Bethlehem and later to Egypt? Why didn't the older sons accompany Joseph and Mary to the Passover Feast? These and other queries raise unanswered issues about the concept that Joseph was a widower.[81]

Was Jesus reared with brothers and sisters born of Mary?

This question opens the Christian debate about the doctrine of perpetual virginity (see Matt. 1:23). This doctrine, which purports that Mary was a virgin all her days, has been debated by Christian scholars and theologians throughout the ages. The logic and reasoning surrounding the theme of virginity has varied from theologian to theologian and scholar to scholar, as have opinions about the veracity of the doctrine.

It should be noted that the doctrine of perpetual virginity is not contained in the writings of Matthew, Mark, Luke, or John. The Gospel writers mention the names of sons born to Mary—James, Joses (Joseph), Simon, and Judas—as well as female offspring (see Matt. 13:55; Mark 6:3).

Other New Testament writers suggest that the siblings of Jesus united with the early Christians (see 1 Cor. 15:7; Acts 1:14). His brother James became an Apostle (see Gal. 1:19).[82]

Is anything else known about the youthful years of Jesus?

The Joseph Smith Translation of Matthew 3:24–26 adds precious details about the youth of Jesus:

"And it came to pass that Jesus grew up with his brethren, and waxed strong, and waited upon the Lord for the time of his ministry to come.

"And he served under his father, and he spake not as other men, neither could he be taught; for he needed not that any man should teach him.

"And after many years, the hour of his ministry drew nigh."

4

Preparing the Way

In a society where class distinction, fine-twined linen, and a self-serving embrace of the sacred were all too apparent, there was a lone voice in the wilderness. John the Baptist began preaching in the wilderness of Judea far from the soft garments and flowing robes of the Jerusalem aristocracy. Repent was his clarion cry. Turn from the blatant ills of the Palestinian society was his urgent plea. Embrace the sacred (the covenants between Jehovah and the fathers of Israel) was his pressing invitation.

Is there any record of John preaching in a synagogue or on the Temple Mount in Jerusalem?

Gospel writers do not mention John preaching in a synagogue or within temple courts when Tiberius Caesar ruled Rome and Herod Antipas was tetrarch of Galilee. Even though Gospel writers tell only of his preaching in the wilderness of Judea, multitudes of Jews from Jerusalem and adjacent rural areas journeyed to the wilderness to listen to him. Perhaps more listened to John than to the scribes, rabbis, or doctors of the law who taught in synagogues and on the Temple Mount.[83]

Why did John the Baptist wear a "raiment of camel's hair, and a leathern girdle about his loins" while preaching (Matt. 3:4)? Is it not true that the "messenger should match the message"?

John's clothing matched his simple, yet poignant message. His desert attire was in direct contrast

Camel hair being shorn

to the soft garments and flowing robes worn by the Jewish aristocracy. His camel-hair garment was held in place by a clasp or knot in the girdle. The leather girdle, fashioned for use by both men and women, served as a pocket or purse. John preferred goat's hair to spun linen, flax, cotton, and the wool cloth worn by Pharisees.[84]

Why was repentance the central message of John's preaching?

An easy answer to that question comes from reviewing the blatant ills of the Palestinian society in which John lived—extortion in the tax-collecting process, abuses heaped on women, poverty suffered by children, and so on.

Such an obvious answer misses the central purpose of his message. To repent is to return (the Hebrew word *Isashuv* is translated "to return"), and when used in its scriptural context implies to come back to the covenant agreement between God and Israel. By repenting, Jews returned to the covenants between God and their ancient fathers—Abraham, Isaac, and Jacob. The word repent was also the first word spoken by Jesus as He began His ministry in Galilee (see Matt. 4:17).[85]

Was John the Baptist a Nazarite?

By the broadest definition, a Nazarite was any male or female who voluntarily vowed to sacrifice in service to God. Whether the vow was for a limited time or for life, the one who committed to God was known as a Nazarite (see 1 Sam. 1:27; Judg. 13:7).

In its restricted Essene definition, a Nazarite must not only make vows of sacrifice and service, but also vows of abstinence, which was a protest against the segment of Jewish society that had forgotten Jehovah.

By using either a broad or a restricted definition, it is possible that John the Baptist was a Nazarite.[86]

Can it be assumed that John really ate "locusts and wild honey" (Matt. 3:4)?

The meat of the locust may refer to insects or to carob pods. The scriptural reference is more likely to the small insect. If the reference is to insects, John would not be the first or the last to consume locusts, or what ancient Israelites called "an instrument of God's curse." To native tribes in the Near East and Africa, eating locusts was a connoisseur's delight. According to the Mosaic law, "[The Hebrews] may eat of every flying creeping thing . . . the locust after his kind."

Pods of the carob tree, referred to as locusts, are abundant in the eastern Mediterranean region. Pods are high in sugar content and valued as fodder for cattle and as a basic staple for the poor. In the Jerusalem area today, carob pods are referred to as Saint John's Bread in remembrance of John the Baptist eating locust as a meat substitute.

The scriptural passage also records that John ate wild honey. According to rabbinic sources, wild honey was a thick, heavy syrup made by boiling dates or grapes. It may also refer to the honey or product of bees.[87]

Desert locust

Was John referring to the Pharisees and Sadducees as a "generation of vipers" or as scorpions (Matt. 3:7)?

John the Baptist and Jesus referred to antagonists as vipers (see Matt. 12:34; 23:33). Although it is well known that a viper is a snake, the eastern Oriental text of Matthew reads, "O generation of scorpions" (Matt. 3:7). Eastern theologians suggest that the Pharisees and Sadducees, like scorpions, were spiritual orphans without parental or divine guidance. The Western translation of the Matthew text argues that John was referring to Pharisees and Sadducees as vipers.

A viper reflects not only the thinking of western Christian theologians, but Hebrew lore. According to folklore, the snake represents Satan's slanderous grasp on man. As the snake grows stronger with age, so the clasp of Satan grows stronger with time and destroys spiritual longings.

Because the land of Palestine boasts "thirty-five species of snakes and fifteen species of scorpions," it is difficult to know whether viper or scorpion was the word John used to describe Pharisees and Sadducees. If viper is the correct answer, it is interesting that of the snakes indigenous to Palestine, none is more dangerous or poisonous than a viper. When its front fangs grasp a victim, poison is secreted from its glands into the wound. The poison gives the victim a temporary feeling of well-being before the venom builds in "lymph vessels and then slowly courses through the tissues destroying cells and rupturing capillaries." The victim becomes paralyzed before a massive, internal hemorrhage causes death.[88]

Did the baptism of John differ from Jewish rites of immersion?

Jews participated in an immersion rite long before John began baptizing in Bethabara. Mosaic law dictated that the Levitically defiled or unclean be immersed before offering a sacrifice to Jehovah. It also dictated that Gentiles be immersed to become "proselytes of righteousness." A proselyte of righteousness acknowledged through immersion the symbolic removal of moral defilement that corresponds to Levitical uncleanliness. Rabbis illustrated the need for a cleansing immersion by stating, "All the baths of lustration would not cleanse a man, so long as he continued holding in his hand that which had polluted him." The immersions of John differed from those performed according to Mosaic law. John taught that all Jews should be immersed in a baptism of repentance. Because of the uniqueness of John's immersions, he was called John the Baptist.[89]

Was Bethabara the only baptismal site used by John?

Christian tradition suggests that there were three baptismal sites used by John the Baptist. The first was in Bethany near Jericho in the wilderness of Judea (Revised Standard Bible Version). The second was known as Aenon and was located on the border between Samaria and Judea. The third and most famous was Bethabara, meaning "place of crossing," located on the east bank of the Jordan River (King James Version).[90]

John said, "I indeed baptize you with water; but one mightier than I cometh, the latchet of whose shoes I am not worthy to unloose" (Luke 3:16). What did he mean by this statement?

According to scholars D. Kelly Ogden and Andrew Skinner, "John

Proposed location where John baptized Jesus Christ

understood his role and his place. There was no vying for superiority. He knew that Jesus was greater than he and that Jesus was the long-promised Messiah. His humility is demonstrated in his expression that he felt unworthy to even unloose the latchet of Jesus' sandals."

Sandals were worn outdoors by men and women during the Roman rule of Palestine. The sole of the sandal was made of leather, cloth, felt, or wood. Occasionally, the sole was covered with iron to increase its durability.

Sandals were not worn indoors. The unloosing of a sandal or its latchet was the responsibility of the lowest household servant or slave. To be given such a responsibility was a sign or mark of the servant or slave's inferior domestic station.[91]

"Then cometh Jesus from Galilee to Jordan unto John, to be baptized of him" (Matt. 3:13). Does the Jordan River have any distinctive features?

Of the three rivers referred to as holy in the Mideast—Ganges, Nile, and Jordan—the Jordan or Yarden, meaning the "descent of Dan," is the smallest. It has the distinction of being the only river in the world that flows most of its course below sea level. The river begins at the base of Mount Hermon and flows downward through the Sea of Galilee before emptying into the Dead Sea. It is the "lowest spot on earth where anyone could be baptized in fresh water."

As it winds and twists on its route to the sea, it journeys through the deepest valley in the world. The distance of its course is nearly two hundred miles. But as a bird flies, the distance is only sixty-five miles. The average width of the river is a hundred feet.

Near the river is the Wadi Kherar cave, suggested by sixth-century Christian scholars as the probable shelter Jesus used prior to his baptism.[92]

Is it symbolic that the baptism of Jesus was in the lowest river on the earth?

Symbolically, the baptism of Jesus represents the depth of his humility. Elder Russell M. Nelson wrote, "By example, He taught us that He literally descended beneath all things to rise above all things." By accepting baptism Jesus acknowledged the importance of John's baptism as a covenant with God for the remission of sins (see Matt. 28:19). By so doing, He fulfilled all righteousness.[93]

> **When Jesus was baptized, the Spirit of God descended like a dove (see Matt. 3:16). Why did the Spirit descend like a dove?**

Ancient Jewish rabbis would have found this curious; to them, the dove was a symbol of Israel as a nation but not the Spirit of God. But to Christians, the dove has symbolized the Holy Spirit. Perhaps a discussion of the actions of doves when attacked will partially answer why Christians associate this bird—but not the 350 other species of birds found in the Palestine region—with the Spirit.

"The dove has no means of defense except swift flight," wrote scholar Byron R. Merrill. When its young are attacked and wounded, the dove flutters above them, mourning the suffering of its offspring. Similarly, the Spirit of God mourns the loss of every soul. Perhaps the Spirit, like the dove, awaits recovery and an opportunity to be reunited with a wounded soul.

The dove was given as a sign for the two most important baptisms in the world—the baptism

Baptism of Jesus Christ

of Jesus and the baptism of the earth. John witnessed the Spirit of God descending like a dove as a sign that Jesus was the Son of God (see Matt. 3:16). Noah saw the dove as a manifestation that God had "made peace with the earth" (see Gen. 8:8–12).[94]

> **After Jesus was baptized, He went "into the wilderness, Being forty days tempted of the devil" (Luke 4:1–2). Was the wilderness Jesus entered a wasteland?**

The wilderness was not a wasteland like the Sahara or Arabian deserts. The wilderness of Judea is about ten miles wide and lies west of the Dead Sea, extending northward to the Jordan River. It is known for its desert-like terrain, animal life, and flora. The desert wilderness contrasts dramatically with Jerusalem, which averages between twenty-two and twenty-five inches of rain each year. It also contrasts with the fertile valleys, rivers, and seaside coasts found in Israel today.

The traditional Christian site of the temptations is Jebel Qaruntul, a chalk mountain northwest of Jericho. Its name, a Latin word meaning "forty," refers to the forty-day fast of Jesus. Through the centuries, so many religious ascetics have meditated at Jebel Qaruntul that it is now known as the "nursery of souls." A few Christians suggest that the site of temptation was not Jebel Qaruntul, but the wilderness area near Bethabara, and that Jesus was led westward into the Judean wilderness (see Luke 4:1).[95]

Did Jesus go into the wilderness to be tempted by God?

Although the wilderness setting is reflective of ancient Hebrew lore that spins tales of God's voice being heard in the mountains and evil spirits lurking in desert wastes, it was not lore or a desire to be tempted that caused Jesus to go into the wilderness of Judea. Jesus went into the wilderness to fast, pray, and commune with God (see Matt. 4:1).

It was after forty days and nights of fasting that Jesus hungered and Satan tempted Him (see Luke 4:2–13). (The phrase forty days and nights has both a literal interpretation and a figurative interpretation; figuratively, it means a "long time.") The insulting assaults of Satan were directed

Temptation of Christ

against the submission of Jesus to the will of God. The Gospel of Mark records Satan's wiles in a single verse, whereas the Gospels of Matthew and Luke present colorful detail, but transpose the second and third temptations. His triumphant victory over the adversary in the wilderness did not exempt Jesus from further satanic assaults.[96]

Jesus "fasted forty days and forty nights" (Matt. 4:2). Was fasting part of Jewish worship during the days of Jesus?

Fasting was a common practice among Jewish people and other Eastern cultures in the days of Jesus. When an Easterner fasted, he was generous in his offerings to the poor, because in fasting the Easterner learned something of hunger. When the Jews fasted, they did not link fasting with giving to the poor. To the Jews, fasting was always associated with worship and "as with prayer, so with fasting. No ostentation."

References to fasting in the New Testament are to "the fast"—that is, the Day of Atonement and weekly fasts (see Acts 27:9). In the days of Jesus, Pharisees

designated forty formal days of fasting each year. Most of the formal fasts occurred between Jewish festivals. For example, during the seven weeks from the Feast of Passover to Feast of Pentecost, fourteen fasts were designated. During the ten weeks from the Feast of Tabernacles to the Feast of Dedication, twenty fasts were designated.

The weekly fasts occurred on Monday and Thursday. The Thursday fast was in remembrance of the traditional day Moses received the Tables of the Law at Mount Sinai, and the Monday fast was in remembrance of the traditional day Moses came down from Mount Sinai and presented the law to the children of Israel.[97]

After Jesus fasted, "He was afterward an hungered" (Matt. 4:2). Would the temptation of bread alone have abated his hunger?

To eat bread or break bread meant "to partake of a meal." The satanic temptation was an invitation for Jesus to succumb to His carnal appetite, and to succumb would be contrary to the teachings of Judaism. In Judaism, everything is in subjection to the spiritual realm—even the necessary act of eating. Ancient rabbis taught, "The eating [of] some foods and refraining from others . . . elevate[s] the act of eating, which in itself is neutral, to a vehicle for godliness."

Jesus did not submit to hunger. He acknowledged the temptation by repeating the words of Moses, "Man doth not live by bread only" (Deut. 8:3). He then declared the source of life: "Every word that proceedeth out of the mouth of God" (Matt. 4:4).[98]

Did stones in the Judean wilderness resemble bread?

According to tradition, ancient Eastern cultures baked round loaves of bread that resembled stones. Hungry travelers, seeing stones in the distance, were known to fantasize that the stones were unbleached loaves of bread. As the fantasy grew, weary travelers pressed forward seeking a house and an opportunity to obtain bread. Upon finding an occupied house, travelers asked the occupants for bread. If his company and conversation inconvenienced those in the house, he was told, "If you come to my house, I will set before you snake bones and stones."[99]

Judean wilderness

Did the devil set Jesus on a pinnacle of the Holy Temple?

Jesus was taken by the Spirit of God to the pinnacle, and then the devil came to tempt Him. Satan did not have power to take Jesus to the pinnacle even though he freely used scriptural verse (see Ps. 91:11–12). Jesus responded to Satan with a verse of His own: "Thou shalt not tempt the Lord thy God" (Matt. 4:7). The Greek word for "pinnacle" is *pterugion,* meaning "little wing." The wing of the temple overlooked the temple courts and the Kidron Valley.[100]

Early Galilean Ministry

Jesus left the wilderness of Judea to raise His voice in sweet Galilee. Along the harp-like shoreline of the sea, He spoke of repentance. Rejecting evil ways was not a new theme to His listeners—many had heard a similar message from John the Baptist. His central message, however—"The kingdom of heaven is at hand"—was new (Matt. 4:17). In those precious words, Jesus announced that His preparatory years had passed. The Messiah now walked among men.

By the seashore of Galilee, "Jesus began to preach, and to say, Repent: for the kingdom of heaven is at hand" (Matt. 4:17). Is there any record of Jesus preaching in the wilderness like John the Baptist?

Jesus did not remain in the wilderness to preach. He began His ministry in villages and cities throughout Galilee before extending His ministry to other Palestinian communities. Although the locale of His ministry differed from the wilderness setting of John's ministry, their messages were the same. Repent was the first recorded word of Jesus' ministry, just as it was the first word uttered by John in his ministry (see Matt. 3:2; 4:17.)[101]

Is it significant that Jesus began His ministry at age thirty?

Thirty was the legal age Levites began their ministry and the age when Jewish males were considered mature enough to be recognized as teachers and rabbis (see Num. 4:3, 47.) If Jesus had not been at least thirty years old when He began His public ministry, His age would have aroused criticism.[102]

Who were the first men to accept the gospel message of Jesus? Who became His first disciples?

Today, the word *disciple* refers to a student, an apprentice, and a follower. This definition suggests that a disciple is in a secondary position to a teacher or leader.

In biblical times, the word *disciple* was defined differently. Because the "streets were so narrow, if two people went together, they had to go in single

Narrow streets of Jerusalem

file. To follow after a person was to go with them" or to be his disciple.

The first recorded disciples to go with Jesus were John, meaning "Jehovah is gracious," and Andrew, meaning "manly." Both men had been followers of John the Baptist before becoming disciples of Jesus.[103]

Who was the first disciple to participate in missionary activities?

Andrew, son of Jona, became the first missionary when he said to his brother Simon, "We have found the Messias" (John 1:41). As Andrew introduced Simon to Jesus, Jesus gave Simon the name Cephas, an Aramaic word for "seer" or "stone" (see John 1:42). The Greek equivalent to Cephas is Petros, meaning "rock."[104]

Why didn't the early disciples of Jesus address Him as teacher or rabbi?

Teachers were known by three distinct titles—rab, rabbi, and rabboni. Rab was an inferior title and the lowest grade of honor. Rabbi, meaning "My Master" or

"My Great One," referred to a teacher at a synagogue or a man studying the law of Moses (see John 1:49).

After the destruction of the Holy Temple in Jerusalem (AD 70), *Rabbi* was an academic title of a recognized scholar. *Rabboni*—meaning "My lord, my master," or "My beloved Master"—was the highest distinction given a teacher. Mary Magdalene addressed the Resurrected Jesus as "Rabboni" (John 20:16.) [105]

Some of the early disciples of Jesus—Andrew, Peter, and Philip—were from Bethsaida. Where was Bethsaida located?

Bethsaida, meaning "place of nets," was a fishing village on the northeast corner of the Sea of Galilee. At the time of Jesus, Bethsaida was an important center for processing fish. At the time of Josephus, it was an agrarian community known for its grapes and figs.

Herod Philip changed the name of the community to Bethsaida-Julia in honor of Livia-Julia, mother of the Roman emperor Tiberius.[106]

Philip said to Nathanael, "We have found him, of whom Moses in the law, and the prophets, did write" (John 1:45). Jesus said to Nathanael, "Before that Philip called thee, when thou wast under the fig tree, I saw thee" (John 1:48). Did Jesus see Nathanael sitting under a literal or a figurative fig tree?

Fig tree

"Under the fig tree" has a literal and a figurative interpretation. Rabbinic teachings point to the literal interpretation, claiming that a proper place to study the Mosaic law was under a fig tree. The figurative interpretation points to the Jewish saying, "Every man under his vine and under his fig tree," meaning the man has a comfortable life and does not wish to change. Nathanael, meaning "gift of God" or "God-given," was from Cana.[107]

The Gospel writer John records that Jesus and his disciples were "called" to a marriage in Cana of Galilee (see John 2:2). Whose wedding did Jesus and His disciples attend in Cana?

Although Christian tradition suggests that Jesus and His disciples attended the wedding feast of a local farmer in Cana, not all scholars agree. A few claim that it was the wedding feast of a family member. Even fewer theologians claim that it was the marriage feast of Jesus. The answer to these speculations is not found in the Gospels. However, "had Jesus not been married, we would undoubtedly read of accusation after accusation against him, because marriage was number one of the commandments God had given from the beginning."

The conjecture over whose marriage it was does not negate the presence of Jesus at the feast or the fact that He "set the seal of His approval upon the matrimonial relationship and upon the propriety of social entertainment."[108]

What Jewish customs occurred at the wedding feast in Cana?

At the time of Jesus, Jewish marriages were elaborate. They required the appointment of a chief groomsman known as the friend of the bridegroom. The groomsman represented the groom in making arrangements for the marriage contract and wedding feast.

The typical wedding feast began when the groom, with a myrtle garland atop his head as a symbol of love, left his home to find his bride. The groom, accompanied by friends who carried lighted torches, found the bride at her parents' home. Upon finding her, the groom lifted her veil to reveal a dowry—a string of shiny coins on a headband. The groom then expressed to his friends an overwhelming joy at the treasure he had found. He took the veil and laid it on his shoulder. Upon seeing his action, his friends shouted, "The government shall be upon his shoulder."

The groom then led his bride in a festive procession to his home. Some in the procession made merry sounds of music while others carried torches, held flowers and myrtle branches, and danced before the bride. Jews observing the procession joined in praise of the bride's beauty, modesty, and virtue.

As the bride arrived at her new home, the words *Take her according to the Law of Moses and of Israel* were spoken. The festive couple was then crowned with garlands, encircled by guests under a wedding canopy, and called king and queen. These titles of nobility were exclaimed because "entrance into marriage was thought to carry the forgiveness of sins."

After the groom signed a legal document promising to honor and care for his bride after the manner of an Israelite and the prescribed washing of hands and benediction had been completed, the marriage feast began. The feast climaxed the happy occasion and often lasted more than a day. For wealthy Jews, the marriage feast lasted for a week or two. When the feast ended, the newlyweds were led by merry friends to the bridal chamber.[109]

In reference to the guests at the marriage feast of Cana, Mary said to Jesus, "They have no wine." Why did Jesus answer her, "Woman, what have I to do with thee? mine hour is not yet come" (John 2:3–4)?

Wedding at Cana

Jesus knew the time to offer Himself as a sacrificial lamb had not come. Yet, He who had triumphed over Satan's temptation to abate His own hunger responded affirmatively to His mother's plea. He provided a luxury for the wedding guests, whose thirst was momentary.[110]

Why was it important to Mary that the wedding guests have wine to drink?

Although water was a precious commodity to desert travelers, it appears that Mary recognized that wine was needed to satisfy the thirst of wedding guests. The common wine of Galilee was a light, sweet, unfermented drink made from the fruit of the vine.[111]

To provide wine for the wedding guests, "Jesus saith unto them, Fill the waterpots with water" (John 2:7). Knowing that the six pots could hold two or three firkins apiece, how much water did Jesus miraculously turn into wine?

If each water pot held two or three firkins—a firkin being about nine gallons—the combined pots held between twelve to eighteen gallons of water. When added together, it appears that Jesus miraculously provided an estimated 150 gallons of wine for what must have been a large wedding celebration.[112]

What is the difference between the water pots of stone and the water pots set aside for purification purposes?

In each Jewish household, six stone jars were reserved for ceremonial washing and purification. At marriage feasts, these vessels were used by the bride and distinguished wedding guests to wash their hands and feet. It is important to note that these stone jars were never to become "ritually impure."[113]

Is there any similarity between Jesus changing water into wine and the mysterious actions of the Greek god Dionysus?

Although Christian tradition suggests that the Gospel of John was written in the Greek city of Ephesus, there is no similarity between the mythical actions of the Greek god Dionysus, who was worshiped for his mysterious ability to create wine, and the miracle of Jesus in Cana. In fact, it was purported that Jesus miraculously provided "fresh wine," a drink that did not lead to drunkenness.[114]

The changing of water into wine is the first recorded miracle of Jesus. How many other miracles are recorded in the Gospels?

Although the exact number of miracles performed by Jesus is unknown, thirty-seven miracles are recorded in the Gospels. Scholar Donald Q. Cannon classified these miracles into six categories: 1) healing, 2) raising the dead, 3) casting out devils or evil spirits, 4) miracles of nature, 5) providing food, and 6) passing unseen.[115]

The village of Capernaum, or Kefar Nahum (anciently known as the village of Nahum), was located on the northern shore of the Sea of Galilee. At the time of Jesus, the lakeside community of Capernaum was on the major trade route between Damascus and Alexandria and boasted a population of five to six thousand residents. The village served as a border station between Herod Philip's territories in the east and land ruled by his brother, Herod Antipas. Roman soldiers were stationed in Capernaum to prevent border conflicts and the rise of revolutionaries. Jesus performed more miracles in this lakeside village than in any other location in Galilee or Judea.[116]

The nobleman was an official of Herod Antipas. Although Antipas was only a tetrarch, he was

Synagogue ruins at Capernaum

addressed as king and his officials were called "noblemen." Jesus said to the nobleman, "Go thy way; thy son liveth" (John 4:50). Healing of the nobleman's son is viewed as the second miracle of Jesus in Cana even though the son lay near death in Capernaum, more than twenty miles from Cana.[117]

In the Holy City

Jesus left Capernaum and journeyed to the Holy City to celebrate Passover with worshipful pilgrims. What he found in the city was not to His liking: In a complex of courtyards on the Temple Mount, money-changers were profiting from the sacred.

> When the "passover was at hand," Jesus left Capernaum to go "up to Jerusalem." In the Holy City, He "found in the temple those that sold oxen and sheep and doves, and the changers of money sitting" (John 2:13–14). Was merchandising occurring in the Holy Temple or on the Temple Mount?

A complex of courtyards on the Temple Mount formed a thriving marketplace that served the needs of religious pilgrims. Market stalls were crowded with sacrificial doves, pigeons, oxen, and lambs to be sold to the highest bidder. The ceremonial fitness of these products was extolled by merchants who charged an exorbitant price to unsuspecting pilgrims.

Near the merchants sat money-changers. These men were eager to make a profit by trading foreign coins—the legal tender used by Jews for temporal purposes—for a half shekel, the only monetary denomination accepted by priests as a temple offering.

"From the unrighteousness of the traffic carried on in these Bazaars, and the greed of their owners, the 'Temple-market' was at that time most unpopular. . . . It is no wonder that, in the figurative language of the Talmud, the Temple is represented as crying

Looking at modern-day Jerusalem from the Mount of Olives

out against them: 'Go hence, ye sons of Eli, ye defile the Temple of Jehovah!'"

Moneychangers and merchants had market stalls near the temple in an outer court called the Court of the Gentiles and at temple porticoes and colonnades. All people were welcomed into the Court of the Gentiles; however, foreigners were forbidden entrance into the inner precincts of the temple complex. Posted on the balustrade—a stone railing about four and a half feet high that surrounded the inner temple precinct—was an inscription in Greek and Latin that read, "No foreigner may enter within the balustrade and enclosure around the Temple area. Anyone caught doing so will bear the responsibility for his own ensuing death."[118]

Why didn't the Roman rulers or Jewish leaders stop Jesus from driving the moneychangers from the Temple Mount?

Jesus improvised a whip of small cords and lashed out against those who were merchandising and profiteering on the Temple Mount. He drove both animals and merchants from the Court of the Gentiles and overturned the tables of the moneychangers (see John 2:14–17). Even though His actions disrupted business and led to a loss of merchandise, there is no record of His being stopped, arrested, or criticized by Roman rulers or Jewish leaders. Only a question of credentials was asked (see Ps. 69:9).

Why? There was negative opinion of merchandising practices on the Temple Mount. It is probable that these practices had evoked such a loud public outcry that the actions of Jesus appealed to popular Jewish sentiment.[119]

Christ driving out the moneychangers from the temple

Christ with Nicodemus

The Talmud mentioned a man named Niqdimon, whose real name was Bunai, the son of Giron. This man was a rich and distinguished Jew before becoming a disciple of Jesus. The story of his life is told through his daughter's frustration at having enjoyed an abundance of wealth and being reduced to a life of abject poverty due to her father's Christianity.

Christian tradition contends that the somewhat legendary Niqdimon was not the Nicodemus mentioned in the Gospels. The Nicodemus spoken of in the Gospels was a seeker of truth.[120]

Nicodemus came to Jesus to ask about the nature of God. The questions of Nicodemus and the answers of Jesus constitute "one of our most instructive and precious scriptures relating to the absolute necessity of unreserved compliance with the laws and ordinances of the gospel, as the means indispensable to salvation."[121]

When Jesus heard that John the Baptist was cast into prison, He sent angels to comfort John. In which Herodian prison was John held captive?

Gospel writers do not name a specific prison. According to the

John the Baptist preaching

Jewish historian Josephus, John was a prisoner in the dungeons of Machaerus, one of the strongest citadels in Palestine. In his text *Antiquities,* Josephus penned, "John was sent in chains to the fortress of Machaerus . . . and there put to death."

Machaerus, located on the mountain slope east of the Dead Sea, was built by the Hasmonean king, Alexander Jannaeus. The citadel was enlarged and strengthened by Herod the Great. Herod used the fortress, as did his son Herod Antipas, as a summer residence.[122]

Why did Herod Antipas imprison John the Baptist?

The imprisonment of John stemmed from his denunciation of the unlawful marriage of Herod Antipas to Herodias (see Matt. 14:3–12). Circumstances leading to the unfortunate union began when Herod Antipas was residing in Rome with his half-brother Philip. In Rome, Herod Antipas became romantically involved with Philip's wife, Herodias—who was not only his sister-in-law, but his niece through Aristobulus, Herod's half-brother.

When Antipas proposed marriage to Herodias, she consented on condition that he reject his wife, the Nabataean queen and daughter of Aretas, King of Arabia. Antipas agreed. Upon learning of her husband's rejection, the Nabataean queen fled to the Perean fortress of Machaerus near the Nabataean frontier, and from there to her father. Five years later, her father defeated Antipas in battle.

Although never divorced from the Nabataean queen, Antipas married Herodias, the lawful wife of Philip. Under Jewish law, their marriage was condemned as adulterous and incestuous (see Lev. 20:21). The union was decried by John the Baptist, who said, "It is not lawful for thee to have her" (Matt. 14:4). For his denunciation of this marital relationship, John was imprisoned. The Joseph Smith Translation of Matt. 4:11 reads, "And now Jesus knew that John was cast into prison, and he sent angels, and, behold, they came and ministered unto him."[123]

Did the disciples of John the Baptist eventually become disciples of Jesus?

Some of the followers of John the Baptist refused to transfer their allegiance to Jesus. They clung tenaciously to the memory of their beloved prophet. They argued that it was John who had baptized Jesus—and, as a result, John was the greater, for he was the forerunner. They spread his message beyond the borders of Judea to Ephesus, where twenty-five years after the martyrdom of John, a congregation boasted of having his baptism. A century later, his followers were found in Alexandria, Egypt, and southern Europe.[124]

Return to Galilee

Jesus did not remain long in Jerusalem. When the Passover festivities ended, He journeyed toward Galilee. As He did so, He passed through Samaria.

At the time of Jesus, why did the Jews deride the Samaritans?

Jews insisted that the Samaritans were a people of mixed blood, meaning they polluted themselves by mingling the blood of Israel with that of Assyrians and other nationalities through marriage. Jews believed Samaritans to be "genealogical half-breeds and historical enemies." Samaritans disagreed. They claimed that they were a pure lineal descent from Abraham, Isaac, and Jacob. As children of the Abrahamic covenant, they were the chosen seed and inheritors of the promised blessings of Jehovah. Jews denounced this heretical belief and summarily dismissed the Samaritans as having a pagan religion that rejected the prophets and the psalms. Jewish leaders declared that the Samaritans revered their own version of the Pentateuch as law, but failed to accept other Hebraic writings.

Bitter hatred between the Jews and Samaritans resulted. Hatred stemmed not only from these misconceptions, but from centuries of conflict that began when the Jews returned from Babylonian captivity and began to build the temple and the walls of Jerusalem. Samaritans offered to assist the returning Jews in their building endeavors. Their offer was rejected. Believing themselves insulted, Samaritans hindered the building process.

Rebuilding of the temple after Babylonian captivity

By the time of Jesus, pious Jews had concluded that the Samaritans were more unclean than gentiles and heathens. They classified Samaritans with heretics and the Prince of Demons.

Rabbis placed legal restrictions on interactions with Samaritans. The restrictions included: 1) the testimony of a Samaritan was not acceptable before a Jewish tribunal; 2) it was an offense for a Jew to eat food prepared by a Samaritan; and 3) produce touched by a Samaritan was unclean and unfit for Jews to eat. These restrictions and other antagonisms led the Samaritans to befriend the Herods and Rome instead of their Jewish neighbors. The Gospel writer John recorded, "Say we not well that thou art a Samaritan, and hast a devil?" (John 8:48).[125]

Did the Samaritans worship with the Jews on the Temple Mount in Jerusalem?

Samaritans did not believe that Mount Moriah was the correct temple mount. They believed that Mount Gerizim was the temple mount of blessings. Their traditions also purported that Mount Gerizim had not been covered by the great flood in the days of Noah (see Ezek. 22:24). To the Samaritans, Gerizim was a holy place, the site where Abraham was willing to sacrifice Isaac and the site where the remains of altars built by Adam and Noah stood.

In 400 BC a Samaritan temple was built atop Gerizim by the priest Manasseh. There Samaritans sacrificed sheep and enjoyed feasting during the Passover festivities. In 130 BC John Hyrcanus destroyed the Samaritan temple.[126]

The Gospel writer John records that Jesus, "being wearied with his journey," stopped at Jacob's well (John 4:6). What is the significance of Jacob's well?

Belief in holy wells was common in antiquity and dates to the Babylonian period. Jews, Samaritans, Moslems, and Christians still associate Jacob's well with the patriarch Jacob. They view the well as holy even though there is no mention of Jacob digging a well in the Old Testament.

Traditionally, the well was used by Jacob and his children. The traditional well is located forty miles north of Jerusalem in the city of Shechem on land referred to as "Jacob's parcel of ground."

Jacob's Well, ca. 1880

Christ with the woman at the well

During the days of Jesus, the rough masonry well was used by both Jew and Samaritan. It was at this well that Jesus openly declared to a Samaritan woman His true identity.[127]

> Jesus said to the woman of Samaria, "Give me to drink" (John 4:7). Was it customary for a Jewish man to speak to a Samaritan woman in a public setting?

The answer depends on the social status of the Jewish man. For example, it was improper for a rabbi to speak to any woman in a public place. In fact, social norms dictated that most women were not to be seen in public places. Then there is the issue of the woman being a Samaritan, an outcast from Jewish society, whose moral integrity was questioned. First-century Jewish philosopher Philo wrote, "A woman, then, should not be a busy body meddling with matters outside her household concerns, but should seek a life of seclusion. She should not show herself off like a vagrant in the streets before the eyes of other men, except when she has to go to the temple."

Since Jesus had attracted disciples who viewed Him as a master teacher, His speaking to the woman at the well was not in accord with His elevated social status. Then there is the matter of her status: To be seen speaking to a woman of Samaria could cast a permanent shadow on Jesus' reputation among His disciples. The disciples seemed to understand the neglected custom presented by the situation at the well. When they saw Jesus, the disciples "marvelled that he talked with the woman" (John 4:27). However, they did not rebuke Him or interrupt His conversation.

Why? The answer may be that they had overheard His request, "Give me to drink" (John 4:7). Oriental hospitality dictated that "a request for water was one that should never be denied if possible to grant."[128]

When Jesus returned to Galilee, He healed the sick. What medical options did the sick have for alleviating afflictions at that time?

Five limited medical practices were available to the Jews at the time of Jesus—folk medicine, cultic healing, a physician, a magician, and a miracle worker.

Folk medicine consisted of traditional remedies passed from one generation to another. Cultic healing was associated with specific locations believed to have healing properties, such as the twin

Christ at the pools of Bethesda

pools of Bethesda. Physicians were available to Jews willing to be treated by a Greek or Roman surgeon. Greek physicians were more respected than their Roman counterparts. The wizardry of magicians was frowned on by pious Jews but was a medical option. Magicians entreated the spirit world with incantations and secret herbs, hoping to cast out the demons that caused the affliction. The final medical option was a miracle worker. For those healed by Jesus, He was a miracle worker.[129]

When Jesus "came to Nazareth, where he had been brought up: and, as his custom was, he went into the synagogue on the sabbath day" (Luke 4:16). What did the Sabbath day mean to the Jews at the time of Jesus?

Sabbath, derived from the Hebrew word *shabbath,* means to "break off," "to desist," and "to rest." On this holy day, devout Jews remembered and observed the goodness of God. Because of its holy nature, rabbis symbolically spoke of the Sabbath as a bride. "All the days of the week," the rabbis claimed, "has God

paired, except the Sabbath, which is alone, that it may be wedded to Israel." Jews welcomed the Sabbath as a groom greets with delight his bride and as a nation rejoices at the advent of its king.[130]

Did the Jews trace their remembrance of the Sabbath day to the creation of the earth?

Ancient Israelites were commanded to remember two themes on the Sabbath day. The first was to remember and commemorate the divine process of creation: "For in six days the Lord made heaven and earth, the sea, and all that in them is, and rested the seventh day: wherefore the Lord blessed the sabbath day, and hallowed it" (Ex. 20:11). On the Sabbath, Jehovah invited the children of Israel to be His partner in the renewal process of creation (see Ex. 20:11, 31:17; Gen. 2:3). "Last in creation, first in intention," the rabbis said. "The Sabbath is not for the sake of the weekdays; the weekdays are for the sake of Sabbath." Israelites accepted the divine invitation by taming and molding nature six days a week—but on the Sabbath they, like the Great Creator, hallowed the day by resting from

Christ creating the world

their earthly labors. "During the six weekdays of productive work, people impose their will upon nature. The Sabbath is to be a time when people refrain from creating changes in nature, and instead participate in the harmony of nature," wrote Jewish scholar Raphael Jospe. Resting from temporal cares gave place for contemplation of Sabbath concepts—perfection, covenant, and completeness.

Second, the children of Israel were commanded on the Sabbath to remember the Israelite redemption from Egyptian bondage (see Deut. 5:15). Freedom from bondage, although a secondary remembrance, is the most repetitive theme in the Hebrew Bible, being mentioned 111 times.[131]

Were there formal aspects of the Sabbath ritual?

Formal aspects of the Sabbath ritual began at sunset on Friday. As a designated hour to begin Sabbath was not appointed, its announcement in Jerusalem came when a priest atop a temple tower blew a ram's horn or trumpet. In other Palestinian localities, Sabbath was announced when a sexton atop a synagogue roof blew six blasts with a horn.

The first blast signaled those laboring in the fields to cease work. Those working in town waited until the second blast to close their shops. The third blast announced the time to kindle Sabbath lights and take pots from the stoves to preserve their warmth. After candles were lit and fires extinguished, three successive blasts heralded the beginning of the Sabbath day.

On the Sabbath fine clothes were worn, delicious meals were eaten, the Torah was studied, and lectures on religious topics were attended. It was a day for praising God. Fasting and mourning were forbidden on the Sabbath, as were claims of fatigue and illness. This was a day of peace and joy, not a day for disharmony or petition. As the day waned and three stars were seen in the sky, the mother of a Jewish household lit a candle and announced, "A good week, a full week, a fortunate week, on us and on all of Israel. Amen." Songs were sung and the Sabbath ended.[132]

What rabbinic rules governed Sabbath during the days of Jesus?

Pharisaic laws regulating Sabbath observance were meticulously divided into thirty-nine categories, with additional subcategories. Strict guidelines or hedges to protect the sanctity of the Sabbath controlled sowing, plowing, reading, binding sheaves, threshing, winnowing, sifting, grading, sifting in a sieve, kneading, baking, shearing the wool, washing the wool, beating the wool, dyeing

The Torah is studied on the Sabbath

the wool, spinning, putting the wool on the weavers beam, weaving two threads, separating two threads, making a knot, undoing a knot, sewing two stitches, and so on.

An example of the strict guidelines is found in the tying and untying of knots. "The camel-driver's knot and the sailor's were unlawful, and it was equally illegal to tie or to loose them. A knot which could be untied with one hand might be undone. A shoe or sandal, a woman's cup, a wine or oil-skin, or a flesh-pot might be tied. A pitcher at a spring might be tied to the body-sash, but not with a cord."[133]

What blessings were promised the Jews for keeping the Sabbath day holy?

Ancient Israelites who remembered and observed the Sabbath day received God's favor. Jehovah sent rain in due season, caused the land to yield an increase, helped His chosen people conquer enemies, brought peace to the distraught, and multiplied a righteous posterity (see Lev. 26:4, 7–9). Jehovah promised, "And I will walk among you, and will be your God, and ye shall be my people. . . . [I will] feed thee with the heritage of Jacob thy father" (Lev. 26:12; Isa. 58:14).[134]

On a Sabbath day in Nazareth, Jesus entered the synagogue. Was the synagogue easy to identify in each Jewish community?

Anciently, a synagogue meant a "group of people." In the days of Jesus, a synagogue was the community building in which Jews assembled and worshiped. Synagogues were built in prominent places in the communities—high ground, street corners, near entrances of towns, and in village squares (see Isa. 2:2; Prov. 1:21). If houses in the community were constructed on higher ground than the synagogue, a tall pole was attached to the roof of the synagogue. Later Jews superstitiously believed that if houses were higher than places of worship, the community was in danger of being destroyed by the wrath of God.

Traditionally, synagogues faced toward Jerusalem and had twelve windows, one for each of the twelve tribes of Israel. Windows conveyed to the worshipers gateways to heaven and symbolically

A modern synagogue in Alexandria

revealed various ways for the tribes of Israel to reach Jehovah.

The size of the structure depended on the number of Jewish males in the community. Most synagogues were small in comparison to the large synagogue built in Alexandria, Egypt, which was so massive that the congregation seated in the rear could not hear the benediction. A waving flag from the front platform alerted those in the back of the congregation to say, "Amen."135

What did the inside of a synagogue look like?

The interior of the synagogue was divided between the Most Holy and the Holy area, much like the plan for Solomon's Temple and the ancient tabernacle of Moses. In the Most Holy area was an ark that held the books of Moses and a raised platform with a reading desk that faced the ark. There was also an eight-branched lamp and chief seats (see Matt. 23:6).

The Holy area had a separate access for men and women. A partition—often a grate—ensured that men and women did not mingle during the worship service. The same strict rules of "decorum, analogous to those enforced in the Temple, were enjoined on those who attended the synagogue. Decency and cleanliness in dress, quietness and reverence in demeanour, are prescribed with almost wearisome details and distinctions."[136]

Was the leading rabbi responsible for the synagogue in each community?

The rabbi was responsible for the synagogue in small villages. In larger communities, a college or council of elders had responsibility for the structure (see John 9:22; 12:42; 16:2).[137]

Were synagogues only used for Sabbath worship?

Although Jews worshiped in synagogues on the Sabbath, the buildings were used on weekdays as centers for education, community affairs, public forums, and judicial proceedings. Historic evidence suggests that synagogues in small villages were also used as public dining halls and inns.[138]

Was there a strict order to worship services in the synagogues?

A typical synagogue service began with two prayers and the recitation of the Shema. Three passages from the Pentateuch were then read and another prayer offered before eighteen eulogies or benedictions were given, followed by additional prayers.

After these formalities, the rabbi or chief of the synagogue lifted the scroll of the Books of Moses from the ark. He then invited seven members of the congregation to read scriptural passages from the scroll at a reading desk located in front of the congregation. The first invited to read was a descendant of Aaron, the second a descendant of Levi, and the remaining five readers descendants of other sons of the House of Israel. Each reading was preceded and followed by a brief benediction.

Next, extracts from the prophetic books were read—"Joshua, Judges, Samuel, Kings, Isaiah, Jeremiah, Ezekiel, or the twelve minor prophets" (see Luke 24:27, 44).[139]

Was it a common practice to invite strangers to read in the synagogue?

When "some great Rabbi, or famed preacher, or else a distinguished stranger, is known to be in the town," it was customary to invite him to read in the synagogue. This courtesy or recognition was granted because the "institution of preaching [was] a way of life among the Jews." Popular preachers were acclaimed and given freedom to teach "parables, stories, allegories, witticisms, strange and foreign words, absurd legends, in short, anything that might startle an audience."[140]

Did Jews in the synagogues read the scriptural passage in Hebrew, Aramaic, or Greek?

Scrolls in the synagogue were written and read in ancient Hebrew. Hebrew, the language of Canaan, is read from right to left and has twenty-two consonants. Written Hebrew is a comparatively pure Semitic language. During the days of Jesus, it was not polluted by the adoption of the Aramaean dialect spoken outside the synagogue.[141]

Why is there a difference between Jesus' reading of the Isaiah passages and the same passages written in the Hebrew Bible?

When Jesus read from the scroll of Isaiah, probably given him by the chazzan or attendant of the synagogue, He targumed the verses (see Isa. 61:1–2). To targum means "to use the oral translations" or "to paraphrase written Hebrew." As Jesus targumed Isaiah's writings, He expanded and interpreted the scriptural passages.

This was not unusual, because each reader was expected to expound upon the scripture as he read. When the reading ended, those seated in the chief seats questioned, criticized, and gave further explanations of the scriptural passages that were read. If the reader was allowed to respond to the criticisms, he did so. By the third century, readers concluded their remarks by saying, "Thou art Jehovah, our God, and the God of our fathers, our King, and the King of our fathers, our Saviour, and the Saviour of our fathers, our Creator, the Rock of our Salvation, our Help and our Deliverer. Thy name is from

Jesus reading in the synagogue

everlasting, and there is no God beside Thee. Blessed art Thou, Jehovah, Who quickenest the dead!"[142]

Was it an affront to the rabbi when Jesus sat down after reading the Isaiah passages?

No. Sitting was the appropriate position for readers when commenting, explaining, or preaching about the scriptural passages read.[143]

"All they in the synagogue, when they heard [the sayings of Jesus], "were filled with wrath" (Luke 4:28). How did Jesus escape their wrath?

Nazarenes were angry with Jesus for claiming to be the Messiah. It is assumed that they intended to kill Him in what was known as a "rebel's beating." The beating did not involve hitting or clubbing the victim, but crowding the victim over a cliff at least twice a man's height.

By simply crowding Jesus to fall from the cliff, no one person in the angry Nazarene mob could be held accountable for the deadly consequence. If Jesus were pushed over the cliff by a single individual, accountability for death under the Mosaic law was mandatory.

According to Jewish/Christian scholar Alfred Edersheim, the notion of a rebel's beating "explains how, when [Jesus] turned sharply round to the right, and passed through the crowd, they did not follow Him," and thus Jesus escaped their murderous designs (see Luke 4:29–30). Scholars D. Kelly Ogden and Andrew Skinner claim, "Jesus had the ability to disappear, to pass unnoticed through a crowd of people."[144]

Did Jesus later return to Nazareth?

According to the Gospel writers, Jesus never returned to the village of His childhood after reading in the local synagogue. When He left Nazareth, He went to Capernaum and resided on the northern shore of Galilee for a time. Yet it was said, "Foxes have holes, and birds of the air have nests; but the Son of man hath not where to lay his head" (Luke 9:58).[145]

> Jesus left Nazareth and went to Capernaum "and straightway on the sabbath day he entered into the synagogue, and taught" (Mark 1:21). Was there more than one synagogue in the busy fishing community of Capernaum?

There was only one synagogue in Capernaum during the days of Jesus. Four future Apostles—Peter, Andrew, James, and John—and their families worshiped in that synagogue. The uncovered basalt foundation of the synagogue dates to the time of Jesus. A portion of the stone synagogue, dating to the fourth century, was unearthed by archaeologists. "Ornamentation over the lintel, consisting of a pot of manna [carved] between representations of Aaron's rod" was the most exciting discovery during the excavation process.[146]

> At the synagogue in Capernaum, a man with "an unclean spirit" cried out, "Let us alone; what have we to do with thee thou Jesus of Nazareth?" (Mark 1:23–24). Was the man possessed by a demon?

Anciently, when Jews lost control of their "body or will, or in both, by evil forces," they were said to be possessed by an unclean spirit or a demon. The word *demon* anciently referred to a minor god or a supernatural force. But by the time of Jesus, demon referred to "spiritual beings at enmity with God who have power to afflict man with disease and to enter and possess him bringing spiritual pollution as well."147

> **Jesus rebuked the man with the unclean spirit, saying, "Hold thy peace, and come out of him" (Luke 4:35). Why didn't Jesus want the demonic man to proclaim His divinity?**

Jesus refused to permit anyone possessed with an unclean spirit or demon to proclaim His divinity. He knew that such a proclamation from one influenced by Satan was not a declaration of converting testimony. Before this event, "The people were impressed with Jesus' teaching; now they were impressed with his miraculous power—even spirits from the other realm obey him. His fame went before him."148

Christ and the man with an unclean spirit

Boat on the Sea of Galilee

As Jesus walked along the seashore of Galilee, He "saw two brethren, Simon called Peter, and Andrew his brother, casting a net into the sea" (Matt. 4:18). Can it be assumed that He saw these fishermen in the daylight hours?

Fishing on Galilee is always better at night. Fish swim deep in the sea during the day, but at night, the fish (predominately carp, sardine, mullet, catfish, and comb fish) swim near the surface of the water, making them an easy catch for fishermen.

It can be assumed that Jesus saw the two brothers fishing in the evening unless they were using a dragnet designed for scooping fish that were swimming near the bottom of the sea. If the brothers were using a dragnet, Jesus saw them fishing during the daylight hours. Either way, He chose men while they were working. The chosen men left their nets and followed Him.[149]

What fishing methods were used on the Sea of Galilee?

There were three main types of fishing methods used on the sea to catch freshwater fish. The first was angling, meaning "casting an hook" (Matt. 17:27). The second was casting a small circular net, eighteen to twenty-five feet in diameter, into the sea from the shore or shallow water and manually hauling in the catch. The third process involved a large dragnet called a seine. The dragnet, a thousand feet long and twelve feet high, formed a vertical wall in the sea. The net, weighted with lead at the bottom and cork floats at the top, spread over a large area and was dragged in by men standing on boats (see Luke 5:4; John 21:6). Once the net produced its catch, the sorting process began.

Whatever the process, unwanted fish—meaning "any fish that didn't have scales or was forbidden to eat" under the Mosaic law—were tossed back into the sea.[150]

Jesus "saw two other brethren, James the son of Zebedee, and John his brother, in a ship with Zebedee their father" (Matt. 4:21). What is known about the fishing partnership of Zebedee and his sons?

Zebedee and his sons were partners with Simon Peter in a fishing business on the Sea of Galilee. Because he had hired servants, we know Zebedee was not a poor fisherman. For him to be laboring beside his sons was in keeping with existing Jewish customs (see Mark 1:20).[151]

Why are the sons of Zebedee referred to as "Sons of Thunder" (Mark 3:17)?

Thunder to the Jewish people was a "symbol of divine power and vengeance" (see Ps. 29:3). The title *Sons of Thunder* or *Boanerges* was given to the Apostles James and John by Jesus. The title, an appropriate use of Jewish symbolism, refers to the zealous desire of these two men "to destroy Samaritan villagers who had refused hospitality" to Jesus (see Luke 9:52–56).[152]

Near the sea, multitudes gathered to listen to Jesus. Among them was a man afflicted with leprosy. Was leprosy a term used to describe all skin diseases?

Although Luke uses the Greek word *lepra,* a technical term for

Christ calling Peter and Andrew

psoriasis, biblical usage did not restrict leprosy to the technical. It broadened the definition to encompass all skin diseases that had common symptoms. The universal symptom of leprosy was a deterioration of the humors in the body that caused limbs to decay and fall off. When an individual reached what was termed full leprosy, the disease affected the entire body and death resulted.

Those afflicted with mild or full leprosy lived in dismantled houses or tombs located east of the villages and cities in Palestine. Lepers were compelled, as if in mourning, to wear rent garments and emblems of death. Lepers were shunned for their physical deformity and what was perceived as uncleanliness brought on by spoken sins. Jews believed that leprosy destroyed the physical body and corrupted the spirit.

Today, the word *leprosy* no longer describes a variety of skin conditions. It is an infection "characterized by the appearance of nodules in the eyebrows, the cheeks, the nose, and the lobes of the ears, also in the hands and feet, where the disease eats into the joints, causing the falling off of fingers and toes. If nodules do not appear, their place is taken by spots of blanched or discolored skin (muscular leprosy)." In advanced stages of the dreaded disease, "nails loosen and drop off, the gums are absorbed, and the teeth decay and fall out; the breath is a stench, the nose decays; fingers, hands, feet, may be lost, or the eyes eaten out."[153]

Why was it important that the cleansed leper present himself before a temple priest?

Before a leper could be pronounced clean and invited back into Jewish society, the leper needed to perform specific rituals in the Court of the Gentiles on the Temple Mount. In the court, the leper reported to a temple priest and offered an asham offering—a fine for "having been unable to serve God because of physical impurity." The offering included "two birds alive and clean, and cedar wood, and scarlet, and hyssop" (Lev. 14:4).

The priest then monitored the shaving of the leper and examined the afflicted for signs of continuing leprosy. If leprosy was not found on the body, the cured leper was quarantined for seven days and then re-examined. If pronounced clean a second time, clothes of the cured leper were washed, required temple sacrifice was offered, and blood of the offering was sprinkled on the altar (see Lev. 14:1–32). The leper was then sprinkled with water from a pure flowing spring and welcomed back into Jewish society. In the case of the healed leper, he "went out, and began to publish it much, and to blaze abroad the matter" (Mark 1:45).[154]

Christ teaching on the Sea of Galilee

Jesus left the multitude and went "into a mountain, and calleth unto him whom he would" (Mark 3:13). From His disciples, He ordained twelve men to be Apostles. Is an Apostle the same as a disciple?

The Greek word *apostle* means "being sent from God" and "empowered and commissioned by God." The word *disciple* means only "to follow" or "to go with."

The process of choosing Apostles differs from the self-appointed choosing of a disciple. Jewish tradition encouraged bright, aspiring young men to choose a teacher and become the teacher's disciple.

Contrary to tradition, the master teacher Jesus chose Twelve Apostles from among His disciples.

Seven of the twelve were mentioned in the Gospels before their call to the Apostleship—Andrew, John, Simon Peter, Philip, Nathanael, James, and Matthew Levi.[155]

Why is there a discrepancy between the names and ordered seniority of the Twelve Apostles?

The Apostles are listed as a group four times in the Gospels—once each by Matthew and Mark, and twice by Luke. Each listing has a different order of seniority,

Christ sends forth the Twelve

but each records Simon Peter as the first Apostle and Judas Iscariot as the last.

Gospel writers also differ in name variations for the Apostles. For example, Judas is called Lebbeus Thaddeus by Matthew; Thaddeus by Mark; and Judas, the brother of James, by Luke.

The writers place the Twelve in three groups of four. The groupings do not designate native origin, because eleven of the twelve were from Galilee and only one—Judas Iscariot—was from Judea. The groupings do indicate a type of seniority. The leader of each grouping is always mentioned first—Peter, Philip, and James of Alphaeus.[156]

> **Jesus instructed the Twelve that "when ye come into an house, salute it. And if the house be worthy, let your peace come upon it" (Matt. 10:12–13). What does it mean to salute a house? Is dusting of feet the opposite of saluting a house?**

To salute a house was to say to the occupants, "Peace be to this house." The dusting of feet was the opposite of saluting a house. The saying *dusting of feet* is attributed to rabbis, who taught that

the land of Judea was the only holy ground on earth. To them, land outside of Judea was heathen, defiled, and polluted. The smallest dust particle from such a land could defile a Jew. Rabbis further taught that the heathen land, with its dust, was like a tomb shrouded in darkness and death. If the dust of a heathen or idolater was brought into Judea, rabbis claimed it did not mix with the dust of the Holy Land. It remained in its unclean, defiled state.

Jesus told the Twelve to confine their ministry to the borders of Judea. If the Judeans rejected their message, the Twelve were to leave them in the same manner the Jews for generations had left heathen lands—shaking dust off their feet. This instruction illustrates that the Jews would be viewed no better than heathens if they rejected the gospel. Their rejection would be comparable to the lowest physical cities in the world, Sodom and Gomorrah.[157]

> **Was the teaching of Jesus to be "wise as serpents, and harmless as doves" a common Jewish saying (Matt. 10:16)?**

His teaching was similar to the Jewish saying, "The holy and blessed God said to the Israelites, Towards Me the Israelites are incorrupt like the doves, but towards the Gentiles they are as cunning as serpents." The dove represented harmless, while the serpent symbolized good and evil (see JST Matt. 10:14; 2 Cor. 11:3). The followers of Jesus are to be wise as serpents but harmless as doves.[158]

> **Jesus warned His disciples about being scourged in synagogues. This warning appears unusual, for synagogues were known as places of worship. Were synagogues also used as places of judgment and punishment?**

In addition to being a community center and a place of worship, synagogues were also used as a court of justice. During a court session, Jewish elders judged religious and secular cases to determine the guilt or innocence of a defendant. Scourging or flogging with a leather whip embedded with sharp objects like metal, bone, and pottery was a punishment pronounced by the court. If the court determined that the guilty party warranted scourging, punishment was administered inside

the synagogue. Scourging was often accompanied by the singing of a psalm.[159]

> **Why did Jesus compare the purchase of sparrows to individual worth?**

Jews enjoyed eating sparrows and could purchase two sparrows in the marketplace for a Greek assarion, a coin still circulating at the time of Jesus. The English translation of assarion is "farthing," which was one-fifteenth of a Roman denarius (a laborer's daily wage). Jesus taught that not even one sparrow is sold at the marketplace without God knowing. Jesus told His disciples, "Ye are of more value than many sparrows" (Luke 12:7).[160]

> **Was the Sermon on the Mount a series of speeches?**

The sermon was not a series of comments or speeches made

White-crowned sparrow

at various locations and combined by Matthew to appear as one speech. The sermon is composed of selected sayings of Jesus following the ordination of the Twelve Apostles. African Bishop St. Augustine believed that the Sermon on the Mount was "the perfect rule or pattern of Christian life."[161]

Why is the Sermon on the Mount referred to as "the Beatitudes"?

The word *beatitude* means "to make happy," "to attain the blessings of heaven," and "to be fortunate." The ten beatitudes in the Sermon on the Mount outline the pathway to eternal happiness. Beatitudes are the characteristics and experiences enjoyed by the exalted.[162]

What is meant by the saying, "The meek shall inherit the earth" (see Matt. 5:5)?

The time period in which Jesus lived cannot be taken out of His teachings. It was customary in Palestine and in other eastern provinces to give land—what the beatitude called "earth"—to the meek. For example, when a Jew-

ish man died without naming a male heir, his property was given to the meritorious meek. This does not mean that it was given to the man who was the most courteous, kind, gentle, or considerate. It was given to the man who had "poise under pressure and patience in the face of provocation." It was given to the man who had self-control (meaning meritorious meekness), for such a man could be trusted with the things of the earth and will one day inherit a celestial earth.[163]

Jesus told His Apostles, "Ye are the salt of the earth" (Matt. 5:13). Were the Apostles familiar with the saving qualities of salt?

Salt was mined at Mount Sedom, a literal salt mountain located on the southern end of the Dead Sea. It was transported from Sedom to towns and villages throughout Palestine. Since salt was plentiful, Jews knew of its saving properties and the command, "Every oblation of thy meat offering shalt thou season with salt" (Lev. 2:13). They knew that "salt does not lose its savor with age," only by contamination with other ingredients. They

Sermon on the Mount

may also have known that among their Eastern neighbors, salt was a sacred token of friendship. When Easterners ate salt together, they pledged to preserve each other's life. Salt was also used by temple priests. Priests sprinkled salt that had lost its savor on stones in the temple courts to reduce the chances of falling on slippery rocks. The old adage, "Salt that has lost its saltiness is trodden under foot of men," was attributed to priests on the Temple Mount.

The salt metaphor was a warning to the Twelve Apostles not to contaminate the word of God with traditions, pagan beliefs, or philosophies of the world. The metaphor was a call to purification and an admonition to become the preserving power of the covenants between God and Israel. As the salt seasoned the meat offering, the Twelve were to "season the world and preserve" the truth.[164]

Was Jesus speaking of Jerusalem when He said, "A city that is set on a hill cannot be hid" (Matt. 5:14)?

If He were referring to a specific city, it was Safed, the highest community in Palestine. Safed was 2,790 feet above sea level, about 300 feet higher than Jerusalem. It could easily be seen at night. If He were referring to His disciples, it was an admonition to be a light for others.[165]

Could a lit candle flicker if placed under a bushel?

A bushel was a common method of measuring seven and a half dry quarts, or one peck. The term bushel in Greek is *modios,* meaning "pan" or "vessel" that holds the requisite number of quarts. Such an instrument would immediately smother the flame of a candle. The metaphor encouraged the Twelve Apostles to share the gospel with others and bless their lives, that they might also glorify God.[166]

What is the meaning of the jot and tittle metaphor: "Till heaven and earth pass, one jot or one tittle shall in no wise pass from the law, till all be fulfilled" (Matt. 5:18)?

A jot or *yod* is the smallest letter in the Hebrew alphabet.

A bushel

A tittle is a tiny literary mark or stroke that distinguishes similar letters from each other. It is also a "decorative flourish that the calligrapher adds to a letter of a word in the Hebrew Bible." In modern English, a jot and tittle are equivalent to dotting an "i" and crossing a "t." The metaphor assures the Twelve Apostles that every word spoken by the ancient prophets will be fulfilled, even the smallest portion of the law, for God is the same yesterday, today, and forever, and will not vary a jot or a tittle (see Matt. 5:18).[167]

What did Jesus mean when He said, "Whosoever shall say to his brother, Raca"? Was he referring to a fool, who "shall be in danger of hell fire" (Matt. 5:22)?

The Aramaic term *raca* or *reyk* means "empty-headed" or "worthless." Angry Easterners often exclaimed, "Raka arek na bapek," meaning, "I will spit in your face" (see Prov. 29:22). Raca in this scriptural context condemns profane and vulgar expressions like "raka arek na bapek" that convey negative impressions of another. Such speaking was forbidden by God.

The word *fool* refers to a wicked and godless man—a rebel.

When inserted in the scriptural passage, it reads, "Thou rebel, shall be in danger of hell fire." Hell fire was the ancient practice of burning trash and sacrificing children in the Hinnom Valley, which was located on the border of the lands of Judah and Benjamin (see 2 Kgs. 23:10; 2 Chron. 33:6).[168]

Why did Jesus challenge the public nature of almsgiving that had blessed the poor for generations?

Almsgiving was a public process devised to relieve the burdens of the poor throughout Palestine. The freewill offering was daily collected in each Jewish community. Collecting alms was done in three ways: 1) men walked through the Palestinian communities asking for alms from both Jew and Gentile and gathered the proffered alms in baskets; 2) synagogue officials asked for alms at Jewish homes and placed the offerings in what was called the "poor man's chest"; and 3) alms were collected on the Sabbath from those worshiping at the synagogue.

Jesus taught, "When thou doest thine alms, do not sound a trumpet before thee," but no literal trumpets were present in any of the three almsgiving processes (Matt. 6:2). Jesus was counseling the Twelve Apostles to give alms in private so that "thy Father which seeth in secret himself shall reward thee openly" (Matt. 6:4).[169]

Jesus didn't want His followers to pray as the hypocrites, who "pray standing in the synagogues and in the corners of the streets, that they may be seen of men" (Matt. 6:5). Did all Jews pray in a standing position?

Although Christians often kneel in the act of prayer and Moslems prostrate themselves on prayer rugs, Jews in the days of Jesus stood facing Jerusalem with heads covered and eyes cast down while they recited a prayer in Hebrew. They prayed each morning, midday, and afternoon in this manner on street corners, in crowded marketplaces, and in synagogues.

At synagogues, the more devout Jews did not participate in public prayers. They stood and uttered aloud private prayers so that

Almsgiving

others would know of their devotion. Those who indulged in such private prayers in the synagogues were also seen through the week standing for hours in marketplaces and on street corners in the attitude of prayer, facing Jerusalem with head covered and eyes cast down.

Jesus admonished the Twelve Apostles not to pray in this ostentatious, hypocritical manner. He said, "Enter into thy closet," meaning "a place of privacy" or "a place of refuge" (Matt. 6:6). A closet was a small adjoining room or inner chamber attached to a Jewish home. It usually contained supplies and valuables.[170]

Was Jesus reproving repeated requests in prayer when He said, "Use not vain repetitions" (Matt. 6:7)?

Jesus decried the heathen's prayer as vain repetition, meaning the prayer had no value. He did not decry repeated prayers. In fact, in the Garden of Gethsemane, He prayed three times for deliverance.

At the time of Jesus, the heathen doctrine of prayer was that the number of prayers, not the sincerity of those prayers, deter-

mined whether a divine answer would be granted. Jews referred to heathen prayers as mere babbling because of their length and precise repetitions. The extreme length was based on mentioning each god to ensure that the prayer reached the god that would answer. Since each god had his own epithet, the right epithet needed to be stated precisely to ensure a favorable answer.[171]

Why are certain phrases so misunderstood in the Lord's Prayer?

One reason given for the misunderstanding is failure to learn about Jewish practices and customs at the time of Jesus. For example, when Jesus asked for forgiveness of debts, He was not speaking of financial obligations, as most Christians believe (see Matt. 6:12). Although Jews trafficked in letters of credit, *debt* was the Jewish word for *sin.* "Lead us not into temptation" refers to legal entanglements or trials in which the Sanhedrin determined truth (Matt. 6:13). It is not a description of God leading His children to temptation and sin. Amen, often thought by Christians to be a benediction or ending, has more to do with a seal or approval.[172]

> Jesus taught, "Lay not up for yourselves treasures upon earth, where moth and rust doth corrupt, and where thieves break through and steal" (Matt. 6:19). Did Jews place their treasures in the earth?

Costly garments were not buried in the ground. They were hidden in secret vaults within a Jewish house. Apparel was not subjected to the dampness of the earth, but was in jeopardy from tiny moths that infested houses.

Another portion of Jewish wealth was gold and silver coins. Jews buried coins in the earth to protect them from robbers. Too frequently, the location of buried treasure was forgotten. Today, ancient coins are being unearthed by shovels and plows throughout Israel.[173]

> Jesus asked, "Which of you by taking thought can add one cubit unto his stature?" (Matt. 6:27). Is the word cubit correctly used in this verse?

Few people want to literally add a cubit—the equivalent of a foot and a half—to their height. A better translation of the verse reads, "Which of you taking thought can add a span to his age?" This translation moves the reader from cubit and stature to life span and age.[174]

> In Western society dogs are known as man's best friend. Why did Jesus equate dogs with swine when He said, "Give not that which is holy unto the dogs, neither cast ye your pearls before swine, lest they trample them under their feet, and turn again and rend you" (Matt. 7:6)?

Jews detested swine, not dogs. Many adult Jews would only talk of swine as *dabhar acheer,* meaning "another thing," so as not to even speak the word *swine.* Jews were mildly annoyed by the scavenger tendencies of the dog, which they did not regard as man's best friend.[175] In the scriptural passage cited, dogs represent an unworthy recipient of the gospel; swine represent any who would trample the word of God. Jesus wanted His disciples to be cautious with whom they shared the gospel.

Why did Jesus caution His disciples to take their journeys on narrow paths?

When Roman appointees ruled Palestine, bandits and robbers often harassed travelers journeying on broad roads. Although these roads were popular highways for pilgrims and caravans, dangers were present. Broader routes located near springs and wells provided modest comforts, yet were hazardous

Christ teaching

for the wanderer who ventured alone.

Wise travelers chose narrow paths. "The road is safe. Everything will be all right. Even your feet will not strike a stone" was an ancient Eastern farewell expressed to those who ventured on narrow paths. To the Easterner, this meant that taking the narrow path would result in a safe arrival at the destination.

The narrow path, unknown to robbers and murderers, was not easy. The route usually took longer than traveling on broad paths and led travelers over steep climes and rocky terrain. Symbolically, the narrow path leads to heaven while the wide highway leads to destruction. Matthew's passage, "Narrow is the way, which leadeth unto life, and few there be that find it" reads in Aramaic, "Oh how narrow is the road and how few are found on it" (Matt. 7:14).[176]

A centurion said to Jesus, "Lord, my servant lieth at home sick of the palsy, grievously tormented" (Matt. 8:6). Was the centurion an officer of the Roman legion stationed at Capernaum?

Capernaum was located near the Via Maris international route and was home to many Roman soldiers. However, there was neither a large contingency of Roman soldiers nor a legion in the community. (A standard Roman legion consisted of six thousand men. Each legion was divided into sixty groups of about a hundred men under the command of a centurion.)

The centurion who spoke with Jesus built the synagogue at Capernaum (see Luke 7:5). He had responsibility for an infantry unit of anywhere from fifty to a hundred soldiers—and estimated at eighty soldiers—stationed at Capernaum. His soldiers had been recruited from the "Samaritans and Gentiles of Caesarea." They were at the disposal of Herod Antipas.[177]

Did the centurion ask Jesus to heal his servant or his slave?

Slaves and servants in the days of Jesus had no legal recourse to right purposeful wrongs. The Greek philosopher Aristotle described a slave as a living tool. Roman writer Varro equated slaves with cattle, and concluded that the only difference between cattle and slaves was that slaves could speak.

If the centurion were asking for his slave or servant to be healed, he was more enlightened than the Greco-Roman society in which he lived. The centurion may be so credited, because each reference to a centurion in the Gospels is a positive. For example, it was a centurion who acknowledged Jesus on the cross as the Son of God, and it was the centurion Cornelius who became the first recorded gentile convert (see Matt. 27:54; Acts 10).

However, before undue social enlightenment is given this centurion, we need to review possible translations of the Greek word for servant as used in this scriptural passage. One translation is "boy" or "young man." If *boy* were inserted into the Matthew passage, it reads, "My boy lieth at home sick of the palsy, grievously tormented" (Matt. 8:6). Another translation is "son," and still another is "servant." Following the later translation, it can be concluded that the centurion was more enlightened for his time than the Greco-Roman society in which he lived. In reference to this centurion, Jesus said that He had

not seen such "great faith, no, not in Israel" (Matt. 8:10).[178]

Did Jesus join with the funeral procession in "a city called Nain" (Luke 7:11)?

As Jesus entered Nain, a village at the northern end of Mount Moreh in the eastern Jezreel Valley, He saw a funeral procession led by women. Jews held the false belief that it was through a woman that death came into the world, and that each time death took a life, women should lead the procession to the burial site.

The body of the deceased was carried behind the women on a bier or wood frame referred to as an "open coffin." Those carrying the bier were to frequently rotate to give many in the family or village an opportunity to perform a last act of kindness for the deceased. Behind the bearers were a minimum of two flute players and, where money was not an issue, hired mourners.

As the funeral procession advanced to the burial site, all who witnessed the sorrowful scene were expected to join the procession. Therefore, it can be assumed that Jesus participated.

When the assemblage reached the grave site—located on the north, south, or east of a village, but never on the west because of prevailing westerly winds in Palestine—the procession halted. If the deceased had not been raised by Jesus, He would have been buried. Jesus, like Elisha before Him at Shunem on the other side of Mount Moreh, raised the widow's son from the dead (see 1 Kgs. 17:21–22). Those who witnessed the miracle greatly feared (see Luke 7:16).[179]

Does the phrase "come into Peter's house" mean that Jesus lived with Peter in Capernaum (Matt. 8:14)?

Jesus lived periodically in the home of Simon Peter at Capernaum. Houses in the seaside village consisted of a series of rooms built around a courtyard. Houses were made of unhewn stones and bricks plastered with a clay or lime facade and set on a rock foundation. Stone steps outside the dwelling typically led to a flat roof made of sticks and packed dirt.[180]

Christ raising the widow's son

Was it inconvenient for Peter's family to have Jesus reside with them?

We can only guess. Housekeeping in the homes of Galilean fishermen was simple, as was the preparation of evening meals. Galileans dined on wheat and barley bread, beans, and other vegetables. Watered wine was drunk, and meat was served only on Jewish feast days. Bedding consisted of an outer cloak or long garment that was worn during the day. Furniture was sparse and luxuries few.

Knowing something of the simplistic living in Capernaum, an additional guest in the house of Peter does not seem an undue burden for the family.[181]

What was the illness that afflicted Peter's mother-in-law?

A violent fever laid Peter's mother-in-law prostrate (see Luke 4:38). References to the disease in the Talmud are only to a burning fever. Jesus took the mother-in-law by the hand, lifted her up, and restored her to health.[182]

What did Jesus mean when He said, "Let the dead bury their dead" (Matt. 8:22)?

"Suffer me first to go and bury my father" is an Oriental phrase, meaning either "my father is an old man and I must take care of him until his death" or "my father is on the side of the grave," which implies the father may soon die. Although giving a proper burial to a kinsman was important to the Jews, Jesus said to His disciple, "Let the dead bury their dead" (Matt. 8:22). The Aramaic word for dead is *metta,* meaning "town." It is conceivable that Jesus replied, "Let the town bury the dead" or "Let the town take care of your father."[183]

Why has the miracle of calming the storm elicited such great opposition in the scholarly world?

This miracle has been the source of continuous debate among Christian scholars for centuries. Many scholars contend that the miracles of Jesus that involved nature were a greater violation of natural law than the healing miracles. Others disagree. Nevertheless, "even the winds and the sea obey him" (Matt. 8:27).

Calming the storm may have involved more than stopping a heavy rainfall or the easterly wind that causes waves on Galilee to soar seven feet and appear like high seas. The Sea of Galilee is known for its sudden westwardly squalls and shaking, occasionally caused by earthquakes.[184]

After Jesus crossed the sea and entered "the country of the Gergesenes, there met him two men possessed with devils" (Matt. 8:28). Were these men living in a cemetery in Gadara or Gergesa?

After Jesus crossed the Sea of Galilee from the west to the east, He was in the Perean region. There, He met a lunatic coming from a cemetery. (The Gospel of Matthew mentions two lunatics, whereas the Gospels of Mark and Luke mention only one.)

The Joseph Smith Translation reads "man" (JST Matt. 8:29). Matthew placed the incident in Gergesa, and Mark and Luke placed it in Gadara. Ancient Greek manuscripts fail to reach an agreement as to the correct

Calming the storm

place; five manuscripts record the incident in Geresa, eight in Gergesa, and seven in Gadara.

Modern scholars disqualify Geresa due to location—it was thirty miles from the Sea of Galilee in the hill country of Gilead. They reason that swine would not stampede that distance (see Mark 5:13). With that same reasoning, they dismiss Gadara. The remaining choice is Gergesa, which is less than a mile from the eastern shore of Galilee. Today excavation and restoration of the site is ongoing.[185]

> When Jesus commanded the devils to "Come out of the man, thou unclean spirit," they came out and "went into the herd of swine" (Mark 5:8; Matt. 8:32). Were the swine owned by Jews, gentiles, or the Roman legion stationed in the area?

The swine, estimated at two thousand, were probably not owned by Jews. If orthodox Jews claimed ownership of the swine, they were operating an illegal trade, because the Mosaic law forbade owning swine in Judean lands. It should be noted that apostate and liberal Jews, who did not abide by the Mosaic law, may have owned the swine.

It is most likely, however, that the swine were the property of Romans. This assumption is based on the demoniac declaration that the name of the unclean spirit was legion, meaning an "indefinite, large number." The name may also have reference to the Roman military unit, or "legion," stationed in the area. The Roman legion in that region had a boar as its insignia.[186]

Was Decapolis near Gergesa?

Decapolis was a federation of ten Greek cities—Damascus, Raphana, Dion, Hippos, Gadara, Scythopolis, Pella, Gerasa, Philadelphia, and Abila—governed by Syria and located between the kingdoms of Herod Philip and Herod Antipas. Scythopolis, the capital of Decapolis, boasted the largest population of the ten cities. Decapolis gained independence in 63 BC. By AD 1 the federation had become a trading and defensive alliance wedged between two powerful Jewish tetrarchs. The visit of Jesus to the federation extended His ministry and, according to Elder Bruce R. McConkie, "prefigur[ed] the Gentile harvest."[187]

Was the "man sick of the palsy, lying on a bed" brought to Jesus in the evening hours (Matt. 9:2)?

The sick in Capernaum and throughout Galilee remained indoors until evening due to an Eastern superstition claiming that the sun was harmful to the sick. In the evening, those who could function arose from their beds and performed necessary tasks. Those too ill to rise from their beds of affliction were brought outdoors and laid on a mat near a wall or fruit tree. (Although shade and decorative trees grew naturally and were valued in Galilee, only fruit trees were planted. Trees that failed to bear fruit were cut down and used for kindling.)

It is assumed that the sick man was brought to Jesus in the evening hours by his four friends, who went up to the housetop and lowered the man down through the tiled roof.[188]

Did Jews believe that palsy was afflicted by Jehovah as a punishment for sin?

Palsy is a type of paralysis that results in loss of voluntary mo-tion and speech. Those afflicted with the disease are usually helpless due to loss of movement. Jews believed that palsy and other forms of illness were God's punishment for sin.[189]

Was Jesus accused of blasphemy for saying to the palsied man, "Thy sins are forgiven thee" (Luke 5:20)?

Scribes prided themselves on their legal understanding of the Mosaic law. They wrote the books of the Torah—Genesis, Exodus, Leviticus, Numbers, and Deuteronomy—on parchment scrolls for each synagogue in Palestine.

During the Ptolemaic rule of Palestine, the Torah served as the civic and religious law of Israel. It was during this era that scribes became not only copiers of the Torah, taking care to ensure that the exact wording remained unchanged, but "guardians and interpreters of the law."

As they created commentaries and searched for deeper meaning in the books of Moses, they gained religious and political influence. Because of their societal status during the Ptolemaic rule, young scribes were admonished by their elders to "be careful in judgment;

set up many scholars, and make a hedge about the law."

At the time of Jesus, the political power of the scribes had diminished. Their religious status as interpreters of the Torah, however, had heightened. As respected interpreters of the law of Moses, scribes felt confident in accusing Jesus of blasphemy, for they knew that only God could forgive sin.[190]

Was Jesus referring to an actual bed when He told the man to "take up thy bed" (Mark 2:9)?

Galilean beds were mats, handwoven rugs, or litters. Jesus was referring to a litter when He said "take up thy bed, and walk" (Mark 2:9).[191]

Jesus saw "a man, named Matthew, sitting at the receipt of custom: and he saith unto him, Follow me. And he arose, and followed him" (Matt. 9:9). What was the receipt of custom?

Receipt of custom was the place of toll, or a tax office where Roman tax was levied on imported

"Take up thy bed, and walk"

114

and exported goods. Since Capernaum was a border town in the territory of Herod Antipas, it served as a point of custom or toll. Toll places were familiar sites on roads and bridges throughout Palestine. Residents of Palestine were expected to pay custom (a tax for road and bridge use) and tribute (an annual tax on houses, lands, and courts of appeal). Hebrew scholar F. C. Grant estimates that "the total taxation of the Jewish people in the time of Jesus, civil and religious combined, must have approached the intolerable proportion of between 30 and 40 per cent; it may have been higher still."

Rome sold the right to collect toll to the highest bidder within each province and principality of the Roman Empire. Within the principality of Palestine, Herod Antipas was the highest bidder. Antipas sold his right to collect toll to the publicans. Publicans had the reputation of exacting more than the allotted toll (see Luke 3:12–13). Accounts of exorbitant collections, bordering on extortion, were common on the international road near Capernaum, where Matthew Levi had his custom office.[192]

Are Gospel writers referring to the same man when they mention Matthew and Levi?

Matthew was also known as Levi, son of Alpheus. The name Matthew is of Hebrew derivation and means "gift of Jehovah." Matthew Levi was selected as one of the Twelve Apostles and was the author of the first evangelical Gospel.[193]

When Jesus "sat at meat" in Matthew's house, "many publicans and sinners came and sat down with him and his disciples" (Matt. 9:10). Was a publican respected in Jewish society?

Although Herod Antipas and Roman appointees viewed publicans as men of high social station, a majority of the Jewish society did not. To the Jews, publicans were men who extracted burdensome taxes, customs, and tolls for Roman overlords. The Jewish contempt for one of their own becoming a publican was unbridled anger. Jews did not allow publicans to hold public office, have communal responsibility, or testify in a Jewish court of law. In fact, the words *publican* and *sinner* appear to have had the same meaning to the Jews at the time of Jesus.[194]

Was a tax collector always a publican?

Not always. Rome sold the right to levy and collect taxes, customs, and tolls to the highest bidder. Publicans purchased that right, but often resold it to others who assessed and collected Roman levies.[195]

How did the Pharisees know that Jesus was eating with publicans and sinners?

Houses in Palestine were not protected from intrusion. It was not unusual for visitors and even strangers to enter a house at meal time, observe the dining arrangement, and talk to dinner guests without receiving an invitation. Because of the public nature of private dwellings, rights of privacy were almost unknown. Jews could enter the house of other Jews at any time, but were restricted from entering a gentile house. Rabbinic law denounced gentile houses as unclean and defiling to a Jew.

Since Matthew was a Jew and not a Gentile, the Pharisees, although not invited to dine, walked in and observed the proceedings. They witnessed Jesus mingling with men they perceived as outcasts from Judean society.[196]

Followers of John the Baptist asked Jesus, "Why do we and the Pharisees fast oft, but thy disciples fast not?" (Matt. 9:14). Was the manner of fasting the same for Pharisees as it was for disciples of John?

John's followers were a community of believers comparable on the issue of fasting to the disciples of Pharisaic teachers. John apparently imposed fasting as a doctrinal duty upon his followers. It is not known whether they fasted Monday and Thursday of each week like the Pharisees, but there is a scriptural basis for assuming that they fasted twice a week, for it is written, "Why do we and the Pharisees fast oft" (Matt. 9:14).

When fasting, the Pharisees did not wash or anoint their bodies, shave their faces, or wear sandals. They purposely disfigured themselves with ashes so that their fasting would be a matter of public discussion.[197]

Was Jesus referring to Himself when He said to the followers of John, "Can the children of the bridechamber mourn, as long as the bridegroom is with them?" (Matt. 9:15). Was he speaking in parables at the time?

Speaking in parables was a common teaching method of Jesus and contemporary rabbis. Parables of Jesus were of ordinary incidents that illustrated an indirect principle not expressed in the story. The principle gleaned had application in the lives of the listeners. For example, when Jesus spoke of Himself as a bridegroom, His listeners could recall the joyous nature of the bridegroom at the wedding feast, the happiness of his friends, and perhaps the words of Isaiah, "Thy Maker is thine husband" (Isa. 54:5). Therefore, if Jesus were viewed as a bridegroom, it would be inappropriate for John's disciples to expect the sons of the bride chamber to fast in His presence.

It does appear, however, on occasion the followers of Jesus fasted, for He told them that evil spirits "goeth not out but by prayer and fasting" (Matt. 17:21).[198]

Why would Jesus speak symbolically about the doctrine of the kingdom as an old garment and a new garment?

Although old garments were valued by Jews, old garments were subject to the destructive rending of a tiny moth. If old garments were bound to new garments, invariably a tear would appear. Jesus taught that the new doctrine of the kingdom would not be put in the old garment of Judaism.[199]

Jesus said, "Neither do men put new wine into old bottles" (Matt. 9:17). Can new wine be stored in old bottles?

In the days of Jesus, the juice of the grape was drawn from vats and poured into wineskins (goat skins) or stone containers. If new wine were stored in old bottles, problems resulted. An Eastern wine bottle was made from goat-skin drawn from the carcass of a goat, "tanned with oak bark, and seasoned in smoke" before it was used as a bottle or bag for wine, milk, or other liquids. The skin that had covered the goat's neck formed the neck of the bottle. The skin that once covered the goat's torso became the container. This type of bag stretched, became brittle, and deteriorated with time. The reason for not putting new wine in an old bag was not only the stretching and aging of the bag, but the very nature of new wine. Fresh wine continues to ferment after it is placed inside a bag. If placed in an old bag, it will take on the taste of the old. Further, expansion during fermentation leads to bursting or leakage of the bag.

Drinking new wine was preferred by Jews. Wine older than six months was unacceptable because it had lost its fresh flavor and become vinegar inside the goatskin container.

The Christian interpretation of this parable is that Jesus did not package new fruit from the vine, meaning "the gospel from the True Vine, in the old and already stretched skin of Judaism." It also meant that Jesus' doctrine was too powerful to be held in the old confines of Judaism. Luke wrote of the new wine being difficult, for "no man . . . having drunk old wine straightway desireth new: for he saith, The old is better" (Luke 5:39).[200]

Did the first year of Jesus' ministry end with the parable of new wine in old bottles?

The exact length of Jesus' ministry is subject to debate. There were three phases of His ministry, not three years. Phase one ended after Jesus gave the parable of new wine in old bottles. Phase two began as Jesus journeyed from Galilee to Jerusalem to attend the Feast of the Passover. Phase three began with the miracle of feeding the five thousand.[201]

Did Isaiah prophesy that the Messiah would comfort the bruised reed and the smoking flax?

Wineskin

Isaiah (*Esais,* the Greek spelling of *Isaiah*) prophesied that the Messiah or suffering servant would be sent to comfort the weak: "A bruised reed shall he not break, and the smoking flax shall he not quench" (Isa. 42:3; Matt. 12:20). A reed is a tall, hollow-stemmed grass growing near lakes and streams. Flax is a linen fiber used to make wicks for candles and lamps. Smoking flax is a sign that the flame of the wick has diminished. A bruised reed and a smoking flax symbolically represent men who are weak in the faith.[202]

There was "a certain woman, which had an issue of blood twelve years" (Mark 5:25). What is an issue of blood?

It is assumed that the woman suffered from "menorrhagia, a continuous menstruation." Menorrhagia was not uncommon in Judea. The Talmud prescribed astringents, tonics, and "carrying the ashes of an ostrich egg in a linen rag" as treatments for the ailment.

A woman with hemorrhages was unclean according to Levitical law. It is suggested that she approached Jesus from behind so as not to defile him (see Mark 5:27).[203]

Why did the woman with the issue of blood want to touch the garment of Jesus?

Anciently, Jews were commanded to border or fringe their outer garments with blue cloth so that the children of Israel might "look upon it, and remember all the commandments of the Lord, and do them" (Num. 15:39). In the days of Jesus, most Jews failed to border their clothing, even though they continued to reverence hems of outer robes. The woman's desire to touch the hem of Jesus shows her knowledge and remembrance of the commandments of God. Perhaps it also shows that she associated the fringe of the garment with religious power. It was her faith that healed her affliction.

Why were Jewish leaders angry when Jesus healed the afflicted woman on the Sabbath?

Strict Sabbath observance was enforced among the Jews from the days of Moses to the days of Jesus. For a man seen gathering sticks on the Sabbath, Moses

Woman with the issue of blood touches the hem

pronounced death by stoning (see Ex. 31:14–15; 35:2; Num. 15:32–36). Nehemiah, a witness to the careless observance of Sabbath by the Israelites, exclaimed, "Ye bring more wrath upon Israel by profaning the sabbath" (Neh. 13:18). Ezekiel, seeing similar desecration, chastened his fallen people (see Ezek. 20:13).

Between prophetic warnings, inspired guidance, and ardent Pharisees, Sabbath observance developed along two lines: 1) the restrictive or keeping, and 2) the spiritual or remembering. The restrictive elevated the earlier formalism of the law to levels of religious piety. The restrictive included everything from gathering kindling to extinguishing a fire. Explaining the reasons for the restrictive nature of Sabbath observance, scholar Abraham Heschel wrote, "In the tempestuous ocean of time and toil there are islands of stillness where man may enter a harbor and reclaim his dignity." Sabbath was one of those islands. Scholar Truman G. Madsen added that within the island, "somehow God sees fit to send an extra spirit . . . which lifts a man above his ordinary evil inclinations and spells peace."

Jesus did not challenge the spiritual joys of Sabbath, but He did challenge the pharisaic rules that constricted Sabbath observance. He affirmed the lawful right to do good on the holy day and the principle, "The sabbath was made for man, and not man for the sabbath" (Mark 2:27).

Seven healing miracles on the Sabbath day are attributed to Jesus:

—Healing a man with a withered hand (see Matt. 12:10–13; Mark 3:1–5; Luke 6:6–10)
—Healing a man afflicted with dropsy (see Luke 14:2–4)
—Healing a woman with an infirmity (see Luke 13:11–13)
—Healing a blind man (see John 9:1–7)
—Healing a man near the pools of Bethesda (see John 5:2–9)
—Healing Peter's mother-in-law (see Matt. 8:14–15; Mark 1:30–31; Luke 4:38–39)
—Casting out an evil spirit (see Mark 1:23–26; Luke 4:33–35)[204]

When Jesus went up to Jerusalem to observe Passover festivities, He stopped north of the Temple Mount at the Pool of Bethesda. What is the significance of this body of water?

Only two of the ten pools in Jerusalem are mentioned in the Gospels—the Pool of Siloam and the Pool of Bethesda. The double

Pool of Bethesda is the more famous of the two. The pool—or twin pools of Bethesda—is located outside the north city walls near the temple courts. At the time of Jesus, a sheep market was located near the pools known as Sheep Gate (in Greek, *probatike*). Through this gate, sheep were led to the Temple Mount to be sacrificed. According to Eusebius, sheep were washed in the twin pools of Bethesda before being sacrificed.

The word Bethesda is of Aramaic derivation, meaning "house of mercy." According to Jewish superstition, the name had reference to an angel entering the pools and disturbing the water, giving momentary power to the water to heal the first person who entered. In actuality, the disturbance of the water came from an intermittent, flowing stream.[205]

Why was Jesus charged with blasphemy for healing "a certain man" at the Pool of Bethesda, who had "an infirmity thirty and eight years" (John 5:5)?

The charge of blasphemy was based on healing the infirm man on the Sabbath, commanding the man to arise and take his bed, and giving credit to God for

Pools of Bethesda

the healing. The reply of Jesus to the pharisaic charge is one of the most renowned sermons in the Gospels.[206]

According to the Gospel of Mark, Jesus "went through the corn fields on the sabbath day; and his disciples began, as they went, to pluck the ears of corn" (Mark 2:23). Can it be assumed that the disciples of Jesus ate corn from the cob on this occasion?

The question is complex because three Greek words—*sporimos, sitos,* and *stachus*—have been designated by biblical interpret-

ers as corn. Yet none of the three Greek words has reference to corn that is eaten off the cob. *Sporimos* means "planted field," *sitos* means "wheat grain," and *stachus* means "head of grain." The King James Version suggests that *corn* means "grains of all kinds."[207]

Were disciples of Jesus legally accountable for taking a portion of the harvest from the field?

For their actions to be illegal, disciples had to cut sheaves of wheat with a sickle or carry wheat in a vessel from the field. According to the Mosaic law, those passing through another's vineyard or field had the right to eat grapes and corn to abate hunger. Corners of fields and sheaves beyond corners were purposely left by landowners as a gift to the hungry and poor.

Although disciples of Jesus were not guilty of theft, they may have violated rabbinic law against threshing and winnowing on the Sabbath. When they rubbed out an ear of wheat with their hands, they were threshing. When they

Disciples havesting wheat

blew away chaff to eat the kernels, they were winnowing or separating grain from the husks. According to Deuteronomy 23:25, their actions were not against the law.[208]

Did disciples of Jesus violate rabbinic law by walking through wheat fields on the Sabbath day?

It is assumed that the disciples of Jesus didn't violate rabbinic law by walking through a wheat field. A Sabbath day's journey was a distance of two thousand cubits, which is three thousand feet or three-fifths of a mile. The distance was based on the interpretation of "let no man go out of his place on the seventh day" (Ex. 16:29).

By the days of Jesus, rabbis had rationalized an extension of the Sabbath journey to four thousand cubits. The extension was based on establishing a temporary residence two thousand cubits from home before Sabbath began. A temporary residence was established by burying food. On the Sabbath day, a Jew could walk the initial two thousand cubits, stop at the temporary residence, uncover and eat the buried food, and proceed another two thousand cubits.[209]

Heads of wheat

Pharisees asked Jesus why His disciples did "that which is not lawful" on the Sabbath day (Mark 2:24). Jesus illustrated the correctness of their actions by speaking of King David and his men eating shewbread. What is shewbread?

Shewbread, meaning "bread of the presence" or "bread placed in the presence of Jehovah" at the temple altar, symbolized communion with God. Shewbread, made from the finest flour and passed through eleven sieves before being pronounced good, was only to be eaten by priests.[210]

Why did Jesus heal the man with the withered hand when He knew that healing on the Sabbath would lead to further charges of blasphemy?

Biblical scholar Alfred Edersheim stated, "Christ would not witness a disease without removing it—or, as we might express it, that disease could not continue in the Presence of Him Who was the Life." Whether the man was a pawn of the scribes and Pharisees or present at the synagogue on his own volition is not known. Gospel writer Mark reports that

Jesus, although "being grieved for the hardness of their heart," healed the man (Mark 3:5).

In the apocryphal Gospel of the Hebrews, written between AD 65 and 100, the man with the withered hand is referred to as a mason by trade. In the Hebrew account, the man said to Jesus, "I was a mason earning my living with my hands. I pray Thee, Jesus, restore me my health, that I may not disgracefully beg my bread."[211]

Why were the Pharisees so determined to destroy Jesus when He said to the man with the withered hand, "Stretch forth thine hand. And he stretched it forth; and it was restored whole, like as the other" (Matt. 12:13)?

There are many reasons why the Pharisees sought to destroy Jesus. One reason is that the Pharisees rejected all non-Jewish influence in Judea. They wanted a true Israel, a pure Israel. The Pharisees' dream was a nation free of sinners, harlots, publicans, and Sabbath violators. They perceived Jesus of Nazareth as a threat to their definition of a true Israel. As His influence grew with each healing on the Sabbath day, Pharisees concluded that Jesus must be destroyed to protect Israel. As pharisaic opposition mounted, Jesus taught more often in parables.[212]

How many parables are attributed to Jesus?

Matthew records fourteen parables, Mark five, and Luke twenty. Many of the thirty-nine parables attributed to Jesus contradict the accepted norms of His society. "Bad servants are rewarded, and good servants seem to be punished. His heroes are sometimes unsavory characters—an unjust judge, neighbors who do not want to be neighborly, a man who pockets someone else's treasure by purchasing his fields, a steward who cheats his master, a sinful woman, and other socially unacceptable characters."[213]

Does the Gospel of John contain the parables of Jesus?

John did not record the parables of Jesus. The synoptic writers—Matthew, Mark, and Luke—are credited with recording the parables. These writers reveal that Jesus did not use parables in the beginning of His ministry. He adopted this teaching method as pharisaic opposition mounted (see Matt. 13:3).[214]

Why is the parable of the sower referred to as the parable of the soil?

Sowing of seeds was an elaborate process governed by the Mosaic law. Seeds were ceremonially cleansed before being thrown on the ground during the sowing season (see Lev. 11:37–38). The sowing season lasted from October until the end of February. Mosaic regulations controlled the exact date in the season each type of seed could be sown. The mixing of seeds while planting was prohibited by law (see Deut. 22:9).

According to Jewish custom, a vessel or basket containing seeds was held in the left hand while seeds were scattered with the right hand. An accepted alternative was to put seeds in a sack placed on the back of a farm animal. As the animal moved across the field, seeds were dispensed from holes in the sack.

Parable of the sower

The type of seed used in the parable is not identified. However, the seed is always good, for it symbolizes the word of God (see Luke 8:11). The variable in the parable is the type of soil that the seed falls on— good soil, stony portions of land, on the roadway, and under thick vegetation (see Luke 8:5–8, 13–15; Mark 4:5, 8, 16). Whether the seed sprouts and becomes a plant depends, in part, on the soil (see Gal. 6:7). Thus, the parable of the sower is referred to as the parable of the soil.[215]

Was Jesus referring to a specific form of measurement when He said, "Take heed what ye hear: with what measure ye mete, it shall be measured to you" (Mark 4:24)?

In the New Testament, three types of measures are mentioned. Luke refers to a measure of wheat flour and a measure of oil (see Luke 13:21; 16:6–7). The book of Revelation refers to a measure of barley (see Rev. 6:6). It is assumed that Jesus was referring to the common wheat measure, "a square wooden box about two feet wide and fourteen inches deep."

The wise buyer measured wheat with his own wooden box or wheat measure because he wanted to be sure that the farmer was not selling him a smaller portion than was agreed on. The dishonest person bought wheat with one measure and sold it with another.[216]

What does Jesus mean by the statement, "Take heed therefore how ye hear: for whosoever hath, to him shall be given; and whosoever hath not, from him shall be taken even that which he seemeth to have" (Luke 8:18)?

"In the Jewish schools the rabbi sat in his chair, and whispered" in an interpreter's ear the words he wanted his students to hear. The interpreter, who had heard the rabbi's message in Hebrew, proclaimed aloud in Aramaic what the rabbi had said. The possible interpretation of the phrase *What ye hear in the ear* is that the Apostles should proclaim to all people what Jesus had told them (see Luke 8:18).

Jesus was opposed to secret doctrines, like those espoused by the Essenes, who revealed their inner thoughts only to intimates.

The Apostles were to proclaim the gospel from the housetops and from city to city much like the man who ascended a pinnacle and announced with trumpet blasts the arrival of the Sabbath day.[217]

Was Jesus referring to an Eastern sickle when He spoke of a man putting "in the sickle, because the harvest is come" (Mark 4:29)?

A Palestinian sickle was a crescent-shaped metal tool. During the harvest season, a farmer held the sickle in one hand and clutched stalks of grain with the other hand. With a sweep of the sickle, a farmer could cut grain. Stalks of cut grain were gathered and bound together in bundles or sheaves. Sheaves were then spread flat on a threshing floor to dry.[218]

Are tares a form of bearded rye grass?

The answer depends on whether the Gospel reader prefers the Aramaic or Greek translation of Matthew (see Matt. 13:24–43). In Aramaic the word for uncultivated tares is *zivaney,* a

Sickle

form of *zana,* meaning "to commit adultery." In Greek the word *zizanion* refers to tares as weeds in grain. By accepting the Greek translation, it is assumed that the tares mentioned by Jesus were the semi-poisonous, bearded darnel or weed grass known as *lolium temulentum.* This weed resembles wheat in early stages of growth. As the weed grows with the wheat, the roots of the weed intertwine with the roots of the wheat, which may account for the Aramaic translation of adultery.[219]

Do tares naturally grow in wheat fields?

During the Roman rule of Palestine, it was not unusual for one farmer to throw degenerate seeds of tares into another farmer's field to avenge past wrongs. The wronged farmer took tare seeds in a little bag or in his pockets and scattered the seeds on the enemy's field during the night. Tares easily overcame the wheat if not eradicated quickly. To rid a field of tares took years of toil, much to the delight of the avenger and sorrow of the offender.

Palestinian farmers were constantly on guard to protect their fields from enemies with tare seeds during the sowing season. As farmers tired of nightly standing guard, they made amends

Ryegrass (not the same as rye, which is a grain)

with their enemies to save their wheat fields. The general interpretation is that tares represent apostates who are among the righteous wheat.[220]

Why did Jesus teach that a man with his hand to the plow must not look back?

Plowing, the process of breaking up soil in rows for planting, was done in Palestine by using a hardwood plow. The iron-tipped plow was pulled by donkeys or oxen. If the farmer looked back while leading his animals, the five-inch furrows dug by the plow would not be straight. Adding to the dilemma was the Jewish practice of plowing the field a second time to cover the seeds with soil.[221]

Jesus likened the kingdom of Heaven "to a grain of mustard seed" (Matt. 13:31). Was the mustard seed viewed as the smallest seed at that time?

The mustard seed is not the smallest of seeds. "Small as a mustard seed" was a proverbial saying of rabbis when speaking of the smallest amount, such as the tiniest raindrop or a particle of dust.

The saying connotes strength inherent in the smallest particle.

When nourished, the mustard seed grows into a large plant in the Palestinian climate. Birds are attracted to its branches and enjoy its seeds (see Luke 13:19). Palestinian farmers left mustard seeds for the birds to eat due to an Eastern superstition that linked the seeds to insanity. Ancient medical practitioners ignored the superstition and used the seeds for medical purposes, flavoring, and aroma.[222]

Jesus likened the kingdom of God to leaven by saying, "It is like leaven, which a woman took and hid in three measures of meal, till the whole was leavened" (Luke 13:21). In what way is the kingdom of God similar to leaven?

Leaven produces fermentation (like yeast and baking powder), which increases the size of dough used to make bread. Before baking bread each day, Jewish women saved a small portion of the dough in hot water. The saved portion was used in the next day's bread. Flour mixed with the remaining portion formed a larger dough. Thus, the process of leavening or fermentation went forward on a daily basis, much like the kingdom of God.

Anciently, Easterners believed that bread dough raised because it contained a sacred, hidden family blessing. Leaven was deemed holy and was spoken of in reverent terms. Leaven was so valuable to an Easterner that no one could borrow or even touch the leaven of another. If leaven were accidentally touched by those outside the family circle, bread made from the leaven could not be eaten. To curse a life was to say, "Beware of him; he has grown up eating bread made of bad leaven"; "his leaven is bloody"; or "his leaven is defiled."[223]

Matthew wrote of Herod's birthday celebration. Was it a Jewish custom to celebrate birthdays of rulers?

Celebrating birthdays was a Greek custom. Jews viewed

Leavened bread

birthday feasts as a form of heathen worship. Herod Antipas announced a feast to celebrate the anniversary of his ascension to the office of tetrarch, not his birthday. The celebration may have been held at Machaerus east of the Dead Sea near the Transjordanian Mountains. According to apocryphal accounts, the feast was attended by lords (a title given captains of Roman mercenaries) and leading Levites.[224]

At the celebration, the daughter of Herodias danced. Was the type of dancing she performed a Greek custom?

Licentious dancing was a Greek custom adopted by Roman society. The custom mixed dancing with nudity that often led to immoral relationships. Herod, who easily succumbed to physical passions, welcomed the dancing of his stepdaughter Salome (whose name was recorded by Josephus). It is presumed that Salome, the daughter of Herodias, danced nude before the invited lords at the elaborate feast. Her foolish abandonment of the sacred led directly to the death of John the Baptist. According to Jewish lore, Salome married her uncle, Herod Philip. The marriage ended when she fell on ice and died.[225]

What was the Galilean reaction to the death of John the Baptist?

Angered by news of John's death and rumors of Herodias' ordering his "headless trunk to be flung out over the battlements for dogs and vultures to devour," Galileans threatened insurrection against Rome and its appointees. They decried the execution of John without a trial and the manner of his demise. This twofold breach of Judaic law was intolerable to the Galilean Jews. His disciples took his body and properly buried his remains, but their anger was not abated.

Fearing the masses, Herod superstitiously looked for John the Baptist to be a rising savior-god. In the Greco-Roman world there were accounts of savior-gods rising like "Tammuz, Bel-Marduk, Adonis, Sandan-Heracles, Attis, Osiris, the Cretan Zeus, and Dionysus." These pagan deities never lived a mortal existence. They were not martyrs nor did they have a righteous following.[226]

Why didn't Jesus celebrate Passover in Jerusalem after the death of John the Baptist?

Jesus would have placed His life in great danger if He had celebrated Passover in Jerusalem. With the Galilean area threatening insurrection, it would not have been safe for any Galilean to attend festivities in the Holy City. It would have been particularly dangerous for Jesus and His large following of Galilean disciples.

Instead of going to Jerusalem, Jesus journeyed to the secluded area of Bethsaida-Julias near the eastern border of Galilee. There He was safe from Herod Antipas, who had fantasized that Jesus was John the Baptist risen from the dead and "desired to see him" (Luke 9:9). He was also safe from Pontius Pilate, who had ordered the killing of Galilean pilgrims threatening rebellion. By retreating to the eastern border, Jesus moved beyond Herod's domain to land ruled by his more benevolent brother Herod Philip. At this solitary place, Apostles reported their missionary labors to Jesus.[227]

Is the only miracle of Jesus written in all four Gospels the feeding of five thousand men?

132

Presenting the head of John the Baptist

The feeding of the five thousand men—in addition to women and children—was recorded by all of the Gospel writers. It took place in a grassy meadow on the plain of Bethsaida-Julias. It is assumed that the simple peasant meal of two small fishes and five barley loaves (barley being a staple grain of the poor) was a fulfillment of the Jewish tradition that the Messiah would signal His advent by repeating the miracle of manna. Rabbis taught for generations, "'As the first Saviour—the deliverer from Egyptian bondage' caused manna to fall for Israel from heaven, so the second Saviour—the Messiah—will also cause manna to descend for them once more."

Seating the multitude in companies and ranks of fifties and hundreds was reminiscent of an earlier day in the wilderness when Moses organized the children of Israel (see Mark 6:40). Eating barley bread and opsarion, a dried or pickled fish relish sauce, was reminiscent of manna.[228]

Why were the disciples constrained to leave Bethsaida-Julias?

Jesus perceived that the multitude in Bethsaida-Julias wanted to crown Him King of Judea, and His disciples concurred (see John 6:15). Scholars D. Kelly Ogden and Andrew Skinner wrote, "They were so inclined because, by popular tradition, the Messiah would come during Passover, and having witnessed so many healings and now the miraculous multiplication of loaves and fishes, they recognized that he must be their long-awaited Messiah."

The disciples did not want to get into a boat and cross the Sea of Galilee, but they complied out of obedience to Jesus. Those who boarded other boats were "offended by Jesus' refusal to accept a crown." As for Jesus, "he went up into a mountain apart to pray" (Matt. 14:23).[229]

When Jesus was ready to join His disciples again, they were "in the midst of the sea" (Mark 6:47). How far did Jesus walk on the sea before entering the ship of His disciples?

The Gospel of John states that the disciples had "rowed about five and twenty or thirty furlongs" from the shore when Jesus was seen walking on the sea (John 6:19). This means that Jesus had walked a distance of "fifteen to eighteen thousand feet, or three to four miles" on water. The distance places the disciples in a boat in the middle of the sea when they saw Him approach. "It is I; be not afraid," Jesus admonished them (Matt. 14:27).

Jesus reached His disciples at some point during the fourth watch, sometime between three and six in the morning. Night watches were divided into three-hour increments—6–9 P.M., 9–12 P.M., 12–3 A.M., and 3–6 A.M.[230]

Jesus and His disciples came to the land of Gennesaret near Tiberias. Was Tiberias a gentile city?

Gennesaret, known as "the garden of riches," was a "fertile plain on the northwest shore of the Sea of Galilee" near Tiberias. The name Tiberias is a Greek adaptation of Chinnereth (see Num. 34:11). Tiberias, the capital of Lower Galilee, was originally known as Sepphoris, meaning "bird perch." The name had reference to a city built on a hill.

It was renamed Tiberias in honor of the Roman emperor and was established by Herod Antipas about AD 18.

In an attempt to explain why he kept the Herods in office, Tiberius related a fable about a wounded man lying on the side of a road covered with blood-sucking insects. When a compassionate traveler tried to brush off the insects, the man begged him to stop, saying, "These flies, are already sated with blood, and are causing me no trouble now; but if they are driven off, a fresh swarm of hungry ones will take their place and I shall not survive their attentions."[231]

Christ and Peter upon the sea

Why did the Bread of Life sermon cause popular opinion of Jesus to wane?

The antagonism and division raised over the Bread of Life sermon marked the first time that popular opinion of Jesus waned. The masses turned aside, as did His disciples, who were offended by His "hard sayings" (see John 6:60–62).

The division was never mended. Former friends left Jesus seeking truth in conflicting sects. These sects or ideologies included the conservative Hebraic Jews, Hellenistic Jews, communal Essenes, Pharisees, Sadducees, and Zealots—each touting a claim to superior holiness. "No wonder the Savior, seeing such division among the people, prayed to the Father so earnestly in behalf of his own little [remaining] flock to keep them 'one as we are one.'"[232]

Why did so many disciples turn away from Jesus at this time?

Jesus proclaimed himself to be the Messiah in the Bread of Life sermon. His words of "living water" and "living bread"

disturbed and divided many congregated at the synagogue in Capernaum. According to biblical scholar Cunningham Geikie, "Those who had hoped to find a popular political leader in Him saw their dreams melt away: those who had no true sympathy for His life and words had an excuse for leaving Him. None who were not bound to Him by sincere loyalty and devotion had any longer a motive for following Him. Fierce patriotism burning for insurrection, mean self-interest seeking worldly advantage, and vulgar curiosity craving excitement, were equally disappointed. . . . A lowly and suffering Messiah thus unmistakably set before them was revolting to their national pride and gross material tastes. . . . Outward glory and material wealth were the national dream: he spoke only of inward purity."[233]

Why were scribes and Pharisees of Jerusalem at Capernaum? Were they also seeking Jesus?

The reason is simple and forthright: "The Jews sought to kill [Jesus]" (John 7:1). Jewish leaders sent Pharisees and scribes to Capernaum, hoping that they might find legal cause to accuse Jesus of a fault worthy of death.[234]

> Scribes and Pharisees asked Jesus why His "disciples transgress the tradition of the elders? for they wash not their hands when they eat bread" (Matt. 15:2). Why was the washing of hands such a major issue to the scribes and Pharisees?

Upon learning that the followers of Jesus had eaten bread and fishes in the meadow of Bethsaida-Julias with unwashed hands, scribes and Pharisees accused Jesus of failure to comply with the rabbinic interpretation of the Mosaic law regarding the washing of hands. Failure to participate in the ceremonial washing, literally a baptism before dinner, was a criminal offense equal to apostasy and murder as taught by the Pharisees, but not by the law of Moses.

To ignore the ceremonial washing was abhorrent to the Pharisees, for it was written in the Talmud, "It is better to go four miles to water than to incur guilt by neglecting hand-washing. He who does not wash his hands after eating is as bad as a murderer." It was written in the book of Sohar, "He who neglects hand washing deserves to be punished here and hereafter." Famed Rabbi Jose penned, "He who eats bread without hand-washing is as if he went in to a harlot." Zealots, Herodians, and Sadduces did not share this extreme view.

Jesus turned the question back to the scribes and Pharisees by asking, "Why do ye also transgress the commandment of God by your tradition?" (Matt. 15:3).[235]

> What was the ceremonial ritual of hand-washing?

The Schulchan Aruch detailed twenty-six rules governing the morning hand-washing ritual alone.

During the washing, the fist of one hand was placed in the hollow of the other hand. When the washing was completed, finger tips were joined together and raised so that the remaining water on the hands could trickle down to the elbows. The hands were then turned downward, being careful not to let water run off the knuckles or drip to the ground. Fresh water was then poured on the hands, and the process repeated again and again.

The water vessel was held first in the right hand and then in the left. The water was poured first on the right side and then on the left. After every third pouring, these words were spoken: "Blessed art Thou who hast given us the command to wash the hands."[236]

What was the reason or reasons why scribes and Pharisees put the law above the Messiah?

Scribes and Pharisees were so taken with the minutiae of the law that they failed to recognize the Messiah. They decried the failure of Jesus to keep rabbinic laws governing hand-washing, the Sabbath day, purification rites, and fasts; by so doing, they were blinded by their own expertise. Jesus said, "Howbeit in vain they do worship me, teaching for doctrines the commandments of men. . . . Full well ye reject the commandment of God, that ye may keep your own tradition" (Mark 7:7, 9).[237]

Synagogue wash basin

8

Ministry to Decapolis, Perea, and Judea

Jesus expanded His ministry to northern Galilee, an area known for its pagan cities, such as Tyre and Sidon. In these cities and others, Jesus healed the afflicted. His fame spread and many were blessed by His miracles.

Did Jesus have followers in the pagan cities of Tyre and Sidon?

Jesus journeyed to the coasts of the cosmopolitan cities of Tyre and Sidon because of the multitude that had come from these cities to hear Him and be healed of their afflictions in Galilee. Other than this one recorded visit to Tyre and Sidon, there is

Ruins at Tyre

no further record of Him journeying along the coast of the Mediterranean Sea (see Mark 7:24–31).

In Jesus' day, both communities boasted of a large Jewish population. Tyre was larger than Sidon and probably exceeded Jerusalem in population.[238]

> On the coasts of Tyre and Sidon, a woman cried out, "O Lord, thou Son of David; my daughter is grievously vexed with a devil" (Matt. 15:22). Was the woman a Phoenician?

The woman was a Canaanite by birth, a Greek by heritage, and a Syro-Phoenician by nationality (see Mark 7:26). Elder Bruce R. McConkie wrote that "she was a Gentile of the Gentiles, a pure Gentile, who could claim no descent from Abraham."[239]

Most of the residents of Tyre and Sidon were Gentiles and reveled in the pagan worship of Ashtoreth and Baal. Ashtoreth was revered as a goddess of sensual love and as a sacred prostitute. Baal, meaning "lord" or "master," was worshiped as the pagan god of the Asiatic. Residents of Tyre and Sidon offered gifts and sacrifices to these imaginary gods, even child sacrifices, to appease their shifting whims.

Jews called the pagan worship in these cites *elilim,* meaning the "worship of nonentities" or the "figments of a distraught mind."[240]

> Jesus answered the pleading woman, "It is not meet to take the children's bread, and to cast it to dogs" (Matt. 15:26). Were dogs household pets in gentile cities? Does the woman's metaphor of crumbs and dogs fit with mealtime practices in Tyre and Sidon?

In Phoenicia, tables were not used at mealtime. Food, the staple being bread, was served on trays and pieces of cloth. When bread was lifted from the tray or cloth, crumbs fell to the floor. Household pets known as kunariois, meaning "little dogs," waited near the trays or cloths for crumbs to fall. If a household dog was not present, crumbs were carefully gathered and given to beggars.

Jesus healed the woman's daughter.[241]

The healing process of the deaf man with a speech impediment seems most unusual, as Jesus "put his fingers into his ears, and he spit, and touched his tongue" (Mark 7:33). Was Jesus applying a Jewish remedy in this instance?

Using saliva to heal an eye disease was an ancient Jewish healing method. However, this may not have been the reason Jesus used saliva in the healing process. It may be that "Jesus made use of the language of signs, because the man was deaf. He put his fingers in His ears, indicating that He would pierce through the obstruction. He touched his tongue, indicating that He would remove the impediment in his speech." He then said "Ephphatha," an Aramaic word meaning "to be opened."[242]

How did feeding the four thousand in Decapolis differ from feeding the five thousand in Bethsaida-Julias?

Jesus fed His Jewish followers on the plains of Bethsaida-Julias. But on the occasion in Decapolis, Jesus fed those living in the ten cities of Decapolis, regardless of whether they had a Jewish or Abrahamic heritage. At the meadow in Bethsaida-Julias, he laid the foundation for the Bread of Life sermon. According to Jewish/Christian scholar Alfred Edersheim, the feeding of four thousand at Decapolis laid the foundation for the future ministry of the Apostles to the gentile nations.[243]

Why did Jesus call the Pharisees and Sadducees of Magdala hypocrites?

On the western shore of the Sea of Galilee in the town of Magdala, meaning "tower," Jesus spoke of heavenly signs that the Pharisees and Sadducees knew well. They knew, for example, that lightning, storm clouds, and rain came from the west, and that snow mixed with hail was a rare occurrence. These leaders were aware of seismic disturbances running north and south along the Rift Valley. They knew, among other things, that a red sky at night meant fair weather. Jesus contrasted their ability to recognize signs of nature with their inability to see the hand of God. Jesus said to them, "O ye hypocrites, ye can discern the face of the sky; but can ye not discern the signs of the times" (Matt. 16:3).[244]

> The blind man at Bethsaida said, "I see men as trees, walking. After that he put his hands again upon his eyes, and made him look up: and he was restored, and saw every man clearly" (Mark 8:24–25). Why was the healing of the blind man done in two stages?

Biblical scholar James Harpur reasons that the miracle was a learning opportunity for the disciples. Jesus used the "miracle to embody the progressive enlightenment of the 'blind' disciples."[245]

> Is there any significance to the fact that Jesus referred to establishing His church upon a rock near the pagan community of Caesarea Philippi?

The teachings of Jesus often matched the dominant feature in His surroundings. Jesus was standing at the base of the largest rock formation in Palestine, near the city of Caesarea Philippi, when he spoke of establishing a church. Anciently, the formation was known as Mount Hermon to the Jews. On the south foot of Mount Hermon in the Hellenistic period was the town of Panias. The name Panias was given to the town in honor of the pagan god Pan, whom Greeks believed governed forests, meadows, flocks, and herds and roamed mountain slopes and caves as a half-man and half-goat.

The reference to establishing a church matched the nearby Greco-Roman community of Caesarea, first built during the reign of the Roman Emperor Augustus. Augustus gave the city to

Christ heals the blind man

142

Mount Hermon

Herod the Great, who willed it to his son Herod Philip. Philip rebuilt the city and named it in honor of Augustus and himself—Caesarea Philippi. The city had a river flowing through it. The river seems appropriate to Jesus' teachings at the site, for "revelation must be continuous and flowing, like the river."[246]

Why did the people assume that Jesus was Jeremias? Was it prophesied that Jeremias would return?

The answer is found in Jewish folk tales, which depict Jeremiah hiding the ark of the covenant in a cave on Mount Nebo to protect the ark from the unhallowed clutches of Nebuchadnezzar. Poets sing of Jeremiah and Elijah returning to earth to bring the ark of the covenant and the Urim and Thummim from the cave to the Holy of Holies in a

new temple to be built in Jerusalem before the coming of the Messiah. Folk tales also speak of Jeremiah calling forth ancient patriarchs and Moses from their tombs and lamenting with them over the destruction of the Holy Temple.[247]

Is it true that after Simon Peter announced, "Thou art the Christ, the Son of the living God" (Matt. 16:16), Jesus instructed His Apostles with greater plainness?

"From the time of Peter's confession," Jesus spoke with greater clarity to the Twelve Apostles about His ensuing death and resurrection. He spoke plainly of the persecution and abuse that would be heaped upon Him by Jewish leaders and of His resurrection.

Jesus gave the Apostles keys, meaning "right to lead" and

"right to bind and loose"—rabbinic terms for permit and forbid. These rights would enable them to continue their gospel ministry after the death and resurrection of Jesus. [248]

Were the events that led to Peter's rebuke—"Be it far from thee, Lord"—the reason why Jesus referred to him as Satan (Matt. 16:22)?

At that moment Peter wanted his will to be done instead of the will of God. In his attempt to dissuade Jesus from His appointed course, Peter appealed to His human nature by proposing a change in the eternal plan of life—the plan of salvation. According to Elder Bruce R. McConkie, Peter was suggesting that the "things of the world be given preference to the things of the Spirit." "Temptation from the lips of a faithful friend and confidant is even worse than from the mouth of the arch-tempter himself. Are not a man's worst foes they of his own household when they seek to dissuade him from the course of duty and right? . . . [Peter] saw only the cross and not the crown."

That Jesus looked upon His disciples may suggest that Peter's inappropriate statement expressed the thoughts of others, for although the rebuke was directed toward Peter, it may have been inclusive.

It is perhaps not a coincidence that the phrase *Get thee behind me, Satan* is the same phrase spoken by Jesus in the wilderness setting when the arch-deceiver tried to thwart Jesus' earthly mission (Matt. 16:23; see also Matt. 4:10). Scholars D. Kelly Ogden and Andrew Skinner claim that Jesus was not referring to Peter as Satan, meaning "Lucifer." They reason that Peter had placed himself in an adversarial role with Jesus.[249]

Where was Jesus when He was transfigured "and his face did shine as the sun, and his raiment was white as the light" (Matt. 17:2)?

The traditional site of the Transfiguration of Jesus is a dome-like mountain in the Jezreel Valley known as Mount Tabor, meaning "mountain height." The mountain creates a natural corner or division between the ancient lands of Naphtali, Issachar, and Zebulun. It ascends 1,843 feet above sea level and is located six miles east of Nazareth.

Mount of Transfiguration

The traditional site is discounted by scholars who point to a fortified city atop the Mount Tabor summit during the days of Jesus. The presence of a city suggests that the mount was not suitable for the Transfiguration, for it was not secluded. Using this reasoning, scholars suggest that the snow-capped Mount Hermon, the highest peak in the country, was the site of the

Transfiguration. With confidence, they point to the scriptural passage in Matthew that reads "high mountain" (Matt. 17:1).[250]

What is transfiguration?

The basic definition of the Latin *trans figura* is "to change to another form." Elder Bruce R. McConkie said, "*Transfiguration* is a special change in appearance and nature which is wrought upon a person or thing by the power of God. This divine transformation is from a lower to a higher state; it results in a more exalted, impressive, and glorious condition."

During the transfiguration of Jesus, a bright cloud overshadowed Him. It was "not a watery cloud, but what the Jews called the Shekinah or Dwelling cloud, the cloud which manifested the presence and glory of God." The cloud was reminiscent of an earlier cloud that rested upon Moses' tabernacle and a foreshadowing of a cloud that would cover Jesus as He ascended to heaven (see Num. 9:15–22, 11:25; Ex. 33:9; Acts 1:9).[251]

At the Mount of Transfiguration, Peter, James, and John were given keys of the kingdom and a vision of the earth in its paradisiacal state. As they came down from the mount, Jesus charged them to "tell the vision to no man, until the Son of man be risen again from the dead" (Matt. 17:9).

"A certain man, kneeling down to him," said, "Lord, have mercy on my son: for he is lunatick, and sore vexed" (Matt. 17:14–15). What was the definition of a lunatic in the days of Jesus?

Ancient Easterners believed that lunatics suffered from an epileptic malady due to demonic forces that caused periodic changes in the moon. This absurd notion took centuries to eradicate. As for the man's son, Gospel writers say that he suffered from "dumbness" or "lunacy" (Mark 9:17; Matt. 17:15). It was not unusual for a father to seek relief for an ailing son.

It was not unusual that the boy had fallen into a fireplace. Such accidents were common in the East, since most homes contained "one or several ovens dug in the floor."[252]

Jesus said, "If ye have faith as a grain of mustard seed, ye shall say unto this mountain, Remove hence to yonder place; and it shall remove" (Matt. 17:20). Were His words a common Jewish saying or were they a literal interpretation?

The phrases tearing up or removing mountains were proverbial expressions uttered by Jewish rabbis. A renowned rabbi was often referred to as a man who uprooted mountains—and the phrase *uprooting mountains* had reference to the rabbi's ability to accomplish a seemly impossible task.

For many faithful Christians, "remove this mountain" has a literal interpretation (Matt. 17:20).

The figurative meaning is to overcome personal difficulties.[253]

Jesus instructed Peter to go "to the sea, and cast an hook, and take up the fish that first cometh up; and when thou hast opened his mouth, thou shalt find a piece of money" (Matt. 17:27). What variety of fish could have held a coin in its mouth?

The Sea of Galilee has a variety of types and sizes of fish that date back to the time of Jesus. Edible fish that date to antiquity are represented by three surviving groups—musht, barbel, and sardine. The best known and tastiest is the musht fish, known as Tilapia Galilea or "Saint Peter's Fish."

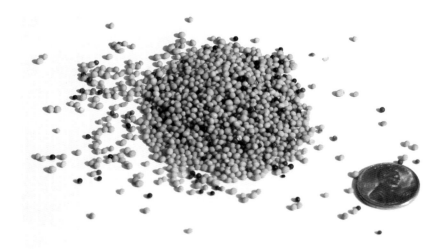

Mustard seed, compared in size to a penny

It acquired its nickname long after Peter obtained the requisite tribute money (see Matt. 17:27). The Tilapia Galilea uses its mouth as a receptacle for fish eggs. This fish "has been known to carry pebbles, bottle caps, and other foreign objects in its mouth."[254]

Was Jesus' counsel to not offend a child difficult for His disciples to accept?

The disciples of Jesus were influenced by their Judaic culture, which held that children were inferior to adults. Jesus admonished His disciples to "take heed that ye despise not one of these

Christ with the children

little ones" or offend them (Matt. 18:10). An offense was an action that caused a child to falter in faithfulness due to the poor example or false doctrine taught by an adult. An offense too often led innocent children and ultimately their posterity to lose their position in the House of Israel. Such offense was greater than "death by the hand of God," for it was a "cutting off" that extended into the eternities.

The penalty Jesus suggested for offending a child was placing a millstone, a heavy grinding stone, about the offender's neck and tossing him into the sea. This penalty was not a Jewish practice, but a Roman and Greek punishment for crimes of peculiar enormity. St. Jerome wrote of Roman soldiers inflicting this punishment on leaders of an insurrection led by Judas of Galilee.[255]

What is the meaning of "seventy times seven" (Matt. 18:22)?

Rabbis and Jewish leaders found the subject of forgiveness a favorite topic of discussion. At the time of Jesus, rabbis taught "three offenses were to be pardoned," but no more. Jesus expanded forgiveness to an infinite number, the meaning of "seventy times seven" for the repentant. For those who failed to repent, Jesus taught that judgment rests with God.[256]

In what ways are the parables of the lost sheep, lost coin, and prodigal son similar?

Jesus was accused of associating with sinners. In response to the accusation, He gave three parables presenting different views of being lost and efforts made to recover what was lost. The parable of the lost sheep, spoken at least twice by Jesus (once in Capernaum and a year later in Perea), is about a sheep that strayed. The true shepherd left the ninety-nine to search for the lost sheep and returned that sheep to the fold.

The parable of the lost coin depicts an initial neglect or carelessness, followed by a diligent search to recover the loss. The vigorous sweeping of the house signifies that the woman realizes the value of what was lost and "turn[s] the world upside down" in her quest to recover the coin (see Luke 15:8).

The parable of the prodigal son is of a son who becomes lost through willful rebellion. The son's demand of his inheritance while his father is "alive and in good health" is equivalent to wishing his father dead. His actions are unprecedented in Jewish literature. Bible scholar Kenneth Bailey wrote, "[It is] difficult to imagine a more dramatic illustration of the quality of love, which grants freedom even to reject the lover, than that given in this opening scene" of the parable.

Although the willful son enjoyed a season of riotous living in a gentile country, the law of the harvest unfolded in his life. As he ate husks—leathery horn-shaped pods from a carob tree—he remembered his home and his father's servants (see Luke 15:16). Humbled by his own foolishness, the son returned.

If Eastern customs prevailed in the parable, a crowd would have gathered near the returning son to mock, taunt, and abuse him for his past rebellion. The father, seeing his returning son in the distance, prevented the abuse by running to greet him. By his actions, the father turned the mocking crowd on himself— for to be seen running was to be publicly humiliated.[257]

Jesus and His disciples went to the Holy City and there attended the Feast of the Tabernacles. What was the Feast of the Tabernacles?

There were three great feasts celebrated in Jerusalem each year—Feast of the Passover, Feast of the Pentecost, and Feast of the Tabernacles. Of these feasts, the Feast of the Tabernacles or "Feast of the Ingathering" was the most cosmopolitan (see Ex. 23:16). Through the centuries, it attracted more pilgrims from distant lands than Passover or Pentecost. There were several reasons for the greater attendance at the Feast of the Tabernacles: 1) the feast was linked to the Day of Atonement and had many ceremonial rituals that were a type and shadow of the coming of the Messiah; 2) the feast was conveniently held after the harvest season to enable agrarian Jews to attend; and 3) the feast had a unifying effect on all Israelites, for pilgrims came in the spirit of thanksgiving.

Those who attended the celebration believed that "It is better to spend one day in God's courts than a thousand days elsewhere." Pilgrims built temporary shelters of wadded boughs, known as booths or tabernacles, to commemorate the makeshift accommodations of ancient Israelites in the wilderness. The booths were erected in fields, on rooftops, and in courtyards throughout the Jerusalem area. Participants of the festivities lived in the booths during the celebration. They burned lamps brightly inside their booths as a reminder of the pillar of fire that led Moses and his people in the wilderness. Public sacrifices for the salvation of Israel and private sacrifices for the forgiveness of sins and reconciliation with God were offered on the Temple Mount.

Unfortunately, some who came to Jerusalem to celebrate did so with revelry in their hearts. To them the feast was a vintage festival that degenerated into immoral acts. Jewish leaders decried this degrading behavior.[258]

Is feasting a form of worship?

Feasting, like fasting, is a form of worship. Both forms are designed to bring worshipers closer to God. In the case of feasting, lectures were given for thirty days before each of the great feasts to prepare worshipers for ceremonial events. Those who attended the lectures were known as Beney Rigla. This title should not be confused with Beney Khallah, a designation given those who attended Sabbath lectures at local synagogues.[259]

What rituals were associated with the Feast of the Tabernacles?

The ceremonial rituals of the eight-day Feast of the Tabernacles were elaborate and required the services of "not fewer than 446 priests and an equal number of Levites." The most memorable ritual occurred each morning after the appointed Levite laid sacrifices on the Holy Temple altar. Surrounded by throngs of worshipers waving palm branches, the Levite walked to the nearby Pool of Siloam to draw water. He drew about two pints from the pool before pronouncing it "living water." He then poured the water into a golden ewer. Carefully carrying the ewer, he returned to the temple altar. On his return, he was followed by a procession of worshipers who waved palm branches. When they arrived at the altar, the Levite gave the ewer to a priest who poured the water into a silver basin on

Pool of Siloam

the west side of the altar. Another priest poured wine into a silver basin on the east side of the altar. Those in the processional then joined the Levite in chanting the Hallel (see Pss. 113–18). During the chant, worshipers exclaimed, "Hallelu Yah," meaning "Praise ye the Lord" (Ps. 117).[260]

> **Was it near the climactic end of the festival that Jesus said, "If any man thirst, let him come unto me, and drink" (John 7:37)?**

Jesus made this statement on the last day of the Feast of the Tabernacles. On that day, known as "Day of the Great Hosanna," "Day of Willows," and "Day of Beating the Branches," multitudes praised Jehovah by waving palm branches with such enthusiasm that "all the leaves were shaken off the willow boughs, and the palm branches beaten in pieces by the side of the altar." After water was drawn from the Pool of Siloam and poured over the temple altar, multitudes circled the great altar seven times, reminiscent of Joshua and the children of Israel circling the walls of Jericho.

Many circling the altar hoped that Judea would be free from

Roman dominion and that the walls of heathen rule, like the walls of Jericho, would tumble to the ground. Near these climactic moments, Jesus called the Jews to come unto Him—the "living water" (John 7:37).[261]

Is it coincidental that the appointment of seventy men to go "two and two before his face into every city and place" (Luke 10:1) was the same number chosen by Moses when he appointed the first Sanhedrin?

It is a type and shadow. It appears that Jesus was instituting a new Sanhedrin of elders, meaning "old men" with the responsibility to preach the gospel beyond the borders of Palestine and to cast out devils (see Luke 10:1–20).

The selection process of the seventy men is unknown except that Jesus chose them from among His disciples. The selection process of Moses is known. Moses chose his seventy by inviting seventy-two men, six from each Israelite tribe, to pick a lot from an urn. Seventy lots were inscribed with the word *zaqen*, meaning "elder," and two were blank. Those who drew a lot inscribed with the word *zaqen*

became a seventy. As such, they presided over Israel with Moses (see Ex. 24:1, 9–10; Num. 11:16).[262]

Jesus upbraided "the cities wherein most of his mighty works were done, because they repented not" (Matt. 11:20). Which cities failed to repent and come unto Jesus?

There were many villages, towns, and cities in Palestine that failed to repent of their wickedness during the days of Jesus. A listing would appear like a gazetteer of the Palestinian province. It is assumed that the question is focused on the scriptural passages found in Matthew (see Matt. 11). In these passages, Jesus refers to three villages on the shoreline of the Sea of Galilee—Capernaum, Chorazin, and Bethsaida.

Chorazin was located in the black basalt hillside two miles north of the seaside village of Capernaum. Bethsaida was situated at the northeast corner of the Sea of Galilee. Jesus said of these cities, "Woe" (Matt. 11:21). The saying may have been a recognition of future suffering, affliction, and calamity that would befall the towns. Today Capernaum and Chorazin are a pile of rocks and partially restored ruins. Even less remains of the fishing village of Bethsaida.[263]

> **Was Jesus speaking metaphorically when He said, "Take my yoke upon you, and learn of me . . . for my yoke is easy" (Matt. 11:29–30)?**

The word yoke had three common definitions at the time of Jesus. The first was a wooden beam made by a carpenter and fastened with leather or rope straps to two animals. According to the Mosaic law, the yoking of two different types of animals, such as an ox and an ass, was forbidden. An unequal pull caused the weaker animal discomfort and pain.

The second definition was Yoke of the Law. This definition was a common rabbinic phrase used to describe the burden of legal requirements and ordinances. Rabbis believed an act of piety was to request that the Yoke of the Law be as heavy as possible.

The third definition was an Aramaic expression describing discontent over taxation, levies, and other financial burdens extracted by overlords.

Jesus assured His disciples that His yoke, meaning "Yoke of the Law," was easy and not a "multitude of burdensome ordinances like that of the Law and of the Pharisees."[264]

> **"A certain lawyer stood up, and tempted him, saying, . . . And who is my neighbour?" (Luke 10:29). What was the Jewish interpretation of the word *neighbor*?**

By the second century, Jews had a contracted interpretation of the word *neighbor,* which meant "only a Jew." Rabbinic laws dictated, "We are not to contrive the death of the Gentiles, but if they are in any danger of death we are not bound to deliver them, . . . if any of them fall into the sea you need not take him out, for such a one is not thy neighbour."

Rabbinic laws also dictated that "an Israelite killing a stranger-inhabitant doth not die for it by the Sanhedrin, because it is said, If any one lifts up himself against his neighbour."

Jesus broadened the definition of neighbor to mean "all of God's children" (see Lev. 25:35–36).[265]

The wounded man to be helped by the good Samaritan

Would the priest or Levite have been pronounced unclean if he had assisted the wounded man in the Parable of the Good Samaritan?

The road between Jerusalem and Jericho was called the "Red Way" and "Bloody Path" because of the violence committed by robbers or thieves on unsuspecting travelers along the road. If the victim in the parable had been dead and the priest or Levite touched him, according to rabbinic law that priest or Levite would be ritually unclean. For the next seven days, the priest or Levite would have participated in the rite of purification to cleanse themselves.

The Samaritan was not bound to Jewish purification laws.[266]

In the parable of the good Samaritan, the Samaritan had compassion on the afflicted, "bound up his wounds, pouring in oil and wine" (Luke 10:34). Was it acceptable in the Jewish culture for a Samaritan to show compassion toward a Jew?

If the wounded man had been a Jew, he would have been restricted as to the application of wine to disinfect his wounds and oil to sooth his abrasions. These restrictions included: 1) a Jew was forbidden to accept oil and wine from a Samaritan; 2) to accept oil and wine was to incur an obligation to pay a tithe on the products; 3) a Jew must be assured that the wine used in a compassionate manner was purchased on the Temple Mount in Jerusalem; and 4) a Jew must know if the oil had come from olive trees grown in Judea or Perea, and if the olives had been crushed in Jerusalem.[267]

During the Feast of the Tabernacles, did Jesus reside in the leafy booth erected on the property of Martha and Mary?

Two-story booth used for the Feast of Tabernacles

It is probable that Jesus lodged in a temporary booth built in a courtyard or near His friends' home. It was the religious duty of all Jews to live in a leafy booth or tabernacle during the Feast of the Tabernacles. The roof of the structure was covered with branches, the floor with fine sand, and the walls decorated with drawings of fruits and flowers.

These temporary structures were a reminder of the wilderness journey of the children of Israel. Philo, an ancient philosopher residing in Alexandria, Egypt, wrote of an additional purpose: "[They] were erected to bring evidence of misfortune at a time of good fortune, and a reminder of poverty to those who were wealthy."268

Were watch towers erected during the Feast of the Tabernacles?

Watch towers were permanent structures built in fields. From the towers, men guarded fields from predators, such as wild animals and thieves. Towers were also used as storage bins for harvested produce.269

Is the parable of the wounded man and the rich man the only parable in which characters are given names?

It is more correct to assume that the characters were not given proper names, but labels designating their circumstances. The wounded man was named Lazarus, meaning "God is my help." From the word *lazarus* comes the word *lazar,* meaning a "leper"—perhaps the reason the beggar had sores on his body. *Dives* is a Latin term meaning "rich man" (see Luke 16:19–31).270

Is the parable of the unjust judge and the importunate widow contrary to rabbinic teachings on prayer?

According to rabbinic doctrine, three prayers a day sufficed. "If a man comes to address you every hour, you say that he holds you cheap," said the rabbis, "the same is true of God, whom no man ought to fatigue by praying every hour." Jesus countered this rabbinic doctrine with a parable that teaches the importance of continually calling upon the Lord in earnest prayer.[271]

Why did the scribes and Pharisees ask Jesus if the woman taken in adultery should die by stoning when they knew that stoning as a penalty for adultery had stopped years before?

Under Roman rule, Jewish courts could order the execution of Jews under certain conditions, but adultery was not one of those conditions. Although the law of Moses "decreed death by stoning as the penalty for adultery," such punishment was abandoned by the Jews long before the time of Jesus and was forbidden under Roman law (see Lev. 20:10).

It seems clear that the scribes and Pharisees wanted to entangle Jesus in a legal foray between the law of Moses and the laws of Rome. If Jesus concluded the woman should suffer death by stoning, He defied Roman law. If He concluded the woman should not suffer death by stoning, He appealed to the Jewish populace but not to the law of Moses.

By writing on the ground, a symbolic action signifying an unwillingness to make a decision or discuss the matter, He distanced himself from the issue. By stating, "He that is without sin among you, let him first cast a stone," He avoided legal issues (John 8:7; see also Deut. 17:7).

Did the healing of the blind man have both spiritual and physical connotations?

Spiritually, the disciples and perhaps the blind man labored under the Jewish misconception that physical affliction was associated with sin and that children inherited the sins of their parents. When Jesus said, "Neither hath this man sinned, nor his parents," He taught the true nature of illness and sin (John 9:3).[272]

The blind man was told to "Go, wash in the pool of Siloam" (John 9:7). What was the significance of the Pool of Siloam?

The Pool of Siloam received its water from the Gihon Spring, also known as Virgin's Fountain via Hezekiah's Tunnel. For seven days during the Feast of the Tabernacles, a Levite carried water from the Pool of Siloam to the Temple Mount. The carried water, referred to as "living water," was a reminder of the water that flowed from a rock during the days of Moses. It was also a symbol of the future Messianic deliverance (see Num. 20:8–11; Isa. 12:3).[273]

Jesus said to the Pharisees, "He that entereth not by the door into the sheepfold, but climbeth up some other way, the same is a thief and a robber" (John 10:1). What did a sheepfold look like?

A sheepfold had high walls with thorns placed atop it to prevent wolves and robbers from climbing into the enclosure. The only entrance into the enclosed sheepfold was a door or gate. Shepherds led sheep through the door during the evening hours (see John 10:1). Sheep readily followed shepherds, but would not follow a stranger into the enclosure. Only one shepherd remained inside the sheepfold for the night. This shepherd was a gatekeeper who was paid by the other shepherds to guard their

Sheepfold

sheep while they returned to their homes. In the morning, the returning shepherds went to the sheepfold to claim their flocks and lead them to the fields. The analogy is that the sheepfold is the kingdom of God; Jesus is the door or gatekeeper and knows His sheep.[274]

Jesus referred to Himself as "the good shepherd" (John 10:14). What is the difference between a good shepherd and a hireling?

A good shepherd is the opposite of a hireling. Even though rabbinic law assured shepherds that they need not expose themselves to danger to protect their flocks, a good shepherd would lay down his life for his sheep. A hireling did not own the sheep and did not fulfill all the duties of a shepherd. He often fled when danger lurked, leaving sheep in harm's way. Hirelings were known to sell sheep in the marketplace and pocket the money, claiming wolves devoured the animals.[275]

When the Pharisees asked, "Is it lawful for a man to put away his wife for every cause?" (Matt. 19:3), was their question in reference to the unlawful marriage of Herod Antipas?

Pharisees may have plotted to entrap Jesus into decrying the divorce and unlawful marriage of Herod Antipas in hopes that His words, like those of John the Baptist, would lead to His demise.

Pharisees may have raised the issue of divorce also in hopes of hurling Jesus into the debate that raged between the Jewish schools of Hillel and Shammai (contemporary schools from 60 BC to AD 20). Students of Hillel argued in favor of a husband divorcing his wife for any cause—even if the husband found another woman more appealing. Students of Shammai argued that divorce was only lawful for offenses against chastity—marital unfaithfulness. If Jesus sided with either school, additional hostility would have risen against Him.[276]

What is known about the young man who called Jesus "Good Master" (Matt. 19:16)?

Tradition suggests that the young man was either a ruler, a presiding official in a local synagogue, or a member of the Sanhedrin. The young man's acknowledgment of Jesus as "Good Master" is strongly questioned by scholars. No mention is made in the Talmud of a young man or student "addressing a Rabbi as *good*. It simply was not done in that day," wrote Elder Bruce R. McConkie. The young man "seeks a middle ground, one that will honor Jesus more than the mere title Rabbi, and yet one that will avoid ascribing to him divine Messianic status." While scholars question the terminology, there is no debate over the rejection of the unsolicited praise (see Matt. 19:16).

When the young man confessed that he had kept the commandments all his days, implying continual righteousness, Jesus invited him to give away his riches and become a disciple. Renouncing riches to devote oneself to religion was an old Eastern custom. The custom and invitation were rejected by the young man, whose heart was not centered on God, even though his outward actions appeared to be righteous.[277]

Was the phrase "it is easier for a camel to go through the eye of a needle" (Mark 10:25) a Jewish idiom?

There is nothing in Judaism or Aramaic literature to suggest a correlation between a camel and a needle. However, an old Jewish proverb says that "even in a man's dreams he will not see an elephant pass through the eye of a needle."

Since the ancient Patriarchs, a camel has symbolized wealth to the children of Israel: "A man with more camels can carry more merchandise." Whether the word *camel* is the correct interpretation or a hyperbole is questioned. Scribes may have mistakenly used the Greek word for camel *(kamelos)* instead of the Greek word for rope *(kamilos)*. If rope were placed in the scriptural passage, it would read, "It is easier for a rope to pass through the eye of the needle." This translation correlates with an ancient saying of Eastern women in the marketplace. When such women shopped for thread and wanted to refuse a merchant's product, they would say, "It is a rope, I cannot use it," meaning "the thread is too thick for my needles."

There were three sizes of needles used in Palestine during the days of Jesus. The smallest needle was used for fine embroidery, the common needle was used for household sewing, and the five-to seven-inch needle was used for sewing large bags, rugs, and tents.[278]

> Jesus said, "The kingdom of heaven is like unto a man that is an householder, which went out early in the morning to hire labourers in his vineyard" (Matt. 20:1). What type of laborer was needed in the vineyard?

Although grape vines are hearty, the attention of many laborers was needed in ancient times to keep them fruitful. Pruning vines in the spring and burning withered branches in the fall were two necessary procedures to ensure a good crop (see John 15:6). To guarantee a fruitful harvest, the owner or lord of the vineyard employed a steward. He in turn employed wine dressers or workers of the land. Last, but most important, a watchman was employed to guard and protect the vineyard from thieves and arson.

The steward went to the marketplace, the commercial center of the community, to find laborers to employ for a day's wage. He thoughtfully hired laborers and sent them to the vineyard. At the vineyard, several laborers were

Vineyard

assigned to work in the fields located on the hillsides. Additional laborers were assigned to the winepress or wine vat, and at least one laborer was assigned to the watch tower erected inside the hedge or stone walls enclosing the vineyard.[279]

Why was the same wage given to laborers hired at different times throughout the day?

Since Easterners were unaccustomed to clocks, it was impossible to calculate the exact hour that the householder, steward, or laborers would be in the marketplace. Morning, noonday, and evening were the divisions best understood by the rural Jewish populace. Laborers went to work when they awoke, and householders remained in the marketplace until they employed all that were needed to work in the vineyard or field that day.

For a day's work, laborers received denaries (penny or pence). The wage was so small that benevolent field and vineyard owners disregarded the time worked and paid each laborer the same amount. This was not because the owner had a partiality toward those hired later in the day—it was because no time records were kept, and the laborer depended on his wage to support himself and his family.

Although this generous accounting system caused friction and dissension between the laborer and the householder, it was a long-standing Jewish tradition among the more benevolent employers. Workers hired early in the day complained about equal pay given to those hired later in the day, but the tradition lasted for centuries.[280]

Jesus attended the Feast of the Dedication. What was that feast?

Between two and three months after the Feast of the Tabernacles, Jews celebrated the wintry Feast of Dedication, also known as Hanukkah or Feast of Lights. The feast was not one of the great feasts that Jewish men were required to attend, but it was a favorite feast and a time of national rejoicing. Festivities of the feast occurred over an eight-day period in which elaborate meals were eaten, extra synagogue services were held, and lamps were kept burning in Jewish homes.

These festivities were held in remembrance of the victorious end of the bloody warfare between the Jews and their Greek ruler Antiochus Ephiphanes. Antiochus was hated for his attempts to stop the worship of Jehovah. He sacrificed swine to Zeus on a Greek altar in the Holy Temple and constructed heathen altars throughout Judea. He demanded that Jews worship heathen gods or suffer death, and ordered the burning of all copies of the Mosaic law. His attempt to suppress centuries of Judaism led to the Maccabean revolt. Judah Maccabee and fellow revolutionaries refused to give homage to Greek gods or to honor other pagan demands of Antiochus. With religious zeal, they waged a three-year war to gain control of Jerusalem, purify the temple, and restore the worship of Jehovah.[281]

Did a temple priest lead a scapegoat through Solomon's porch?

On the Day of Atonement, the holiest day of the year to the Jews, a temple priest led through the Porch of Solomon a goat with a red sash tied to its horns and a placard around its neck that read "La-Azazel." Solomon's porch was an eastern colonnade or row of porticoes in the outer courtyard on the Temple Mount enclosure. Jewish historian Josephus claimed the porch was a cover for the original temple wall built by

Scapegoat

Solomon. Jewish tradition suggests the porch was actually part of Solomon's Temple and not a later building project.

After passing through the porch, a priest took the scapegoat out the eastern gate to the Mount of Olives, and from there into the wilderness—thus fulfilling the scripture that tells of the goat being sent "away by the hand of a fit man into the wilderness" and that "he shall let go the goat in the wilderness" (Lev. 16:21–22). The goat in the wilderness symbolically represented the sins of Israel vanishing.[282]

Where did Jesus end His public ministry?

Jesus left Jerusalem to journey to Perea, located on the east side of the Jordan River in the region where John first baptized. In Perea, Jesus concluded the last months of His public ministry. Many of His followers came to Perea to hear Him preach.[283]

Why did Jesus say, "We go up to Jerusalem" (Matt. 20:18)?

Although the answer could easily evolve into a geographic discussion of Jerusalem being 2,500 feet above sea level, such a discussion would be trite when speaking of the Holy City. To leave Jerusalem was always to go down. To enter the Holy City was always to go up. To the Jews, Jerusalem was the pinnacle, the highest place on earth—Salem.[284]

Was it Doubting Thomas who said, "Let us also go, that we may die with him" (John 11:16)?

Thomas or Didymus—a Greek word meaning "twin"—has been ridiculed and maligned for initially doubting the resurrection of Jesus. In this scriptural passage, Thomas was supportive of returning to Jerusalem, and if need be, "we may die with him" (John 11:16).[285]

As Jesus was passing "through the cities and villages, teaching, and journeying toward Jerusalem," a Pharisee admonished Him to "Get thee out, and depart hence: for Herod will kill thee" (Luke 13:22, 31). Why would a Pharisee warn Jesus about Herod's plot?

Not all Pharisees sought the life of Jesus. In this scriptural

Jericho

account, Jesus ate bread at the Pharisee's house and cured a man of dropsy, an ailment caused by fluid retention.[286]

On His journey to Jerusalem, Jesus passed through Jericho. Did priests reside in Jericho during the days of Jesus?

Jericho, eight hundred feet below sea level and the lowest city on the earth, was in antiquity home to as many priests as was Jerusalem. By the days of Jesus, the number of priests in the city had diminished. The city was rebuilt close to the an-

cient site by Herod the Great. It became an oasis or resting place for travelers and pilgrims as they journeyed between Galilee and Judea (see Luke 19:1). Anticipating their arrival in Jericho were the physically impaired of the community, who sat near the city entrance hoping that one of the pilgrims would cure their afflictions.

During the middle ages, Jericho became a favorite oasis for the religiously inclined who referred to the community as "Date City" and "City of the Palms."[287]

Did the blind men in Jericho make the first public acknowledgment that Jesus was the Messiah?

The call of the blind men, "Have mercy on us, O Lord, thou Son of David," was the first public acknowledgment of Jesus as the Messiah (Matt. 20:30). Until then, only the disciples of Jesus and those possessed with evil spirits expressed knowledge or conviction of His true identity. Those harboring unclean spirits were silenced by Jesus. Disciples were admonished to keep their witness to themselves. When the blind men addressed Jesus as "Son of David," He accepted their public recognition (Matt. 20:30).[288]

Why was Zacchaeus, "chief among the publicans," in the priestly town of Jericho (Luke 19:2)?

Jericho was not only home to priests and religious seekers, it was an official residence of publicans and collectors of custom. Chief among the publicans was Zacchaeus (variation of the Hebrew name Zacharias). In an effort to see Jesus, Zacchaeus climbed an evergreen sycomore tree. Sycomore trees flourished in the Jordan Valley, growing to more than fifty feet in circumference. These trees produced a species of fig.[289]

Had the mourning rituals for Lazarus ended when Jesus and His disciples arrived in Bethany?

When Jesus and His disciples reached Bethany, a small village on the southeastern slope of the Mount of Olives, Lazarus had lain in the grave for four days. A popular belief at the time was that "the spirit remained near the body up to three days, but by the fourth day the spirit was irretrievably gone."

As part of the traditional mourning ritual, noisy lamentations from bereaved family members and hired mourners accompanied by flutes, pipes, and other musical instruments would still be piercing the air. Chairs and couches in the family home would probably still be turned over and mourners seen seated on low stools. Lamentations would have continued in this manner for twenty-six more days. Sorrow and misery in the home would have ebbed and flowed for an additional thirty days. During those days Mary and Martha would have worn torn garments as a sign of their sorrow had not Jesus raised Lazarus from the tomb.[290]

Why did the raising of Lazarus cause such anger among the Jewish leaders?

Jewish leaders tenaciously guarded Judaism and the law, and did not believe in the miracles of Jesus. They believed that the influence and power of Jesus threatened their way of life. They believed that His followers had been seduced by miracles and that they might rebel against Rome if Jesus were not stopped.

Power and concern for public order dominated Jewish thought as their "council" met. The high priest Caiaphas concluded that for public safety, "It is expedient for us, that one man [Jesus] should die for the people, and that the whole nation perish not" (John 11:50). From that council forward, plans were laid to put Jesus to death.

Knowing of the mounting malice directed toward Him, Jesus left Bethany and journeyed to Ephraim, an isolated hillside town about fifteen miles northeast of the Holy City (see John 11:54). There He "found respite before his final journey to Jerusalem."[291]

Christ raising Lazarus

The Last Week

Although He knew the trials that awaited Him the last week of his mortality, Jesus did not turn from His appointed destiny. He moved confidently forward to fulfill the will of His Father.

Did Jesus make His entry into Jerusalem from Bethany or Bethphage?

The last week of Jesus' life, a subject that occupies more than a third of the Gospel narrative, began in the town of Bethany, meaning "house of dates." Bethany was adjacent to the village of Bethphage, meaning "house of figs." Bethany was located on the eastern slope of the Mount of Olives. Jesus started from Bethany and stopped at Bethphage to mount the ass.[292]

When Jesus had "come to Bethphage, unto the mount of Olives," He sent two disciples to go into the village and "find

a colt tied, whereon never man sat; loose him, and bring him. And if any man say unto you, Why do ye this? say ye that the Lord hath need of him; and straightway he will send him hither" (Matt. 21:1; Mark 11:2–3). **Can it be assumed that the owner of the colt was a generous man?**

During the festive season of Passover, hospitality was generously offered to friends and strangers. Jews hung curtains in front of their doors to signal travelers that all were welcome in their homes. Jews were prepared to offer bed and board to strangers and to loan animals for hire or upon request. During Passover

Two ass colts

week, holy men and Jewish leaders were granted the use of any animal upon request. "Take it, kill it if you wish, it is yours," the animal owner would shout. "You don't need to ask me."

Perhaps the owner of the colt (ass) recognized the disciples of Jesus as holy men. If that were the case, the owner would have believed himself honored that the disciples had chosen his colt (see Matt. 21:2–3; Zech. 9:9). Perhaps the owner was a follower of Jesus.

Matthew was the only Gospel writer to mention both an ass and a colt, meaning the "male off-spring of an ass."[293]

Why didn't Roman soldiers stop the triumphal entry of Jesus?

When Jesus entered the Holy City riding an ass, Roman soldiers did not stop the procession or think Him a revolutionary, an aspiring king, or a fanatic planning religious anarchy. Only when Roman power was challenged or public order threatened would soldiers have interfered with the pomp and ceremony of the Passover week.

Roman soldiers suppressed the Druids for practicing human sacrifice, Phoenicians for casting children into sacrificial fire, and messianic claims. To them, a man on a donkey laden with garments did not appear a threat. Therefore, the entry of Jesus into Jerusalem went seemingly unnoticed by Roman soldiers.

It appears the soldiers did not know the ass was symbolic of royalty to the Jews and a man riding an ass laden with cloths was symbolic of a Jewish king—the Messiah. If Jesus had ridden a horse into the Holy City, His actions would have appeared to

Triumphal entry into the Holy City

the soldiers to be a symbol of war against Roman occupation. It may have triggered bloodshed.[294]

> As Jesus entered Jerusalem, "a very great multitude spread their garments in the way; others cut down branches from the trees, and strawed them in the way" (Matt. 21:8). Did the followers of Jesus cut down palm branches as He entered the Holy City?

The issue of where the multitude cut the branches has produced at least two opinions, because palm trees were not found on the Mount of Olives. The first and most plausible opinion is that the branches were cut and gathered from nearby Bethany, a small village known for its date trees. Date trees produce large leaves called branches (see John 12:13; Rev. 7:9).

The second opinion is that palm branches were brought from Jericho to Jerusalem for the Passover festivities. Although Jericho is known for its palm trees and is only seventeen miles from Jerusalem, it is more plausible that the followers of Jesus spontaneously cut and gathered date leaves from nearby Bethany.

Since the Hasmonaean period, the waving of branches has been a symbol of Jewish patriotism and triumph over foreign oppressors.[295]

> Was the shout of hosanna reminiscent of the shout heard at the Feast of the Tabernacles?

The public exclamation of hosanna—"save us" or "deliver us, we beseech thee"—was the high point of the Hosanna Day celebrated during the Feast of the Tabernacles. On that day, worshipers waved palm branches and shouted hosannas in remembrance of the Israelite exodus from Egypt and the wilderness homes of their ancestors.

The adulation given Jesus was called the Hallelujah Psalm: "He is blessed who comes in Yaweh's name; From Yahweh's house we bless you!" (see Ps. 118:26). The united shout acknowledged Jesus as King of the Jews.[296]

> Why did Jesus weep after His triumphal entry?

Luke records Jesus' weeping as He thought of the past and future of the Holy Temple and the city of Jerusalem. Jesus knew that the temple, with its large stones (some more than 37 feet long, 18 feet wide, and 12 feet thick), would fall and that the great city would be destroyed. Perhaps some who honored Jesus that Palm Sunday would live to see Jerusalem brought low by Titus and his Roman soldiers. Eighty thousand held siege against the city for months before torching it in AD 70. For these poignant reasons, Jesus wept.[297]

Figs

Why did a few Greeks, who had come up to Jerusalem for the Feast of the Passover, approach Philip saying, "We would see Jesus" (John 12:21)? Was Philip a Greek by birth?

The name *Philip* is of Greek derivation and means "lover of horses." By knowing the origin of his name, it should not be concluded that Philip was a Greek by birth. Why certain Greeks approached him and not another is unknown.[298]

Why did Jesus curse the barren fig tree?

Cursing the fig tree was unique among the recorded miracles of Jesus. All other miracles brought a blessing or benefit, but this miracle was an act of judgment. Although

it was spring and Jesus knew that fig trees in Palestine did not produce fruit in the spring—only in June, August, and during the winter—He hoped that this tree was an exception. Its leafy facade gave the appearance of having borne fruit. But there were no kermouses or fruit hidden under the broad leaves (see Luke 13:7).

Cursing the fig tree symbolically represented the anger of Jesus with Israel. The very next day, Jesus spoke the parable of the fig tree—a tree in rabbinic lore that symbolized the nation of Israel—a nation that Jesus had watered, nourished, pruned, and expected to bear fruit.[299]

Was it on the third day of the Holy Week that the chief priests and elders asked Jesus, "By what authority doest thou these things? and who gave thee this authority" (Matt. 21:23)?

On the third day, while Jesus was teaching in the temple, He was confronted by Jewish leaders—chief priests, scribes, elders, and Pharisees. He responded to their queries with three parables: the parable of the two sons (see Matt. 21:28–31), the parable of the wicked husbandmen (see Matt. 21:33–44), and the parable of the marriage of the king's son (see Matt. 22:1–14). The marriage of the king's son was the last parable uttered by Jesus in a public setting. He shared two other parables with His Apostles on the Mount of Olives: the parable of the ten virgins (see Matt. 25:1–12) and the parable of the talents (see Matt. 25:14–30).[300]

Why did the Pharisees league themselves with the Herodians?

Herodians were a political faction whose purpose was to ensure that power and rule remained in the Herod family. They believed that through continual Herodian rule, the status of the Jewish people would be maintained; they also believed that Herodian rule fulfilled messianic prophecy. Since the Herods were subject to the appointment processes of Rome, Herodians were supportive of Roman rule over Palestine.

The political purposes of the Herodians were in direct contrast to the political leanings of the Pharisees, who wanted a separate Judea free from foreign domination. Yet when it came to Jesus of Nazareth, Herodians and Pharisees laid aside their verbal disputes and partisan politics to find fault with Jesus and put Him to death.[301]

Herodians asked Jesus, "Is it lawful to give tribute unto Caesar, or not?" (Matt. 22:17). Was Jesus exempt from paying Roman tribute?

Under Roman rule, priests and rabbis were exempt from paying Roman tribute. Although Jesus was recognized by His disciples as a rabbi, He was not recognized as such by Jewish leaders. Therefore, He was obliged to pay taxes and tribute to Rome. The Greek coin didrachma, equivalent to the Tyrian half shekel, was the

Roman coins

Half shekel, ca. AD 70

expected tribute. The didrachma was stamped with an image of Caesar. The Tyrian shekel was pressed with an etching of grape clusters and palm trees (see Ex. 30:13–15).

If Jesus had answered the Herodians that it was appropriate to give tribute to Rome, He would have been viewed as a disloyal son of Abraham to orthodox Jews.[302]

> The Sadducees asked Jesus, "If a man die, having no children, his brother shall marry his wife, and raise up seed unto his brother. . . . in the resurrection whose wife shall she be?" (Matt. 22:28). Why did the Sadducees ask such a question?

The Sadducees—like the scribes, Herodians, and Pharisees—sought to entrap Jesus with His own words. The case of marrying a brother's childless widow was obviously an imagery pre-

sented for the purpose of debate (see Deut. 25:5).

The Sadducees, a religious party in Judea, not only lost a verbal round with Jesus, but through years of Roman rule lost much of their religious influence to the Pharisees. Their belief in the strict observance of the Torah, their rejection of Judaic traditions, and their denial of the resurrection were not popular with the people (see Acts 23:8).

While the Sadducees struggled to keep a religious hold on the Jews, the more popular Pharisaic beliefs attracted followers. By the time of Jesus, when questions of Jewish rituals arose, people turned to the Pharisees for answers. By the time of the Jewish revolt against Rome (AD 66–70), the Sadducees had little influence. They lost all remaining influence in AD 70, when Titus and his Roman soldiers destroyed Jerusalem.[303]

> What is the meaning of Jesus' accusation that the scribes and Pharisees sit in Moses' seat and "make broad their phylacteries" (Matt. 23:5)?

The seat of Moses was a "chair of judgment and instruction in the synagogue.

During prayers, phylacteries were worn by devout Jewish men. A phylactery consisted of a small leather cubical box held in place by thongs on the forehead (before their minds) or on the inner left arm (next to their hearts). Inside the box were four small compartments containing tiny rolls of parchment inscribed with scriptural passages—Ex.13:1–17, Deut. 6:4–9, and Deut.11:13–21. The purpose of the phylactery was to help the wearer remember the laws of God.

Pharisees found many occasions in public places to wear phylacteries on their arms or foreheads. To ensure their piety was noticed, they pridefully enlarged the borders or size of the one-and-a-half-inch leather box.[304]

Were Pharisees ordained priests?

In synagogues throughout Palestine, Pharisees assembled to instruct Jews in the ways of religious piety. Their lectures undercut priestly authority while extolling their own ritual purity and devout conduct. In many respects, Pharisees acted as if they were ordained priests. They strolled through the marketplace wearing enlarged phylacteries and fine clothing and expected to be greeted by the title rabbi, meaning "master."

During synagogue worship Pharisees sat in the chief seats that in the past had been reserved for the rabbis and rulers of the synagogue. The seats were located in front of the congregation near the ark. As the congregation faced the ark, those in the chief seats looked down on the congregation from a raised platform. Despite their outward piety at the synagogue and in the marketplace, Pharisees were not ordained priests.[305]

Why did Jesus link scribes and Pharisees with hypocrites?

Hypocrisy goes beyond words or mere pretense. Pharisees thought of themselves as the religious leaders of Judaism and wore priestly attire, which was worn anciently only by ordained priests. Jesus decried this action as hypocritical—a pretense. He

Phylacteries

further denounced the pharisaic and scribal command of legal minutiae and persistence in pursuing nagging details of ritual. Such command and persistence had led them to boast and act as if they were devout, when they were actually polluted within. Jesus taught, "He that is greatest among you shall be your servant" (Matt. 23:11).[306]

> Mark tells of Jesus sitting "against the treasury" on the Temple Mount (Mark 12:41). Which court on the Temple Mount contained the treasury?

The temple treasury was located in the Court of the Women. Inside the treasury were thirteen trumpet-shaped receptacles that held monetary gifts donated by faithful Jews. Each receptacle was labeled—temple expenses, sacrifices, oil, wine, incense, sacred vessels, and so on.[307]

> Were the widow's Greek coins an acceptable offering at the temple treasury?

Jewish women could give freely of their means to the treasury without trading foreign coins (such as Greek and Roman coins) for Tyrian shekels. The widow, so named because she was wearing clothes of mourning, gave two mites—the smallest circulating denomination in Palestine. The contribution of a single mite was unacceptable to the treasury because its value was so low (see Mark 12:42; Luke 21:2).[308]

> Jesus said to the Pharisees and scribes, "Ye pay tithe of mint and anise and cummin, and have omitted the weightier matters of the law, judgment, mercy, and faith" (Matt. 23:23). On which herbs did the Pharisees and scribes demand a tithe?

Scribes and Pharisees were so enamored by the details of the law that they demanded a tithe on common, inexpensive Judean herbs—mustard, mint, rue, anise, dill, and cumin. These garden herbs were used for their aromatic, culinary, and medicinal value.[309]

> Jesus pronounced scribes and Pharisees "as graves which appear not, and the men that walk over them are not aware of them" (Luke 11:44). Were graves easily seen in Palestine?

In the days of Jesus, it was impossible to pass a grave or tomb in the daylight hours without noticing it, because each burial site was whitewashed every spring. The purpose of whitewashing was not to guard the remains of the dead, but to guard and warn the living from coming too close to a tomb and being defiled. The words of Jesus—"men that walk over them are not aware of them" (Luke 11:44)—probably referred to walking in a cemetery at night and falling into an open grave by mistake.[310]

Was Jesus referring to an actual hen or another bird when he said, "How often would I have gathered thy children together, even as a hen gathereth her chickens under her wings, and ye would not" (Matt. 23:37)?

The issue centers on the Greek word *ornis,* from which the word *hen* is derived. The literal translation of ornis is "bird" or "fowl."

Hen fits the context of the analogy, however. For example, just as the Lord calls to His people through many holy prophets, the hen communicates with her young through tonal variations. She gathers her chicks for feeding

Hen gathering her chicks

and watering with a low clucking sound. She uses high-pitched tones to warn her chicks of encroaching danger; chicks respond to the high pitch and gather under the hen's protective wings. The hen then fluffs her feathers so as to appear larger in hopes of frightening away danger. If danger persists, the hen will attack to save her young.

Jesus wanted to gather and save Israel as a hen gathers her chicks and saves them, but Israel would not be gathered.[311]

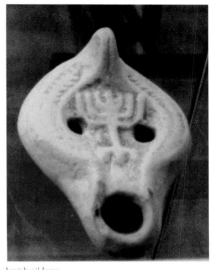

Jewish oil lamp

In the parable of the ten virgins, the foolish virgins "took no oil with them" (Matt. 25:3). Why was it important that the virgins bring oil to the wedding feast?

Friends and family received two invitations announcing a forthcoming wedding. The first was an announcement to prepare for the wedding feast, and the second announced the feasting period. To decline either wedding invitation was to insult the bride and groom.

Wedding festivities began in the evening, when the bride was escorted to the house of the bridegroom. Due to the late hour, each wedding guest was expected to carry a lamp to illuminate the festivities. Lamps consisted of a wick placed in a hollow clay cup or deep saucer that was fastened to a long wooden pole. Guests were to carry vials of oil to keep their lamps lit.

An ancient Bezae manuscript claims that the foolish virgins hung opaque vials from their fingers, pretending to take extra oil for their lamps.[312]

Jesus taught that "he shall separate them one from another, as a shepherd divideth his sheep from the goats" (Matt. 25:32). Did shepherds place goats and sheep in the same flock?

Sheep and goats roamed together in flocks on the hillsides of Palestine. Shepherds referred to sheep as "white sheep" and goats as "black sheep." Sheep supplied wool for clothing, while goats supplied hair needed to make tents, bags, and ropes.

Though sheep and goats were both important to the pastoral economy of Palestine, the Hebrew Bible depicts sheep as highly favored of God, while goats are depicted as rebellious and wayward. In the future, sheep will be on the right hand of God—a favored position. Goats will be on the left hand of God—out of favor with the Great Jehovah.[313]

Why was a known sinner allowed to enter Simon's home and wash the feet of Jesus?

It was expected that the leading Pharisee in a given community would invite visiting rabbis to share a meal. To a Jew, eating or sharing a meal was a form of intimacy.

Simon omitted socially expected courtesies when sharing a meal with Jesus. For example, he failed to kiss Jesus as He entered Simon's home. The customary kiss recognized that the guest held a higher place in society than the host; to not kiss Jesus was a sign of Simon's belief that Jesus held an inferior social station and was a display of open contempt.[314]

Flock of sheep and goats together

As to why a known sinner was allowed into Simon's home at will, the answer lies in the fact that the owner of a Jewish house did not have the right to cast out a friend of his guest. Although Simon knew the woman who entered the house was a sinner, she freely entered the home and bathed the feet of Jesus with her tears. She anointed His feet with oil and wiped them with her hair. Her tears may not have been abhorrent to Simon, but the letting down of her hair was socially unacceptable to the Pharisee and all familiar with Jewish law. According to the law, a peasant woman was forbidden to let her hair down to any man except her husband. It was a great humiliation to the woman and to her kin if she were seen with her hair disheveled. In fact, the Talmud suggests that a husband could rightfully divorce his wife for such an action.

This woman boldly ignored the social and rabbinic disgrace and performed an act of kindness for Jesus. Simon rebuked the act by saying, "Toucheth him," which means she should cease embracing or defiling Jesus (Luke 7:39). Jesus, knowing the Pharisee's thoughts, said, "Simon, I have somewhat to say unto thee" (Luke 7:40). This phrase, used in villages and towns throughout Palestine, meant that Simon was to be reproved for his thoughts and/or actions.

Jesus praised the woman for her kindness and derided Simon for ignoring common Jewish courtesies. His words were contrary to the prevailing social customs that prohibited a man from praising a woman in public and encouraged a guest to speak with exaggerated appreciation of his host.[315]

Who anointed Jesus with costly spikenard?

There were possibly two occasions when this happened. Gospel writer John records that Jesus was anointed by Mary, the sister of Lazarus (see John 11:2). In his account, Luke records that Jesus was anointed by "a sinner" (Luke 7:37). Luke and John wrote that the feet of Jesus were anointed, while Matthew and Mark wrote that his head was anointed. To anoint his head "was to do him honor." To anoint his feet was to display singular regard, a "reverential homage rarely rendered even to kings" on their coronation day.

What is clear in all of the Gospel accounts is that the woman came to Jesus carrying an alabaster box—a sealed flask or cruse made from a translucent stone. When the seal was broken, a costly spikenard ointment—probably imported from the Himalayas—poured forth (see Mark 14:3–9). The estimated market value of the ointment was more than a year's wage of a common laborer.[316]

> **Did the chief priests have more than "thirty pieces of silver" (Matt. 26:15) at their disposal with which to pay Judas?**

Chief priests encouraged the betrayal of Judas and offered to financially reward him (see Matt. 26:15). With the entire temple treasury at their disposal, they could have given a thousand silver pieces or more for the betrayal. Judas received a promise of only thirty pieces of silver (see Zech. 11:13; 12:10; 13:6, 7).[317]

> **On the first day of the Feast of the Unleavened Bread, the disciples asked Jesus, "Where wilt thou that we prepare for thee to eat the passover?" (Matt. 26:17). Was that feast the same as the Feast of Passover?**

In the days of Jesus, the Feast of Passover and the Feast of Unleavened Bread were a single celebration. The purpose of the feast was to remember that the angel of death passed over the homes and flocks of Israel, and to remember Jehovah, the Great Deliverer of Israel. All ceremonial rituals in the festivities centered on these two themes.[318]

> **Jesus told His disciples, "Behold, when ye are entered into the city, there shall a man meet you, bearing a pitcher of water; follow him" (Luke 22:10). Was it unusual for a man to carry a pitcher of water in a public setting?**

Jesus instructed Peter and John to follow a man bearing a pitcher of water drawn from the Pool of Siloam, a pool that originated from the Gihon Spring. Women traditionally carried water from this pool. A man doing a woman's work near the pool would be easy to detect. The man is believed to have resided in the "semi-monastic Essene community" of Jerusalem in the Upper City.[319]

Traditional food of the Passover

Was it unusual to lend an upper room to strangers during the Passover festivities?

During Passover festivities, a devout Jew would never claim a home as his own. All homes were open and available to pilgrims with no payment asked. However, it was customary for pilgrims to offer their host the skin of the lamb they had sacrificed on the Temple Mount. On the night of Seder, a Hebrew word meaning "arrangement or order," Jews purposely left their doors open, hoping to bring good fortune to themselves by entreating a pilgrim or stranger to enter.

Peter and John followed the man carrying the pitcher of water to his house, which was located on a hill (known today as Mount Zion). The man was obviously pleased that these pilgrims had chosen his home for their feast. He didn't make a typical Jewish offer to Peter and John—the use of a hostelry or hall opening to the *khan,* where "beasts of burden were unloaded," shoes and staffs kept, and dusty garments laid down. Instead, the man offered a large upper chamber or guest-chamber located on the roof of his home—a choice secluded setting for the Passover feast that was reached by climbing outside stairs.[320]

How was the upper room furnished?

The upper chamber was prepared by Peter and John and the good man of the house for the festive occasion. The room probably contained rugs and a separate divan or pillow for each of the thirteen guests. The pillows would be used by the guests to recline on while eating the Paschal Supper, for they were to eat in a relaxed manner as free men. Traditionally, the guests would lie on their left side and lean on their left hand while eating the meal.

After the guest chamber was made ready and the lamb roasted on a pomegranate spit, other preparations were still needed. Lighting the lamps, baking the unleavened cakes, and preparing bitter herbs were necessary before all was ready. Each preparation pointed to similar preparations made in the days of Moses and was symbolic of the promised Savior, the Messiah.

When everything was in readiness, Peter and John left Jerusalem to find Jesus and lead Him and the other Apostles to the Upper Room.

Generations before, those attending the feast dressed for travel by wearing sandals on their feet and carrying a staff in their hand as a remembrance of the Israelites' hurried escape from Egypt. Such customs had ended by the time of Jesus.[321]

Who sat next to Jesus in the Upper Room?

Some of the Apostles, like the Pharisees and Sadducees clamoring for the chief seats in the synagogues, quarreled over who would recline next to Jesus.

It was a Jewish custom for the host of the Passover feast to have his choicest friends seated or reclined next to him. Judas received the place of honor, which was on the left side of Jesus. The youngest Apostle, "the disciple whom Jesus loved" (John 21:20), received the second place of honor and was seated on the right side of Jesus.

If slaves were present in the Upper Room, they remained standing as a symbolic gesture of their continued servitude.[322]

Is it true that sharing food was an important symbol in the farewells of Jesus?

Interesting, and perhaps symbolic, are the number of occasions in the ministry of Jesus when food played an important role in His farewells. His Galilean ministry closed with the feeding of five thousand. His ministry to the gentile federation of Decapolis ended with His feeding of the four thousand. His Judean ministry ended with the Passover feast.

In the closing of the Judean ministry, there was a new beginning. "The final Passover was, in reality, two events rather than one: a formal celebration of the annual Passover supper and the first observance of the Lord's Supper in commemoration of the atoning act of Jesus Christ."[323]

Did Jesus follow all of the customary Passover rituals in the Upper Room?

Despite centuries of study, neither theologians, scholars, nor historians claim with certainty that Jesus followed with exactness the customary Passover rituals. However, it is clear from the Gospel passages that portions of

The Savior and the Twelve at the Last Supper

the Passover rituals were instituted in the Upper Room.[324]

Formal Passover procedures have varied through the centuries. It cannot be said with certainty that each step of the feast is an exact replication of the experience of Jesus and the Twelve Apostles. However, it is assumed that the feast proceeded in the following manner until Jesus washed the feet of the Apostles:

First Cup. The host took the first of four cups of wine and said, "Blessed art Thou, Jehovah our God, who hast created the fruit of the vine!" (see Luke 22:17). He then passed the cup to the gathered men and invited them to drink from it. After the cup had passed among the group, the host washed his hands as he recited, "Blessed art Thou, Jehovah our God, King of the Universe, who hast chosen us from among all people, and . . . sanctified us with thy commandments, and hast enjoined us concerning the washing of our hands."

After the washing of hands, the Paschal Lamb, bitter herbs, unleavened bread, and a mixture of dates, raisins, and vinegar were then placed before the host. The host dipped an herb in the date mixture and offered a benediction before passing the remaining herbs to his guests.

Second Cup. The second cup was filled with wine, but was not immediately drunk. First the guests had to receive the flesh of the Paschal Lamb, a piece of unleavened bread, and a bitter herb from the host. According to an ancient Jewish custom, the first mouthful was presented to the honored guest seated at the left of the host as a sign of their close relationship (see Ps. 41:9). Note that Jesus offered the first mouthful to Judas.

Inquiries from the youngest at the feast followed the eating of sop. "Why is this night different from all others?" he asked. "Why do we eat only unleavened bread, bitter herbs and roasted lamb? Why are the herbs dipped twice rather than only once?" In response to his queries, the host recounted the delivery of the Israelites from Egyptian bondage and the giving of the Mosaic law.

A prayer was then offered and all present sang the Hallel and offered a benediction: "Blessed art

Thou, Jehovah our God, King of the Universe, who hast redeemed us and redeemed our fathers from Egypt" (see Pss. 113–14). The second cup was then drunk, hands were washed again, and one of the unleavened cakes was broken and passed to the guests to eat.[325]

> Jesus said, "Behold, the hand of him that betrayeth me is with me on the table. . . . He it is, to whom I shall give a sop" (Luke 22:21; John 13:26). Is *sop* the broth of the meat?

When the meat dish of the Paschal Supper was served, it was customary to place the broth and meat in a bowl. Meat was taken from the bowl with fingers, not utensils. Thin pieces of unleavened bread, symbolizing the haste with which the Israelites fled Egypt, were held in fingers like a makeshift spoon and used to soak up the broth. The dipped or soaked bread was called *sop.*

During the Passover feast, it was an honor for two friends to dip their sop in the same bowl. It was a greater honor for the host of the feast to dip a piece of bread in the broth and offer it to another.

Jesus gave sop to Judas. Judas accepted the sop, yet did not finish the Passover feast, for "Satan entered into him. Then said Jesus unto him, That thou doest, do quickly" (John 13:27). It appears that the other Apostles were unaware of Judas's intention. They may have supposed that as the treasurer of the Twelve, he left the feast to purchase a gift for the poor—a Passover custom.[326]

> Did Jesus and His disciples finish the feast after Judas left the Upper Room?

It was not until the sop was eaten that the Paschal feast, with its symbolic rituals, was over. All that remained was to drink the third and fourth cup, sing the second part of the Hallel, and offer two prayers (see Pss. 115–18).[327]

> When did Jesus introduce the Lord's Supper in the Upper Room?

After Judas left the Upper Room and while those who remained were still eating, Jesus said, "With desire I have desired to eat this Passover with you before I suffer" (Luke 22:15). He then took the round unleavened bread "and blessed it, and brake it, and gave it to the disciples, and said, Take, eat; this is my body," or as Luke reports, "This do in remembrance of me" (Matt. 26:26; Luke 22:19; see JST Matt. 26:22).

At this point, He would have raised the third cup, known as the "cup of the blessing." On this cup, the host was invited to express a blessing upon his guests. In this case, the host—Jesus—would have taken the cup, "and gave thanks, and gave it to them, saying, Drink ye all of it; For this is my blood of the new testament, which is shed for many for the remission of sins" (Matt. 26:27–28; JST Matt. 26:24–25).

When Jesus said, "This is my blood of the new testament," He was referring to a new covenant, new emblems, and a new sacrifice (Matt. 26:28). Jesus then promised the Twelve, "But I say unto you, I will not drink henceforth of this fruit of the vine, until that day when I drink it new with you in my Father's kingdom" (Matt. 26:29).[328]

Christ washes the feet of the disciples

Was Jesus acting the part of a slave when He washed the feet of the Apostles?

To be girded with a towel was to be acknowledged as a slave. Slaves washed the feet of their masters and, as a courtesy, the feet of their master's guests. Large stones or ceramic basins were placed near the entrances of all but the poorest houses in Palestine so that masters and their invited guests could have their feet bathed as they entered.

Jesus did not wash the feet of His Apostles when they entered the Upper Room. He washed their feet during the Passover feast.[329]

Jesus said to His Apostles, "Peace I leave with you, my peace I give unto you: not as the world giveth, give I unto you" (John 14:27). What is the difference between the peace of Jesus and the common Jewish greeting "shalom"?

Jesus, knowing that His death was near, did not leave His Apostles comfortless. He blessed them with peace, a harmony of life, and a completeness of serenity. It was not the Hebrew greeting of *shalom,* meaning to "wish another peace," but a spiritual gift from God. With this gift came a new commandment—"That ye love one another; as I have loved you, that ye also love one another. By this shall all men know that ye are my disciples, if ye have love one to another" (John 13:34–35). Obedience to the new commandment became the mark of a true Christian.[330]

Why is the prayer of Jesus that begins "Father, the hour is come; glorify thy Son, that thy Son also may glorify thee" (John 17:1) called the Intercessory Prayer?

The prayer is known by two titles—the Great Intercessory Prayer and the High Priestly Prayer. *Intercessory* refers to the pleading of Jesus to the Father for His disciples and those who believe on their words. *High Priestly Prayer* refers to His future sacrifice for the sins and sorrows of the world (see Heb. 3:1).

The prayer has three main themes—1) Jesus offers Himself as a ransom for the sins of the world; 2) Jesus announces the completion of His mortal ministry to His Father; and 3) Jesus pleads in behalf of His faithful Apostles and those who will believe in their teachings (see John 17).[331]

Jesus left the Upper Room and went to the Mount of Olives. Is the Mount of Olives a series of mountains?

The Mount of Olives is a mile-long chain of hills about three hundred feet from Jerusalem (see Acts 1:12). Three prominent summits arise amid the hills— Mount Scopus, Mount Scandal, and Mount Offense.

The Garden of Gethsemane is located on Mount Scopus, which in Greek means "lookout point" and in Hebrew means "mount of the watchman." The armies of Babylon and Rome camped on Mount Scopus during their invasion of Jerusalem. Anciently, Mount Scopus was viewed as a watchtower guarding Jerusalem and the Holy Temple.[332]

Were olive trees indigenous to Gethsemane?

Olive trees have thrived for centuries on the Mount of Olives with little care, even during long periods of drought. Year after year, the trees produce fruit without undue attention.

During harvest season, laborers pick fruit and place it in a

Olive trees on the Mount of Olives

Modern-day Mount of Olives and traditional site of the Garden of Gethsemane

gethsemane, meaning "oil press." Fruit from just one tree can produce fifteen to twenty gallons of oil every other year. Anciently, the olive oil was used for fuel, anointing, sacrifices, and food.

Scholar D. Kelly Ogden lamented the appropriateness of the name *Gethsemane:* "Just as the blood (juice) of the grape or olive is pressed and crushed by the heavy stone in the press, so the heavy burden of the sins of the world that was Jesus' to carry would press the blood out of the body of this Anointed One."

Today the traditional site of the Garden of Gethsemane and the Basilica of the Agony is maintained by Franciscan monks. These monks claim that eight gnarled olive trees in the garden date to the time of Jesus. Scholars discount their claim by pointing to the Roman siege of Jerusalem in AD 70 during which even the area surrounding the Holy City was burned.[333]

Was Jesus in Gethsemane when "He took with him Peter and the two sons of Zebedee, and began to be sorrowful and very heavy" (Matt. 26:37)? Was it the night of Seder?

On Seder, Jesus took Peter, James, and John into a secluded area of Gethsemane and asked them to watch while He went "about a stone's cast" (about a hundred feet) away and knelt in supplication to God (Luke 22:41). "This was Jesus' appointed hour—the hour for which he came into the world; the hour when he would take upon himself the sins of the world. For this purpose was he born; for this purpose had he lived." His agony in Gethsemane hallowed the olive garden on the night of Seder.

The night of Seder is called *Leil Shimurim,* meaning "night of the watchers." On this night, Jews were to stay awake and watch for God to save His people. "Blessed is he that watcheth, and keepeth his garments" was a common saying among rabbis when speaking of temple guards who stayed awake at their posts on that night. If found asleep, guards were beaten and their garments set on fire.[334]

How long was Jesus away from Peter, James, and John?

Jews divided the night into three periods—sunset to midnight, midnight to cockcrow, and cockcrow to sunrise (see Mark 6:48; Luke 12:38). The Greco-Roman world divided the night into four military watches of about three hours each. The first watch began at sundown, about six in the evening. The second watch began when the moon was halfway up in the sky. The third watch began when the moon reached the zenith, and the fourth watch began when the moon was halfway down in the sky, about six in the morning.

Because of the two widely varied systems for counting time, it is difficult to calculate the hours Jesus was away from Peter, James, and John at Gethsemane.[335]

How did Jesus atone for the sins of the world?

"There is no mystery to compare with the mystery of redemption, not even the mystery of creation. Finite minds can no more comprehend how and in what manner Jesus performed his redeeming labors than they can comprehend how matter came into being, or how Gods began to be. . . . We may not intrude too closely into this scene. It is shrouded in a halo and a mystery into which no footstep may penetrate."

Christ in the garden

The word *cup* was a metaphor meaning "that which is allotted by God, whether blessing or judgment" (see Ps. 16:5; 116:13). Jesus accepted the judgment of God and became the Savior and Redeemer of the World.337

How did Judas convince soldiers to follow him to the Mount of Olives?

It was not Judas who assembled the soldiers; it is presumed that it was the Jewish leaders and the Roman appointee over Palestine who caused soldiers to follow Judas. Jewish leaders had power to seek for ecclesiastical and military intervention, and they had temple guards at their command.

There may also have been a band of Roman soldiers. The word *band* found in John 18:3 means a "cohort." It is probable that a Roman cohort of four to six hundred soldiers were commanded by Pontius Pilate to follow Judas. The reason for this assumption is that Jewish leaders could not send a strong detachment out of Jerusalem without the specific approval of Pilate. The granted approval may explain the preparedness of Pilate to sit in

Yet we know that in Gethsemane, Jesus "descended below all things as he prepared himself to rise above them all" (see Matt. 26:39). Jesus "suffered the pain of all men, that all men might repent and come unto him" (D&C 18:11). For as Isaiah prophesied, "All we like sheep have gone astray; we have turned every one to his own way; and the Lord hath laid on him the iniquity of us all. . . . Surely he hath borne our griefs, and carried our sorrows" (Isa. 53:6, 4).336

Was Jesus speaking of the third cup of the Passover feast when He prayed, "O my Father, if it be possible, let this cup pass from me" (Matt. 26:39)?

judgment early the next morning as well as the frightening dreams of Pilate's wife.

It is probable that Judas led the soldiers to the house where he had eaten the Paschal Supper with Jesus, where they found the Upper Room empty. Judas may then have led soldiers to Gethsemane, for he knew that "Jesus ofttimes resorted thither with his disciples" (John 18:2). On the northern side of the Mount of Olives is a burial site known as *Viri Galilean,* in remembrance of Galilean pilgrims who camped near the site during the festivities of the Passover week.[338]

> **Judas told those with him, "Whomsoever I shall kiss, that same is he: hold him fast" (Matt. 26:48). Why did Judas betray Jesus with a kiss?**

It was a Jewish custom to greet friends and guests with a kiss. When Simon the Pharisee did not extend a customary kiss to Jesus, he was rebuked (see Luke 7:45). A kiss in public was unusual, however. When bestowed by a pupil or disciple on a great rabbi, it was a token of respect.

Judas chose a traitor's kiss (in other words, kissed Jesus profusely)

to single out Jesus from among the Galileans gathered on the Mount of Olives (see Mark 14:45). Others in the boisterous crowd could easily identify Jesus, for He had been in the temple courts and had often walked the public streets of Jerusalem. Perhaps He did look like a Galilean Jew in stature and dress, but He had just bled from every pore. The kiss of Judas for identification purposes alone seems unnecessary.[339]

> **When the soldiers laid their hands on Jesus, Peter "drew his sword, and struck a servant of the high priest's, and smote off his ear" (Matt. 26:51). Why was Peter carrying a sword?**

During the Passover festivities, thousands of pilgrims flocked into Jerusalem. Pilgrims brought foreign money to exchange for temple shekels that were then given as an offering to the temple treasury. The wealth of the pilgrims attracted thieves and bandits, who viewed foreign worshipers as easy prey.

To protect themselves from thievery, pilgrims from the Galilean region carried under their upper garment a *gladius* or "short sword" with a blade about twenty

The betrayal of Christ

inches long. Peter wielded such a sword when he cut off the ear of Malchus. Malchus, the Hebrew equivalent of "counselor," was a servant of the high priest, which implicates the high priest in the arrest of Jesus. Jesus said to Peter, "All they that take the sword shall perish with the sword" (Matt. 26:52).[340]

Could the armed guard arrest Jesus against His will?

Jesus consented to the arrest and permitted Himself to be taken prisoner. Elder Bruce R. McConkie wrote, "No more could Jesus be arrested without his consent than could his life be taken unless he willed it." After all, prophecy must be fulfilled. Bound securely by armed men, Jesus explained why they were able to arrest Him: "This is your hour, and the power of darkness" (Luke 22:53).

The arrest was one of many illegalities in the proceedings against Jesus.[341]

Why was Jesus immediately taken to the home of Annas and not to the palace of Caiaphas, the Roman-appointed High Priest?

The events of the evening—from the arrest at the Mount of Olives to the trial before Caiaphas—are difficult to reconstruct, because Gospel writers vary the ordered sequence of events. The Gospel of John explains that after the arrest on the Mount of Olives, Jesus was bound and taken to the house or palace of Annas, the father-in-law of the high priest Caiaphas.

Knowing something about Annas may explain why Jesus appeared before him. Annas, a former Roman-appointed high priest, was the best known and "most influential Jew of his day." Though deposed by Roman rulers in AD 15, he was permitted to retain the title of high priest as a courtesy. Annas wielded much influence over the Jews because of the men who succeeded him as high priest—a son-in-law, five sons, and a grandson. Although his son-in-law, Joseph Caiaphas, was the Roman-appointed high priest from AD 18–36, it appears that Annas retained some religious and political control over him. Historically, Caiaphas is portrayed as a puppet to the whims of Annas.

Annas and his posterity are also remembered for the *chanujoth,* four shops located under the twin cedars of Olivet. In these shops, sacrificial turtledoves were sold after being pronounced legally pure. Jews could buy any dove in Jerusalem for two pence, but if the pilgrim wanted a legally pure dove, he purchased the bird from one of Annas's shops for a gold coin.

There is reason to believe that Annas and his posterity also had vested interest in the marketplace located inside the temple porticoes. Historians claim that moneychangers paid a percentage of their profits to Annas. This claim is enforced by the Talmud reference to market stalls being "the booths of the sons of Annas."[342]

Was the examination of Jesus before Annas a legal proceeding?

Details of the examination do not exist. However, there is a consensus among scholars that the process was illegal because: 1) Jesus was arrested without

196

a charge being lodged against Him; 2) the examination was at night; 3) an examination before only one judge was forbidden under Mosaic law; and 4) Jesus was struck during the examination and the violent act was not reproved.

Annas was not aloof from the other events that led to the death of Jesus. It is assumed that he went with the guards to the palace of Caiaphas and later with the guards to the Antonia Fortress. It is further assumed that he lent his influence and prestige at each trial in support of the conviction and death of Jesus.[343]

> Jesus was led to the palace of "Caiaphas the high priest, where the scribes and the elders were assembled" (Matt. 26:57). Were the assembled Jewish leaders members of the Sanhedrin?

Twenty-three leading elders, scribes, and chief priests were assembled in the palace of Caiaphas awaiting the arrival of Jesus. These men, all members of the Great Sanhedrin (which means "sitting together"), formed a quorum or council of the highest Jewish tribunal.

Normally, the Sanhedrin met in council at the Hall of Gazith, known as the Chamber of Hewn Stone, to judge judicial matters important to Judea. But wherever the Sanhedrin met, they held almost absolute power. For example, they had their own police force, could arrest on both civil and criminal charges, and could pass and impose judgment for wrongdoing. Yet under Roman rule, the Sanhedrin had limited authority to execute a judgment of death. Another limiting factor was the regulation governing trial procedures for a capital offense.

If a prisoner was found guilty of a capital offense, a second trial commenced the day following the first judgment. In preparation for the second trial, members of the Sanhedrin were to fast and pray for divine guidance to make a wise decision. At the second trial, those who had first voted against the prisoner could reverse their judgment, but those who had voted for an acquittal were bound by their initial vote. If all members of the council voted to convict the prisoner of a capital offense, the verdict was void because the accused had no defender.[344]

The trial of Jesus

Was there more than one high priest that tried Jesus in the palace of Caiaphas?

When Palestine became a Roman province, the office of high priest regained much of the recognized authority it had enjoyed under Persian and Hellenistic rule. The designated high priest presided over the Sanhedrin and administered in religious and internal affairs of the Jews. Yet the prestigious religious office given to Caiaphas was only a token appointment by Rome. Caiaphas was subservient to Rome and docile in his religious duties. Assisting Caiaphas in his office were former chief priests or high priests. These men formed a type of Jewish aristocracy.[345]

What were some of the illegal implications of the trial of Jesus before Caiaphas?

Many of the illegal issues of the trial before Caiaphas were the same issues that existed when Jesus as examined before Annas. Illegalities included: 1) The trial was held in the evening. The Mishnah reads, "Let a capital offense be tried during the day, but suspend it at night." 2) The trial was held on the eve of Passover. Rabbinic law states, "Let them not judge on the eve of the Sabbath, or on the eve of a feast day." 3) The accused was not dressed in mourning garments. Jesus was led before Caiaphas in His own clothing. 4) False witnesses gave conflicting testimonies that failed to give proof of guilt.[346]

When the high priest asked Jesus, "Art thou the Christ, the Son of the Blessed?" he answered "I am" (Mark 14:61–62). Why did the high priest then accuse Jesus of blasphemy?

When the high priest asked, "Art thou the Christ, the Son of the Blessed," Jesus answered, "I am," and spoke of "sitting on the right hand of power" (Mark 14:61–62). His response raised the issue of blasphemy. The words *blessed* and *power* were understood by Jewish leaders to mean "God." According to the assembled leaders, Jesus committed blasphemy, which means "claiming for human

or demon power the prerogatives of God, or in dishonoring God by ascribing to Him attributes short of perfection."

To high priests and members of the Sanhedrin assembled that evening, Jesus had committed an enormous crime against Hebrew law. The council exclaimed, "He is guilty of death" (Matt. 26:66). The council then arose and spat on His face, which in Judaism signified their refusal to have any part in His guilt (see Matt. 26:67). They also "buffeted him; and others smote him with the palms of their hands" (Matt. 26:67).

The judgment of blasphemy meant that Jesus was unclean and defiled. Holy men, such as those who feigned to judge the Son of God, would be defiled if they even looked upon the condemned. According to rabbinic law, after the judgment of blasphemy Jesus had to die by stoning and have His body suspended from a tree.[347]

Were Apostles present at the trial of Jesus before Caiaphas?

As Jesus was led to the palace of Caiaphas, many followed. They gathered in small clusters outside the palace to await news of the judicial proceeding. Among them were Peter and John. Of the two, John gained admittance into the trial. "Peter stood at the door without" (John 18:16), unable to gain entrance into the palace.[348]

How did the damsel know that Peter was a Galilean?

For those awaiting news of the trial, "a fire of coals [was made]; for it was cold: and they warmed themselves" (John 18:18). As they gathered around the fire, one damsel noticed Peter and announced to others that he was a Galilean.

It may have been his attire that revealed his Galilean origin, but in the evening hours it was more likely his speech. Most Galileans struggled to pronounce the guttural sounds in the Aramaic language. This failure led Judean Jews to think themselves superior to the Galilean Jews.

As Peter feigned denials of being a Galilean and of even knowing Jesus, support for the damsel's claim came from a servant of the high priest who recognized Peter as a companion of Jesus.[349]

Peter's denial

Was it a rooster's crow that Peter heard?

According to rabbinic law, unclean birds were forbidden in Jerusalem. To touch such birds in the Holy City subjected a Jew to Levitical defilement. Yet the Gospel of John claims that Peter's three denials ended just as the cock crowed (see John 18:27).

Peter may not have heard a rooster crow. It may have been bugle notes coming from the Antonia Fortress. The notes signaled a change of the Roman guard and the close of the third watch. The third Roman watch was called *cockcrow* and ended at three in the morning.[350]

What were the irregularities at the second trial before the Sanhedrin?

Sometime between the third and fourth Roman watch, the second trial began. Members of the Sanhedrin who had participated in the first trial had fewer than three hours to prepare for the next trial. About six in the morning, under a veiled pretense of legality, a full quorum of the Sanhedrin "took counsel against Jesus to put him to death" (Matt. 27:1). Details of the trial are lacking other than the voluntary affirmations of Jesus, the mild question of Nicodemus, and the judgment—a mockery of the legal procedures dictated by the Mosaic code.

Among the many irregularities in the trial was the failure of the judges to: 1) meet after the morning sacrificial offering; 2) gain a certainty of the indictment; 3) allow for publicity so all who wished to testify for or against the prisoner could be heard; 4) guarantee the right of the accused to speak; 5) pronounce a sentence of death only when the Sanhedrin holds its sessions in the appointed place; and 6) assure against false witnesses and possible error of testimony. Ignoring the Mosaic code, the Sanhedrin affirmed the validity of the examination before Annas and the trial before Caiaphas, thereby condemning Jesus to death.

It was Jesus' claim of being the Son of Man that was the deciding factor in the trial. This title, according to the Book of Daniel, is given to "the heavenly being who will be sent by God at the end of [the] world to judge all nations." The uncorroborated confession of Jesus should have been disallowed. According to Jewish law, the condemned could not accuse Himself. Again the Sanhedrin ignored the law and accepted the testimony (or personal accusation) of Jesus. They then judged the Son of Man to be a blasphemer.

After the judgment, Jesus was promptly dragged past curious crowds in the courtyard to the guard room.[351]

Did the chief priests and elders enter the Antonia Fortress to formally charge Jesus with blasphemy?

When Caiaphas declared Jesus was guilty of blasphemy, Caiaphas stood up and rent his outer and inner garments about eight inches in length in a dramatic expression of grief and horror. When witnessing this theatrical display, Jewish law prescribed that members of the Sanhedrin, in sympathy with the high priest, should also arise and rend their garments.

Such actions were specifically forbidden by Mosaic law: "The high priest . . . shall not uncover his head, nor rend his clothes" (Lev. 21:10). Yet such rending was a sign of unity among the Jewish leaders.

Then Caiaphas, the Sanhedrin, the temple guards, and probably Annas led Jesus to the Antonia Fortress, a military headquarters also called the Praetorium. Near the fortress, temple guards turned Jesus over to the Roman soldiers, fearing that if they entered the fortress of a Gentile, they would be defiled. Likewise, none of the Jewish leaders entered the fortress. From outside the structure, they loudly accused Jesus of sedition and treason. The charge of blasphemy, pronounced in the Jewish courts, was missing from their outbursts.[352]

The demise of Judas

Where did Judas hang himself? What did the chief priests and elders do with the thirty pieces of discarded silver?

After Judas "cast down the pieces of silver in the temple" (Matt. 27:5), meaning he flung the money onto the porch leading up to the temple, he went outside the city gates to a clay yard on the southern slopes of the Hinnom Valley. The yard had been the property of a potter and was believed to be the traditional site of Jeremiah's prophesied destruction of Jerusalem (see Matt. 27:8; Zech. 11:12–13). In the yard Judas unwound his long girdle and hung himself on a tree.

As for the actions of the chief priests and elders, they gathered the silver tossed onto the temple porch and held council. At issue was the price of blood (see Matt. 27:6–7)—the silver could not be donated to the temple treasury because the coins were tainted and unlawfully gained (see Matt. 27:5–6). Jewish law dictated that the coins be restored to the donor. The donor was to be encouraged to spend the coins on a public project.

According to the Gospel of Matthew, Jewish leaders bought the clay yard in which Judas committed suicide. They designated the yard as a burial site for foreigners, strangers, and pagans. Early Christian tradition suggests that the remains of Judas were the first to be interred in what became known as Potter's Field or *Aceldama,* meaning "field of blood" or "field of sleeping" (see Acts 1:18).[353]

Did Pontius Pilate have any sympathy or appreciation for his Jewish subjects?

In AD 26 the Roman Emperor Tiberius named Pontius Pilate the sixth Roman procurator of Judea, Samaria, and Idumaea. Although Pilate presided over the province for nearly ten years, he had little sympathy or appreciation for his Jewish subjects. He offended them by his blatant disregard for the sacred in Judaism. For example, he defiled Jerusalem by sending legionaries equipped with standards of war into the Holy City. He used military force to take sacred funds from the temple treasury and killed defenseless Jews.

When a petition outlining his atrocities was signed by four Herodian princes and sent to the

Roman emperor, Pilate was reprimanded for his actions against Jews and Judaism.[354]

Why was Pilate in Jerusalem during the Passover festivities?

Pilate and his cohort of soldiers were stationed at Caesarea, the Roman capital of Palestine. Caesarea, later known as Caesarea Palestine, was located on the Mediterranean shore near the border of Samaria. The city was built by Herod the Great and named for Caesar Augustus. The seaside community was heralded as one of the most beautiful cities in the ancient Greco-Roman world. Evidence of its culture—a hippodrome, amphitheater, theater, and hot baths—has been unearthed by archaeological excavations.

Pilate left the splendor of Caesarea to be in Jerusalem during the great Jewish festivals. He was not in Jerusalem on a worshipful pilgrimage, but was in the Holy City to maintain order. He and his cohort of soldiers made their residence in the Antonia Fortress, the largest military fortress in Jerusalem. Pilate's presence in Jerusalem gave just cause for Jews to fear during the Passover festivities.[355]

Did Jesus appear before Pilate in the Hall of Judgment?

The hearing before Pilate probably occurred in the Antonia Fortress, which was constructed by the Hasmoneans. It was rebuilt and enlarged by Herod the Great and named for Marcus Anthony, Herod's early patron (see John 18:28; 19:13). The fortress was known as a hall of judgment, or what Gospel writer John calls the *gabbatha* or pavement, meaning a "stone enclosed courtyard." It was in the courtyard that Pilate transacted public business and held court. The pavement was larger than the entrance or *gabbatha* typical in Eastern homes. Domestic pavements were typically about four feet in length and three feet wide.[356]

Was Jesus accused of blasphemy before Pilate?

Although Pilate was a pagan and worshiped many gods, the accusation of blasphemy without sufficient evidence that Jesus was leading a messianic insurrection would have been frowned upon by the Roman procurator. Such an accusation would cause Pilate to be angry with Jewish leaders for trying to manipulate him into a religious dispute.

Yet, if Jesus were a reactionary with armed followers seeking the freedom of Judea, Pilate would have moved with vicious swiftness. He had stopped the messianic activities of Judas of Galilee and would not hesitate to stop another revolutionary leader.[357]

> When Pilate heard that Jesus was from Galilee, "He asked whether the man were a Galilean" (Luke 23:6). When he learned that Jesus was a Galilean, Pilate sent him to Herod. Why?

After investigating the case against Jesus, Pilate announced to the crowd gathered outside the Antonia Fortress his acquittal of the condemned: "I find no fault in this man" (Luke 23:4). Jewish leaders were angry at the acquittal and hurled additional charges against Jesus. "The chief priests accused him of many things," but Jesus "answered nothing" (see Mark 15:3).

Frustrated with his Jewish subjects and perhaps looking for an escape from the mounting dilemma, Pilate proposed that the Galilean prisoner be sent to Herod Antipas, the Roman-appointed tetrarch over Galilee and Perea. Herod was in Jerusalem for the Passover festivities. He was probably residing in the old Herodian palace that had been the royal residence of the Herods.

Herod was pleased that Pontius Pilate sent Jesus to him. He had wanted to talk to Jesus since the death of John the Baptist. As he interrogated the Son of God, Herod demanded to be shown a miracle. Jesus did not respond to his demand. Jesus' silence was foretold by Isaiah: "He was oppressed, and he was afflicted, yet he opened not his mouth" (Isa. 53:7).

Jesus had previously spoken of Herod Antipas as "that fox" (Luke 13:32). A fox in Greek literature represented cunning and craftiness; in rabbinic lore, a fox symbolized ignominious contempt. Jesus' reference to Herod Antipas as "that fox" may have signified Herod's craftiness, but to a rabbinic Jew it meant that Herod was contemptuous.

After the interrogation, Herod passed the burden of judgment back to Pontius Pilate. According to the Gospel of Luke, "Pilate and Herod were made friends together: for before they were at enmity between themselves" (Luke 23:12).358

It is assumed that the robe draped across the shoulders of Jesus was a white outer garment. This assumption is based on the fact that white apparel was worn by Jewish nobility during the Roman rule of Palestine and that white festive clothing was worn by Jewish pilgrims during Passover week.359

By tradition, the wife of Pontius Pilate was named Procla or Claudia Procula. She was inclined toward Judaism, and may have been a gentile proselyte of

Christ before Pilate

righteousness before becoming a Christian. She is canonized in the Greek Orthodox Church.360

Was Pilate imitating a Jewish ritual by washing his hands?

Pilate performed two symbolic acts as a public witness that he found Jesus innocent—one a gentile witness and the other a Jewish witness. The gentile witness occurred when he arose from the judgment seat. His gesture of standing before issuing a decree was a gentile symbol of innocence.

The other was washing his hands. "When Pilate saw that he could prevail nothing, but that rather a tumult was made, he took water, and washed his hands before the multitude" (Matt. 27:24). Pilate's act of washing his hands was not a mockery of the Jewish ceremonial ritual, but a witness to the Jews that he disclaimed responsibility for the sentence of death that would be pronounced on the prisoner.

As he washed before the assemblage, Pilate performed a Jewish ritual that symbolized his personal innocence and desire to be freed from the responsibility of shedding innocent blood. According to Mosaic law, if a murder was committed, Jewish leaders were required to slay a heifer, "wash their hands over the heifer," and say, "Our hands have not shed this blood, neither have our eyes seen it. Be merciful, O Lord, unto thy people Israel, whom thou hast redeemed, and lay not innocent blood unto thy people" (Deut. 21:6–8). After the hand washing, Jewish leaders were symbolically forgiven of shedding innocent blood (see Deut. 21:9; Ps. 26:6, 73:13).

Pilate's gesture of standing and symbolic hand washing came before his decree to scourge and crucify Jesus.[361]

> Soldiers took Jesus into the common hall and there "stripped him, and put on him a scarlet robe . . . a crown of thorns, and mocked him" (Matt. 27:28–29). Why was Jesus beaten and mocked by the Roman soldiers?

At the end of a formal Roman trial, it was customary for soldiers to mock the condemned prisoner. If the prisoner had gained significant recognition during the trial, as Jesus had through multiple trials before leaders of Judaism and Rome, mockery was intense and attracted most of the soldiers stationed at the Antonia Fortress.

With Pilate watching, garments worn by Jesus were stripped from Him. He was strapped to a pillar or frame and then beaten with a whip or scourge made of leather thongs; the leather thongs or straps would have been weighted with sharp pieces of stone, lead balls, and sheep bone. Romans had no restrictions on the number of lashes administered to a condemned prisoner. The traditional number of times Jesus was scourged was thirty-nine—thirteen hits across his chest and thirteen hits across each shoulder (see Deut. 25:1–3; 2 Cor. 11:24).[362]

Jesus was attired with a scarlet or purple robe or *sagum*—a short, woolen war cloak worn by Roman officers (see John 19:2). The robe would have been fastened by a clasp or buckle over His right shoulder. While the robe was another abuse heaped on Jesus, it would have been a recognition or symbol of wealth and royalty if such a garment had been placed on a soldier or a foreign king.

The color of the cloak is of particular interest. The ancient world prized color dyes, especially blue, scarlet, and purple. The color purple was made from the morex shellfish (snail) and was a rare commodity in the Holy Land. The crimson dye was made from eggs of the *coccus ilicis* insect. When purple dye was added to crimson dye, a scarlet color was produced.[363]

What shrub was used by Roman soldiers to make the crown of thorns that was placed on the head of Jesus?

Prickly and thorny shrubs grew near the Antonia Fortress; among the more common were the box thorn, acanthus, artichoke, thorny caper, star thistle, and milk thistle. Christian tradition suggests that the *Ziziphus Spina-Christi,* commonly known today as the Christ-thorn, was the shrub used by soldiers to make the crown of thorns.

Soldiers placed the *crown*—meaning a "garland of thorns"—on the head of Jesus. The braided or twisted garland was a Greco-Roman tribute awarded to victors in battle and winning contestants of Olympic games, but for Jesus it was a mockery of His rightful position.[364]

Were Jewish leaders guilty of blasphemy when they shouted, "We have no king but Caesar" (John 19:15)?

Pilate presented Jesus to the awaiting crowd outside the fortress by saying, *"Ecce homo,"* meaning "Here is the man." He added, "I bring him forth to you, that ye may know that I find no fault in him" (John 19:4). This was Pilate's third proclamation of the innocence of Jesus. It is ironic that the Roman procurator, a

Pilate presents Christ to the Jews

heathen who did not believe in Jehovah or His commandments, asked the Jews to spare the life of their God and King.

"We have no king but Caesar" was the response of the angry crowd (John 19:15). "With this cry Judaism was, in the person of its representatives, guilty of denial of God, of blasphemy, of apostasy," the very crimes they claimed were committed by Jesus (see Lev. 24:16).[365]

Why did the Jewish leaders choose freedom for Barabbas instead of freedom for Jesus?

During the Passover festivities, it was a Roman custom to pardon one condemned Jewish criminal (see Mark 15:8). Pilate gave the anxious crowd its choice—Jesus of Nazareth or Jesus Barabbas, meaning "Jesus, son of the Father."

Both prisoners had been accused of treason. Barabbas was also guilty of sedition (see Luke 23:19, 25); he had incited an insurrection and committed murder. Jesus was innocent of sedition, and Pilate knew that the Jewish leaders "had delivered him for envy" (Mark 15:10). It is perhaps not surprising that Jewish leaders preferred the more exciting revolutionary leader Barabbas over the compassionate Jesus.[366]

What happened to the Jewish leaders who demanded the crucifixion of Jesus?

Joseph Caiaphas was deposed in AD 36 after serving eighteen years as the Roman-appointed high priest. The house of Annas lost both power and wealth a generation later to an angry mob. Herod Antipas was exiled from Palestine and died in infamy.[367]

What happened to Pilate after the trial of Jesus?

Within a year of the trial, rumor reached Pilate of a threatened Samaritan rebellion against Roman dominion. Pilate violently reacted to the rumor. He marched his soldiers against unarmed Samaritans and won an easy victory. Samaritans, angered at the bloody loss for spurious reasons, complained to Vitellius, leader of the Syrian province. Vitellius sent Pilate to Rome to answer the Samaritan accusations.

Upon reaching Rome, Pilate learned that his foe Caligula had succeeded to the throne. According to tradition, in AD 36 Caligula either banished Pilate to Vienna, the south of France, or to a mountain near Lake Lucerne. In exile Pilate wearied of his life and misfortunes; he committed suicide.[368]

Did death by crucifixion originate with the Romans?

Crucifixion originated in Mesopotamia. Phoenicians, Persians, Greeks, and Romans later used crucifixion as a method of punishment. This method was described by the Roman orator Cicero as "the most cruel and hideous of punishments." Certain people were crucified in Palestine: criminals without Roman citizenship, rebels against Rome, delinquent slaves, robbers and deserters, and those who committed a barbarous offense.

Roman crucifixion had three phases—scourging, carrying a crossbeam, and hanging on a cross. According to the Mosaic law, to die by crucifixion was to be cursed, for "he that is hanged [upon a tree] is accursed of God" (see Deut. 21:23). According to the Mishnah, strangulation, beheading, burning, and stoning were approved forms of punishment, but crucifixion was not.[369]

How much time lapsed between the scourging and crucifixion of Jesus?

In Rome an interval—ordinarily two days—was permitted between the death sentence and execution of the prisoner. This interval did not apply in Roman provinces, however.

Jesus was quickly led by Roman soldiers from the Hall of Judgment to Calvary (see Matt. 27:31). The escort of soldiers was intended to attract attention, demean the prisoner, and frighten bystanders. A sign or block of white wood, either hanging around the neck of Jesus or carried by a soldier, proclaimed His crime: "Jesus of Nazareth the King of the Jews" (John 19:19).[370]

Set over the head of Jesus was the titulus, "THIS IS JESUS THE KING OF THE JEWS" (Matt. 27:37). In what language was the titulus?

The *titulus* or sign was written by a Roman underling in three languages—Hebrew/Aramaic, Latin, and Greek (see John 19:20). It is most likely that the language on the block appeared first in Latin, then in Greek, and last in Hebrew/Aramaic.

Although the wording "Jesus of Nazareth the King of the Jews" varies slightly from one Gospel writer to another, all agree that it was Pilate who suggested the inscription. When chief priests expressed displeasure at the titulus, Pilate said, "What I have written I have written" (John 19:22).[371]

Were the condemned thieves also in the processional moving toward Calvary?

It is probable that the two thieves were led with Jesus from the Hall of Judgment to Calvary (see Matt. 27:31, 38). If so, Roman soldiers would have walked beside each thief on the route. This official escort, like the one attending Jesus, would have attracted attention and frightened onlookers.

Signs hanging from the necks of the thieves or carried by Roman soldiers announced their crimes. The malefactors, who may have been revolutionaries and insurrectionists, carried their own *patibulum* or crossbar. "And the scripture was fulfilled, which saith, And [Jesus] was numbered with the transgressors" (Mark 15:28).[372]

Did Jesus carry a cross from the Hall of Judgment to Calvary?

According to Roman custom, each condemned prisoner would have carried a *patibulum,* or crossbar. The patibulum was about six feet in length and weighed approximately 125 pounds. Chris-

tian tradition suggests that Jesus carried the patibulum from the Hall of Judgment to the city gate.[373]

What is known about the man who carried the crossbar for Jesus to Calvary?

Watching the processional were a multitude of Judeans and Galileans who were in Jerusalem for the Passover festivities. Soldiers impressed one of the multitude, a Diaspora Jew named Simon, to carry the patibulum for Jesus.

Jesus carrying the cross

When Simon was directed to carry the patibulum, he had just come "out of the country" (Mark 15:21) and may have labored in fields near Jerusalem before entering the Holy City.

Simon was from the Jewish colony of Cyrene, a Mediterranean port on the coast of northern Africa. Cyrene, established in 300 BC by Ptolemeus Lagi, was home to a number of Jewish people for generations even though it was first settled as a Greek city.

The command to carry the patibulum would have been abhorrent to any in the crowd. A Jew would not volunteer to bear a crossbeam, for as Elder James E. Talmage wrote, "Every detail connected with the carrying out of a sentence of crucifixion was regarded as degrading." However, Simon—the father of early Christians Alexander and Rufus (see Mark 15:21)—may have been a willing participant. As Simon carried the crossbar, Jesus walked behind.[374]

Approximately how far was the crossbar carried?

The distance from the Hall of Judgment to Calvary was about one-third of a mile. Along the crowded route, women cried aloud in commiseration and praise of Jesus (see Luke 23:27). A few, like generations of women before them, prepared an aromatic potent called *gall* to ease the pain of the condemned prisoners. Also watching the sorrowful procession were men. There is no record in the Gospels of men protesting or lamenting the burdens of Jesus from the Hall of Judgment to Calvary.[375]

Was Jesus executed at Calvary or Golgotha?

Calvary and Golgotha both mean "skull," and they are one and the same. The name may have derived from the shape of the rock on which the cross was erected or from its purpose—a Roman site of execution and place of burial (see JST John 19:17).[376]

What type of cross did the Romans use in Palestine?

There were three types of crosses commonly used throughout the Roman Empire. One type was shaped like an "X" *(Crux Decussata),* another like a "T" *(Crux Commissa),* and the third like a "t" *(Crux Immissa).* It is not known which type of cross was used in Palestine from AD 30–33, but it is known that the cross was not the lofty structure depicted in artistic renderings. Soldiers would not have wasted much effort in constructing an end bar on Calvary. The bar, no doubt also used for the execution of other prisoners, was made from indigenous wood like olive or sycomore. It was placed low to the ground so that the feet of the condemned would be less than two feet above the ground, enabling passersby to physically and verbally abuse the crucified.[377]

How were the condemned men attached to the cross?

Whether Jesus or the thieves were nailed to the crossbeam while it lay on the ground or after it was placed on the end bar is not known. It is probable that iron nails were hammered into the palms of each hand of the condemned by a mallet and that nails were driven between the bones of each wrist, "probably piercing the median nerve in the wrists and causing intense pain." Whether the condemned were also bound to the bar by ropes is not known.

Christ on the cross

After they were attached to the crossbeam, the beam would have been lifted up by ladders and Y-shaped poles and attached to the end bar. To prevent their bodies from tearing away from the cross, nails were also hammered into their feet. Christian tradition suggests that to further prevent the weight of their bodies from pulling away, a prop was placed between their legs and beneath their feet to form a narrow seat. Early Christian artists depicted the prop as if Jesus were "sitting on a throne" while hanging on the cross. This tradition is discounted by modern scholars.

Above the head of Jesus was nailed the sign, "Jesus of Nazareth the King of the Jews" (John 19:19).[378]

Matthew wrote of Jesus being offered "vinegar to drink mingled with gall" (Matt. 27:34). Was the offer of gall an act of compassion?

As a concession to the Jews, Roman soldiers offered gall to condemned prisoners before attaching them to crosses (see Ps. 69:21). Gall acted as a narcotic, causing heavy sleep. It was a mixture of sour wine or vinegar, myrrh, and other anodyne ingredients. The mixture deadened the sensibility of the victim and eased the pain of crucifixion. By itself, gall—the juice of the opium poppy—was bitter and poisonous, thus the expression "gall of bitterness" (Acts 8:23).

When gall was offered to Jesus, "he would not drink" (Matt. 27:34). The reason for His refusal lies in His earlier statement that He would not "drink henceforth of this fruit of the vine, until that day when I drink it new with you in my Father's kingdom" (Matt. 26:29).[379]

Did crucifixion lead to respiratory failure?

Crucifixion did lead to respiratory failure. As the weight of the body pulled toward the ground, it became increasingly difficult for the victim to exhale. When carbon dioxide is not fully expelled from the lungs, death results from asphyxiation.

To hurry the death process, the victim's legs were broken just below the knee. Having subsequently lost the ability to push himself upright on the cross to ease the breathing process, the crucified suffocated and died.[380]

What were the first words spoken by Jesus from the cross?

Jesus hung on the cross for six hours—from nine in the morning until three in the afternoon. During those agonizing hours, Gospel writers report that He spoke seven times. His first words, "Father, forgive them; for they know not what they do" (Luke 23:34), were an expression of charity. Forgiveness was directed toward the soldiers, "not to Judas or Annas or Caiaphas or the chief priests or the Sanhedrin or Pilate or Herod or Lucifer or any who have rebelled against him."381

What part of the clothing of Jesus was a gratuity given the soldiers?

Jewish men typically wore five articles of clothing: 1) a headdress, 2) shoes or sandals, 3) an inner garment called a tunic or robe, 4) an outer garment or cloak, and 5) a girdle. The personal clothing of the condemned became the property of the soldiers when the condemned was lifted on the cross. Other than the loin cloth worn by criminals at their execution, apparel of the condemned was a gratuity to the soldiers for fulfilling their military duties in the crucifixion proceedings.

It is probable that the soldiers claimed one or more articles of clothing, leaving ownership of the inner garment or tunic to the casting of lots or chance "that it might be fulfilled which was spoken by the prophet, They parted my garments among them" (Matt. 27:35; Ps. 22:18). It is purported that the inner garment "resembled a tallith, the Jewish prayer shawl." It was woven from a woolen cloth "without seam, woven from the top throughout" (John 19:23).382

Were the Roman soldiers performing a Jewish ritual by casting lots?

Casting lots in ancient Israel was always associated with prayer and humble submission to God. When Canaan was divided, Saul and Jonathan reconciled by casting lots. Priestly duties in the temple were determined by the casting of lots (see Josh. 14:2, 18:6; 1 Sam. 14:40–42).

When the Roman soldiers "said therefore among themselves, Let us not rend [the inner garment], but cast lots for it, whose it shall be," they were not in solemn prayer or about to perform a Jewish ritual. The soldiers were proposing to play a game of chance (see John 19:24). To do so, they would have used Roman dice made of bones and would have shaken the dice in their hands. When the contents of their hands emptied on the ground, the soldier who guessed the toss or lot would have won the inner garment.[383]

Was Jesus mocked by those standing near the cross?

Taunting Jesus were chief priests, scribes, and elders, "the same satanic souls who had orchestrated the calls for crucifixion now led the same chorus of voices in chanting a derisive hymn of hate and vengeance against the one who had been crucified."

Joining in the abuse were soldiers and the condemned thieves (see Matt. 27:44). Their derisive slurs were not new. They were repetitive of satanic temptations heard years before in the wilderness (see Matt. 4:1–11). Unwittingly, the evil onlookers fulfilled the psalmist's lament, "Reproach

Many of the Savior's supporters gathered at the cross

[had] broken [His] heart; and [He was] full of heaviness: and [He] looked for some to take pity, but there was none; and for comforters, but [He] found none" (Ps. 69:20).[384]

Jesus said to the penitent thief, "Verily I say unto thee, To day shalt thou be with me in paradise" (Luke 23:43). What is known about the penitent thief?

According to Christian lore, the unrepentant thief was named Gastas and the penitent thief Dysmas. Dysmas, upon hearing Gastas rail against Jesus, said, "Dost not thou fear God, seeing thou art in the same condemnation?" (Luke 23:40). In the lore Dysmas recognizes that his crucifixion and the crucifixion of the unrepentant thief are justified. He also recognized that the crucifixion of Jesus was a mistake, for "this man hath done nothing amiss" (Luke 23:41).

The penitent thief, probably a bandit or an insurrectionist, said to Jesus, "Lord, remember me when thou comest into thy kingdom" (Luke 23:42). Jesus promised him, "To day shalt thou be with me in paradise," meaning the "world of spirits" (Luke 23:43).[385]

Which female disciples witnessed the crucifixion of Jesus?

Listening to the accusations, watching the soldiers cast lots, and hearing Jesus speak to the thief were the following women: 1) His mother Mary, 2) the wife of Cleophas, 3) Mary Magdalene, and 4) Salome, the wife of Zebedee and mother of James and John (see John 19:25).

As Jesus looked down from the cross and saw His mother standing near, He said, "Woman" (John 19:26). The word seems impersonal today, but anciently to be called a woman was a mark of honor and respect. An old Eastern saying clarified, "To every son the mother ought to be preeminently the woman of women."

Jesus directed His mother to turn to John and "from that hour that disciple took her unto his own home" (John 19:27). Mary, the mother of Jesus, is not mentioned again in scripture as standing with the other women near the cross.[386]

Why did the Jewish leaders think Jesus was calling for Elias?

At the ninth hour, meaning three in the afternoon, "Jesus cried with a loud voice, saying, Eli, Eli, lama sabachthani? that is to say, My God, my God, why hast thou forsaken me?" (see Matt. 27:46). This psalmist phrase, found in the messianic prophecy of King David, could not be misconstrued by Jewish leaders to mean Elias (see Ps. 22:1). When they tauntingly said, "This man calleth for Elias," they knew it was not true (Matt. 27:47).[387]

Who responded to the request of Jesus, "I thirst" (John 19:28)?

Early Christian scholar Camerarius suggested that the letters "op" were mistakenly repeated to form *hussopo,* meaning "hyssop." He believed the correct word was *husso,* meaning "javelin." With the translation corrected, Camerarius concluded that it was a Roman soldier who lifted the sponge on his javelin. Roman javelins were six and a half feet long—half of that was the blade.

Theologians claim the sponge was on the end of a tall hyssop branch, a branch that symbolizes humility in Judaism. They point to the hyssop branch being used to apply blood to the doorpost of Israelite houses the night the angel of death passed over. The branch was also used in the purification ceremony of women (see Ex. 12:22; Lev. 14:51).

The psalmist taught, "In my thirst they gave me vinegar to drink" (Ps. 69:21).[388]

It Is Finished

At the death of Jesus, "the veil of the temple was rent in twain from the top to the bottom; and the earth did quake, and the rocks rent" (Matt. 27:51.) Was the temple veil rent by the earthquake?

The Talmud describes the temple veil as actually two veils hanging in front of the Holy of Holies. The veils were sixty feet long, thirty feet wide, and about one inch thick. They were made of fine material and beautifully embroidered with white, scarlet, blue, and gold thread. The veils were so heavy—due to the seventy-two plaited squares sewn onto the fabric—that it took three hundred priests to immerse just one veil before hanging it in the Holy Temple.

If the temple veils were as the Talmud described, an earthquake would not cause them to be "rent in twain," or to be torn from top to bottom. "Indeed, everything seems to indicate that, although the earthquake might furnish the physical basis, the rent of the Temple-Veil was—with reverence be it said—really made by the Hand of God."

When the veils were rent, the Holy of Holies was exposed.

The exposure revealed an empty chamber except for a large stone on which the high priest sprinkled sacrificial blood on the Day of Atonement.

Rending the veil symbolized "the rending of Judaism, the consummation of the Mosaic dispensation, and the inauguration of Christianity under apostolic administration."[389]

Did Jews fear the darkness that shrouded Jerusalem that afternoon?

For centuries, Jews superstitiously viewed the obstruction of the sun as an "evil sign to the nations of the world," not Judea. Jews did fear when the moon was obscured, for it was an evil sign against them.

Darkness at noon on the day of the Savior's crucifixion, however, was different. The hours of darkness (noon until 3 P.M.) and the attending earthquake caused those standing near the cross to greatly fear. Women "smote their breasts" and one of the soldiers cried aloud, "Truly this was the Son of God," or as Luke writes, "Certainly this was a righteous man" (Matt. 27:54; Luke 23:47).[390]

When the soldiers "came to Jesus, and saw that he was dead already, they brake not his legs" (John 19:33). Is it significant that Jesus died without any bones being broken?

As Sabbath approached, Jewish leaders, aware that crucified bodies must be buried before a holy day, "besought Pilate that [the condemned] legs might be broken, and that they might be taken away" (John 19:31; see also Deut. 21:22–23). Pilate agreed to their request and sent soldiers to Calvary to break the legs of the thieves and Jesus. When the soldiers discovered that Jesus was already dead, His legs were not broken (see John 19:33). That fact is significant because Jesus, like generations of slain Paschal lambs, died without a broken bone (see Ex. 12:46; Ps. 34:20).[391]

The darkness at noonday

He Is Risen!

Pilate marveled that Jesus had died so quickly, and did not equate Jesus' death with the darkness that engulfed the land or the great earthquake that rocked the holy city.

How did Joseph of Arimathaea gain an audience with Pilate?

Joseph of Arimathaea, a member of the Sanhedrin, perhaps knew that Roman law permitted an honorable burial for prisoners convicted of political crimes. His direct solicitation of Pilate testifies not only to his courage and willingness to risk his societal reputation, but to his importance in the Sanhedrin. He was a rich, just man, and an honorable counselor. Perhaps for these reasons, he was granted an audience with Pilate.[392]

Why did Pilate allow the body of Jesus to be buried in a private tomb?

It was a common Roman practice to leave corpses on crosses until the corpses were devoured by dogs, rats, or ravens or were rotted by the sun.

Soon after the Roman conquest of Judea, Roman appointees consented to a request made by the Sanhedrin to allow corpses to be removed from crosses and buried before nightfall.

Even though the body of Jesus could be removed from the cross before nightfall, Jesus did not according to Jewish law have the right to an honorable burial. The law stated, "They that were put to death by the council were not to be buried in the sepulchres of their fathers, but two burial places were appointed by the council." Both burial sites would have been offensive to the followers of Jesus.

Jewish law did not prevail in the case of Jesus. Since Jesus was executed for political reasons, according to Roman law He could receive an honorable burial. This law opened the way for Pilate to accept the offer of Joseph of Arimathaea to bury Jesus (see Matt. 27:57–59).[393]

> **What role did Nicodemus play in transporting the body of Jesus to the Garden Tomb? What role did he play in preparing the body for burial?**

It is probable that the cross on which Jesus hung was laid on the ground and the nails were removed from His body to release Him from the wood. Joseph of Arimathaea and Nicodemus, also a "ruler of the Jews," probably wrapped His body in a linen cloth and carried it to a nearby tomb. If such was the case, their actions distanced them from associates in the Sanhedrin. They would be viewed by the Sanhedrin as ritually unclean for the next seven days.

Joseph and Nicodemus then prepared the body of Jesus for burial. The body was washed

Joseph of Arimathaea holding the body of Christ

The tomb where Jesus' body was placed

and then rubbed with oil and sprinkled with perfume. It was Nicodemus who supplied powdered myrrh and aloe to anoint the body (see John 19:39).

The body was then wrapped in grave clothes made of long strips of inexpensive linen called *tachrichin* wrappings or traveling-dress (see Matt. 27:59). Myrrh and aloe were packed between the strips of linen to lessen the stench of death. The wrappings, together with the powdered paste, produced a type of cocoon around the body. Typically, the head was bound with a linen napkin, somewhat like a twisted turban, and the jaw was held in place by a linen strip under the chin. According to Jewish custom, the neck and face were left uncovered.

The body was attired in this manner to symbolically prepare it for a journey into the eternities. It was the prevailing Jewish belief that on the fourth day after death, the spirit of the deceased departed and decomposition began.[394]

There were two types of Jewish burial sites outside the walls of villages and towns in Palestine—private and public. Private sites, property of the upper class, were located in gardens and caves and were surprisingly simple. Public sites were in a specified graveyard, such as the Mount of Olives (see Matt. 8:28; 27:7, 52–53; John 11:30–31).

There are two traditional burial sites in Jerusalem—the Church of the Holy Sepulchre and a Garden Tomb north of the Damascus Gate. Both sites are revered by Christians.

If the burial site were the Garden Tomb, then Joseph of Arimathaea brought the body of Jesus to a private burial site located near Gethsemane. By so doing, his actions may have brought duress to his family. If Joseph had intended the Garden Tomb as a family burial site, it could no longer be used as such, even though there was room inside the main chamber to bury additional bodies, because rabbis forbid the burying of kin in the tomb of an executed criminal.

At the garden site is a Herodian tomb that has two chambers. One chamber would have been used for wrapping the body, and the other chamber for burying the body. Between the two chambers was a low connecting door. The inner chamber had niches carved in stone to receive the dead. The other chamber, known as the anteroom or mourning chamber, was used to prepare the body for burial. After the body was placed on a niche in the burial chamber, a disk-shaped stone was rolled edgeways in front of the entrance to secure the tomb from intruders or wild animals.[395]

Jewish leaders believed the disciples of Jesus would steal His body and claim that He had risen from the dead, and they wanted to prevent such actions. Their plea before Pontius Pilate was unnecessary, however; chief priests had complete access to the services of temple guards and could easily command the guards to seal the tomb, which may have meant to place a stone before the opening. Chief priests also had the legal right to take a guard—a small squad of Roman soldiers—to assist them. To defile themselves by asking for support from Pilate was an over-reaction.[396]

> "Mary Magdalene and Mary the mother of Joses" prepared "spices and ointments" and made plans to visit the tomb of Jesus (Mark 15:47; Luke 23:56). Was it a common practice for Jewish women to visit tombs?

For centuries Jewish women visited tombs. Women were more prone to visit tombs on the

Both Marys came to the tomb

third day. An old semitic superstition claimed the spirit of the "departed returned on the third day to say farewell to the body." The women, who mourned near tombs, wore coarse sackcloth, a heavy fabric that served as a testament of their discomfort. They also put dust and ashes on themselves. When they left the burial site, these women placed a small stone near the tomb as a reminder that the dead was not forgotten.

As the women approached the Garden Tomb, they would have walked barefoot, a Jewish sign of mourning and remembrance of the humble approach of Moses to Mount Sinai. They would also have observed the Jewish custom of not eating, drinking, reading, or walking irreverently near the tomb.

In this instance, the women wanted to examine the wrappings of Jesus' body to ensure they were done in accordance with Jewish burial practices; such was not typical (see Luke 23:55–56; 24:1).[397]

> Was Jesus three days in the tomb?

There are ten passages in the New Testament that speak of the resurrection of Jesus as being on the third day. To understand the three-day concept, a few Jewish practices should be considered. First, the expression of three days and three nights is an idiom covering any part of three days and nights. Second, when the Gospel writers said three days in the tomb, it should not be concluded that it was three full days—Jews counted days from sunset to sunset, not sunrise to sunrise. Therefore, the hour before sunset and the hour following sunset were two different days.

Jesus was interred in the Garden Tomb on Friday afternoon. His body lay in the tomb part of Friday, the first day. His body remained in the tomb from sunset on Friday to sunset on Saturday, the second day. On part of Sunday, the third day, He arose from the tomb and conquered death. Since that glorious day, Sunday has been the Lord's Day and the Christian Sabbath.[398]

What is meant by *the resurrection of Jesus?*

"Resurrection is to rise from mortality to immortality, from corruption to incorruption, to change a natural body for a spiritual body," said Elder Bruce R. McConkie (see 1 Cor. 15:42–53). He continued, "We know not how it is done any more than we know how creation commenced or how Gods began to be. Suffice it to say, man is; and suffice it to say, he shall live again."[399]

Which female disciples saw the resurrected Lord near the Garden Tomb?

Jesus appeared first to Mary Magdalene. Second, He appeared to the women who had come to the tomb to mourn His loss. A few of these women had stood near the cross when He was crucified—Mary, the mother of Joses; Joanna; and Salome, the wife of Zebedee.[400]

Mary Magdalene was first to see the resurrected Savior

Why did the women hold the feet of the resurrected Lord?

In the East, "to hold the feet of a nobleman or a holy man" symbolized humble submission. It was a recognition of homage, respect, and reverence.[401]

Besides the women at the Garden Tomb, who else testified to seeing the resurrected Lord?

Jesus was seen in the Palestine area from time to time for forty days after His resurrection. Only a few of His appearances were recorded by the Gospel writers, who write that He appeared to:

1) Disciples on the road to Emmaus, a village eight miles from Jerusalem (see Mark 16:12; Luke 24:13)
2) Peter, in or near Jerusalem (see Luke 24:34; 1 Cor. 15:5)
3) Ten of the Apostles and others at Jerusalem (see Luke 24:36; John 20:19)
4) Eleven of the Apostles at Jerusalem (see Mark 16:14; John 20:26)
5) Apostles at the Sea of Galilee (see John 21:1–23)
6) Disciples on a mountain in Galilee (see Matt. 28:16–18)
7) Five hundred men (see 1 Cor.

The resurrected Savior

15:6)
8) Eleven Apostles on the Mount of Olives (see Luke 24:50–51)

It is symbolic that Jesus was last seen on the Mount of Olives, where He had once descended below all men to atone for the sins of the world, and now ascended above all men to return to His Father in Heaven.[402]

Those who saw the resurrected Lord could not be restrained from sharing the glorious news of His resurrection even it if meant imprisonment or worse. From city courts to rural byways, disciples spoke of Jesus Christ. The honest in heart listened and rejoiced in the knowledge that death was conquered and Jesus had won the crowning victory.

ENDNOTES

1. Bruce, *New Testament History,* 32; Edersheim, *Life and Times,* 182; Smith, *Bible Dictionary,* 272; Senior, *Gospel,* 29.

2. Ward, *Jesus and His Times,* 14, 40–42, 203; McConkie, *Mortal Messiah,* 1:86; Galbraith, *Jerusalem,* 153–54.

3. Geographic, *Everyday Life,* 296–97; Connolly, *History of the Jewish People,* 16.

4. McConkie, *Mortal Messiah,* 1:362; Pax, *Footsteps of Jesus,* 28.

5. Ward, *Jesus and His Times,* 129, 131; Ogden, *Where Jesus Walked,* 152; Edersheim, *Temple,* 25; Geographic, *Everyday Life,* 298.

6. McConkie, *Mortal Messiah,* 1:304–5; Edersheim, *Temple,* 87; Edersheim, *Sketches of Jewish Life,* 37; Dummelow, *Bible Commentary,* 737; Pettingill and Torrey, *Bible Questions,* 373; Fitzmyer, *Gospel According to Luke,* 1:322.

7. Tinsley, *According to Luke,* 26; Edersheim, *Temple,* 165–66.

8. Pax, *Footsteps of Jesus,* 70–71; Edersheim, *Jesus the Messiah,* 3–4; Edersheim, *Temple,* 167.

9. Dummelow, *Bible Commentary,* 738; Smith, *Bible Dictionary,* 112; Fitzmyer, *According to Luke,* 1:328.

10. Ward, *Jesus and His Times,* 92, 311; Berrett and Ogden, *Discovering the World,* 110; Argyle, *According to Matthew,* 34; Pax, *Footsteps of Jesus,* 11, 24; Talmage, *Jesus the Christ,* 113.

11. Smith, *Bible Dictionary,* 193; Pettingill and Torrey, *Bible Questions,* 373.

12. Talmage, *Jesus the Christ,* 84; McConkie, *Mortal Messiah,* 1:223; Ward, *Jesus and His Times,* 16; Gower, *New Manners and Customs,* 65.

13. Smith, *Bible Dictionary,* 238; *Life and Teachings of Jesus,* 23; Talmage, *Jesus the Christ,* 77; Richard Draper, "He Has Risen: The Resurrection Narratives as a Witness of Corporeal Regeneration," in *Lord of the Gospels,* 40; Jacobs, *Book of Jewish Beliefs,* 174; Pax, *Footsteps of Jesus,* 22.

14. Pax, *Footsteps of Jesus,* 22; Edersheim, *Times of Jesus,* 110; Dummelow, *Bible Commentary,* 739; Ward, *Jesus and His Times,* 17.

15. Rhymer, *Illustrated Life of Jesus Christ,* 12.

16. Ward, *Jesus and His Times,* 16, 76; Talmage, *Jesus the Christ,* 79; Rousseau and Arav, *Jesus and His World,* 275.

17. Edersheim, *Jesus the Messiah,* 11; Edersheim, *Sketches of Jewish Life,* 139; Pax, *Footsteps of Jesus,* 89; Rousseau and Arav, *Jesus and His World,* 39.

18. Smith, *Bible Dictionary,* 35; Pax, *Footsteps of Jesus,* 28; *Life and Teachings,* 28; *Jesus and His Apostles,* 21.

19. Ward, *Jesus and His Times,* 13; Pax, *Footsteps of Jesus,* 29; Talmage, *Jesus the Christ,* 86; *Jesus, the Son of Man,* 8.

20. Edersheim, *Jesus the Messiah,* 13; *Life and Teachings,* 29; Talmage, *Jesus the Christ,* 86; Pax, *Footsteps of Jesus,* 34; Ward, *Jesus and His Times,* 13–14; Brown, *Birth of the Messiah,* 412–18.

21. Edersheim, *Jesus the Messiah,* 11; Edersheim, *Sketches of Jewish Life,* 139; Pax, *Footsteps of Jesus,* 89; Rousseau and Arav, *Jesus and His World,* 39.

22. *Life and Teachings,* 29; *Israel,* 47; Berrett and Ogden, *Discovering the Bible,* 187; Ogden, *Where Jesus Walked,* 32; Ward, *Jesus and His Times,* 23.

23. Ward, *Jesus and His Times,* 18, 20; Smith, *Bible Dictionary,* 157; Pax, *Footsteps of Jesus,* 31–32; Edersheim, *Times of Jesus,* 129.

24. Rhymer, *Life of Jesus,* 26; Talmage, *Jesus the Christ,* 54; Geographic, *Everyday Life,* 326.

25. Pettingall and Torrey, *Bible Questions,* 145–46; Schauss, *Jewish Festivals,* 114, 116–17.

26. Talmage, *Jesus the Christ,* 81–82; McConkie, *Doctrinal Commentary,* 95; Argyle, *According to Matthew,* 24; *Life and Teachings,* 29; Rhymer, *Life of Jesus,* 26; Albright and Mann, *Matthew,* 1–6.

27. Ward, *Jesus and His Times,* 22–23; Smith, *Bible Dictionary,* 371; Metzger and Murphy, *Oxford Annotated Bible,* 80; Grower, *New Manners,* 62.

28. Edersheim, *Sketches of Jewish Life,* 76–77; Edersheim, *Jesus the Messiah,* 15.

29. McConkie, *Mortal Messiah,* 1:347; Roberts, *Outlines of Ecclesiastical History,* 12; Pax, *Footsteps of Jesus,* 34.

30. Rhymer, *Life of Jesus,* 30; Dummelow, *Bible Commentary,* 740; Pax, *Footsteps of Jesus,* 34; Heschel, *Sabbath,* 110; Ogden and Skinner, *Verse by Verse,* 773.

31. Pax, *Footsteps of Jesus,* 37.

32. McConkie, *Doctrinal Commentary,* 99; Pax, *Footsteps of Jesus,* 37; Fitzmyer, *According to Luke,* 1:424.

33. Edersheim, *Jesus the Messiah,* 195; Edersheim, *Temple,* 65; Rousseau and Arav, *Jesus and His World,* 55.

34. McConkie, *Doctrinal Commentary,* 99; Pax, *Footsteps of Jesus,* 37.

35. Ward, *Jesus and His Times,* 132.

36. Edersheim, *Temple,* 48.

37. McConkie, *Mortal Messiah,* 1:133; Edersheim, *Temple,* 107.

38. McConkie, *Mortal Messiah,* 1:135; Smith, *Bible Dictionary,* 397.

39. Cannon, "Miracles: Meridian and Modern," in *Lord of the Gospels,* 136; Smith, *Bible Dictionary,* 397; Edersheim, *Temple,* 110–11.

40. Rhymer, *Life of Jesus,* 31; Brown, *Aramaic Approach,* 153–55.

41. Pax, *Footsteps of Jesus,* 40; Ludlow, *Companion,* 269; Edersheim, *Times of Jesus,* 140; Edersheim, *Temple,* 23.

42. Rhymer, *Life of Jesus,* 26; Argyle, *According to Matthew,* 30; Pax, *Footsteps of Jesus,* 46.

43. Lamsa, *Gospel Light,* 12.

44. Ogden, *Where Jesus Walked,* 3; Smith, *Bible Dictionary,* 87.

45. Ward, *Jesus and His Times,* 29; Dummelow, *Bible Commentary,* 627; Smith, *Bible Dictionary,* 221; Rhymer, *Life of Jesus,* 24; Ludlow, *Companion,* 31; Ogden and Skinner, *Verse by Verse,* 61.

46. Ward, *Jesus and His Times,* 27; West, *Jesus,* 5; Albright and Mann, *Matthew,* 11–16.

47. Pax, *Footsteps of Jesus,* 99.

48. Ward, *Jesus and His Times,* 29; West,

Jesus, 5; Argyle, *According to Matthew,* 31.

49. Dummelow, *Bible Commentary,* 628; McConkie, *Doctrinal Commentary,* 107; Ward, *Jesus and His Times,* 29.

50. Rhymer, *Life of Jesus,* 27–28; Ogden, *Where Jesus Walked,* 134; Smith, *Bible Dictionary,* 111; Brown, *Birth of the Messiah,* 165; Danker, *Greek-English Lexicon,* 594.

51. Ogden, *Where Jesus Walked,* 20; Dummelow, *Bible Commentary,* 628; Edersheim, *Jesus the Messiah,* 27–28; Rhymer, *Life of Jesus,* 34; Berrett and Ogden, *Discovering the Bible,* 91; *Life and Teachings,* 31; McConkie, *Doctrinal Commentary,* 624.

52. Pax, *Footsteps of Jesus,* 52–53; Ward, *Jesus and His Times,* 31; Ogden, *Where Jesus Walked,* 46.

53. Berrett and Ogden, *Discovering the Bible,* 223; Dummelow, *Bible Commentary,* 628.

54. Ward, *Jesus and His Times,* 304; Rhymer, *Life of Jesus,* 32; Edersheim, *Sketches of Jewish Life,* 79; Berrett and Ogden, *Discovering the Bible,* 223, 268; Ogden, *Where Jesus Walked,* 47.

55. Ward, *Jesus and His Times,* 87.

56. Edersheim, *Jesus the Messiah,* 29, 38; Pax, *Footsteps of Jesus,* 55; Bruce, *New Testament History,* 27; Metzger and Murphy, *Oxford Annotated Bible,* 4; Connolly, *History of Jewish People,* 46; Ogden and Skinner, *Verse by Verse,* 760–61.

57. Ward, *Jesus and His Times,* 31.

58. Smith, *Bible Dictionary,* 114; Edersheim, *Sketches of Jewish Life,* 33; Berrett and Ogden, *Discovering the Bible,*

3, 104; Rhymer, *Life of Jesus,* 48; Ward, *Jesus and His Times,* 92.

59. Ward, *Jesus and His Times,* 92; Lamsa, *Gospel Light,* 209.

60. Ogden, *Where Jesus Walked,* 55; Pax, *Footsteps of Jesus,* 97.

61. Crossan, *Historical Jesus,* 15.

62. Metzger and Murphy, *Oxford Annotated Bible,* 4; Smith, *Bible Dictionary,* 254; Ogden, *Where Jesus Walked,* 27; Ward, *Jesus and His Times,* 92; Pax, *Footsteps of Jesus,* 11, 24; Crossan, *Historical Jesus,* 18–19.

63. Talmage, *Jesus the Christ,* 89.

64. Rhymer, *Life of Jesus,* 39; Roberts, *Outlines of History,* 40.

65. Roberts, *Outlines of History,* 35.

66. West, *Jesus,* 12; McConkie, *Mortal Messiah,* 1:223.

67. Edersheim, *Sketches of Jewish Life,* 117, 229; Ward, *Jesus and His Times,* 158–59; Dummelow, *Bible Commentary,* xxiv.

68. Edersheim, *Temple,* 199–201.

69. McConkie, *Doctrinal Commentary,* 110; Schauss, *Jewish Festivals,* 38–39, 57; Ogden and Skinner, *Verse by Verse,* 764.

70. Rhymer, *Life of Jesus,* 38; Talmage, *Jesus the Christ,* 106–7.

71. Pax, *Footsteps of Jesus,* 62; Rousseau and Arav, *Jesus and His World,* 163; Schauss, *Jewish Festivals,* 176–78.

72. Pax, *Footsteps of Jesus,* 62; Connolly, *Time of Jesus,* 46.

73. Talmage, Jesus the Christ, 107; Dummelow, Bible Commentary, 653.

74. Berrett and Ogden, Discovering the Bible, 92; Edersheim, Times of Jesus, 172.

75. Edersheim, Jesus the Messiah, 33; Brown, Birth of the Messiah, 691–93.

76. Ward, Jesus and His Times, 133; Edersheim, Temple, 60; Geographic, Everyday Life, 298; Ogden and Skinner, Verse by Verse, 740.

77. Edersheim, Temple, 48; Ward, Jesus and His Times, 133; Ogden, Where Jesus Walked, 155.

78. Pax, Footsteps of Jesus, 58–59; Ogden, Where Jesus Walked, 98; Lamsa, Gospel Light, 180–81; Dummelow, Bible Commentary, 727; Geographic, Everyday Life, 304; Connolly, Time of Jesus, 64–65.

79. Edersheim, Sketches of Jewish Life, 182; Ward, Jesus and His Times, 76–77, 91, 202.

80. West, Jesus, 18; Rhymer, Life of Jesus, 52; Ward, Jesus and His Times, 235.

81. Edersheim, Times of Jesus, 252; Ward, Jesus and His Times, 235.

82. Ludlow, Companion, 27.

83. Rhymer, Life of Jesus, 40; Talmage, Jesus the Christ, 114.

84. Smith, Bible Dictionary, 125, 368; Lane, According to Mark, 51.

85. Metzger and Murphy, Oxford Annotated Bible, 4; Rhymer, Life of Jesus, 40.

86. Ludlow, Companion, 37; Tinsley, According to Luke, 26.

87. Ogden, Where Jesus Walked, 99, 125; Gower, New Manners, 108.

88. Lamsa, Gospel Light, 16; Ogden, Where Jesus Walked, 121, 124; Merrill, "'Behold, the Lamb of God': The Savior's Use of Animals as Symbols," in Lord of the Gospels, 132.

89. McConkie, Mortal Messiah, 1:396; Edersheim, Times of Jesus, 189, 355; Edersheim, Jesus the Messiah, 41.

90. Edersheim, Jesus the Messiah, 43; Edersheim, Times of Jesus, 193.

91. Smith, Bible Dictionary, 335; Ogden and Skinner, Verse by Verse, 84.

92. Ward, Jesus and His Times, 47, 199; Berrett and Ogden, Discovering the Bible, 82; Pax, Footsteps of Jesus, 78; Rousseau and Arav, Jesus and His World, 8; Ogden and Skinner, Verse by Verse, 88.

93. Woods, "The Water Imagery in John's Gospel: Power, Purification, and Pedagogy," in Lord of the Gospels, 197.

94. Argyle, According to Matthew, 38; Merrill, "'Behold the Lamb of God," in Lord of the Gospels, 135–36; McConkie, Doctrinal Commentary, 124.

95. Ogden, Where Jesus Walked, 11; McConkie, Doctrinal Commentary, 113; Ward, Jesus and His Times, 225–26; Edersheim, Times of Jesus, 209.

96. Edersheim, Times of Jesus, 210; Ward, Jesus and His Times, 225–26.

97. Lamsa, Gospel Light, 21; McConkie, Mortal Messiah, 1:185; Ogden and Skinner, Verse by Verse, 209.

98. Ogden, Where Jesus Walked, 84; Jacobs, Jewish Belief, 132.

99. Lamsa, *Gospel Light,* 21, 54.

100. McConkie, *Doctrinal Commentary,* 128; McConkie, *Mortal Messiah,* 1:413, 415; Ludlow, *Companion,* 43; Smith, *Bible Dictionary,* 303; Metzger and Murphy, *Oxford Annotated Bible,* 5.

101. Talmage, *Jesus the Christ,* 125.

102. Talmage, *Jesus the Christ,* 156; Dummelow, *Bible Commentary,* 745.

103. Ward, *Jesus and His Times,* 227; Gower, *New Manners,* 215.

104. Ogden, *Where Jesus Walked,* 68–69.

105. Talmage, *Jesus the Christ,* 67, 632; Smith, *Bible Dictionary,* 316.

106. Pax, *Footsteps of Jesus,* 108–9; Berrett and Ogden, *Discovering the Bible,* 133; Rousseau and Arav, *Jesus and His World,* 22.

107. *Jesus and His Apostles,* 55; Edersheim, *Jesus the Messiah,* 69; Ogden, *Where Jesus Walked,* 88.

108. Pax, *Footsteps of Jesus,* 89; Berrett and Ogden, *Discovering the Bible,* 112; Talmage, *Jesus the Christ,* 137–38; McConkie, *Doctrinal Commentary,* 135; Ogden and Skinner, *Verse by Verse,* 108.

109. Edersheim, *Sketches of Jewish Life,* 140; Ward, *Jesus and His Times,* 115; Edersheim, *Jesus the Messiah,* 69–71; Harpur, *Miracles of Jesus,* 11; Heschel, *Sabbath,* 108; Gower, *New Manners,* 66.

110. Talmage, *Jesus the Christ,* 138.

111. McConkie, *Doctrinal Commentary,* 136.

112. *Life and Teachings,* 40.

113. Edersheim, *Jesus the Messiah,* 72; Metzger and Murphy, *Oxford Annotated Bible,* 127; Ogden and Skinner, *Verse by Verse,* 110.

114. Harpur, *Miracles of Jesus,* 12–13.

115. Cannon, "Miracles: Meridian and Modern," in *Lord of the Gospels,* 27.

116. Talmage, *Jesus the Christ,* 144; Berrett and Ogden, *Discovering the Bible,* 129; Ward, *Jesus and His Times,* 228.

117. Ogden, *Where Jesus Walked,* 26; Talmage, *Jesus the Christ,* 167; Dummelow, *Bible Commentary,* 783.

118. Ward, *Jesus and His Times,* 132; Ogden, *Where Jesus Walked,* 132, 155; Connolly, *History of Jewish People,* 36; Rhymer, *Life of Jesus,* 129; Talmage, *Jesus the Christ,* 145; McConkie, *Mortal Messiah,* 1:460.

119. McConkie, *Mortal Messiah,* 1:460, 462; Talmage, *Jesus the Christ,* 146; Ogden, *Where Jesus Walked,* 132.

120. Edersheim, *Times of Jesus,* 263.

121. Talmage, *Jesus the Christ,* 152.

122. Bruce, *New Testament History,* 152–53; West, *Jesus,* 52; Talmage, *Jesus the Christ,* 236; Smith, *Bible Dictionary,* 309; Berrett and Ogden, *Discovering the Bible,* 354.

123. Bruce, *New Testament History,* 28; Matthews, *Behold the Messiah,* 56–57; Talmage, *Jesus the Christ,* 236.

124. Dummelow, *Bible Commentary,* 664; Talmage, *Jesus the Christ,* 154; Bruce, *New Testament History,* 161.

125. Talmage, *Jesus the Christ,* 161; McConkie, *Mortal Messiah,* 3:165; McConkie, *Doctrinal Commentary,* 151; Ogden

and Skinner, *Verse by Verse,* 129.

126. Berrett and Ogden, *Discovering the Bible,* 98; McConkie, *Mortal Messiah,* 1:495; Edersheim, *Times of Jesus,* 288; Talmage, *Jesus the Christ,* 163; Rousseau and Arav, *Jesus and His World,* 206; Finegan, *Archeology,* 34.

127. Edersheim, *Times of Jesus,* 321; Pax, *Footsteps of Jesus,* 102; Berrett and Ogden, *Discovering the Bible,* 95; Finegan, *Archeology,* 39.

128. Dummelow, *Bible Commentary,* 782; Talmage, *Jesus the Christ,* 162; Senior, *Gospel,* 66.

129. Madsen, "'Wilt Thou Be Made Whole?' Medicine and Healing in the Time of Jesus," in *Lord of the Gospels,* 122–23.

130. Jospe, "Sabbath, Sabbatical and Jubilee: Jewish, Ethical Perspective," in *Jubilee Challenge,* 85; Edersheim, *Temple,* 177; Heschel, *Sabbath,* 51.

131. Jospe, "Sabbath, Sabbatical, and Jubilee," in *Jubilee Challenge,* 85–86; Jacobs, *Jewish Belief,* 97; Heschel, *Sabbath,* 14.

132. Edersheim, *Temple,* 179; Schauss, *Jewish Festivals,* 13–14, 26.

133. Talmage, *Jesus the Christ,* 201, 215–16; McConkie, *Mortal Messiah,* 1:206.

134. Jospe, "Sabbath, Sabbatical, and Jubilee," in *Jubilee Challenge,* 85.

135. Smith, *Bible Dictionary,* 372–73; McConkie, *Mortal Messiah,* 1:190; Jacobs, *Jewish Belief,* 68, 116, 119; Edersheim, *Sketches of Jewish Life,* 232–33.

136. Edersheim, *Sketches of Jewish Life,* 236, 238.

137. Smith, *Bible Dictionary,* 373.

138. Ward, *Jesus and His Times,* 158.

139. Metzger and Murphy, *Oxford Annotated Bible,* 7; Smith, *Bible Dictionary,* 373; McConkie, *Mortal Messiah,* 2:19; Connolly, *Time of Jesus,* 71.

140. McConkie, *Mortal Messiah,* 2:19.

141. Smith, *Bible Dictionary,* 139; Edersheim, *Sketches of Jewish Life,* 21.

142. McConkie, *Mortal Messiah,* 2:20, 22; Metzger and Murphy, *Oxford Annotated Bible,* 84.

143. Ogden, *Where Jesus Walked,* 27; Talmage, *Jesus the Christ,* 168; Metzger and Murphy, *Oxford Annotated Bible,* 6.

144. Edersheim, *Times of Jesus,* 316; Dummelow, *Bible Commentary,* 746; McConkie, *Mortal Messiah,* 2:27; Ward, *Jesus and His Times,* 235; Kelly and Skinner, *Verse by Verse,* 142.

145. Pax, *Footsteps of Jesus,* 135; Ward, *Jesus and His Times,* 235.

146. McConkie, *Mortal Messiah,* 2:35; Edersheim, *Sketches of Jewish Life,* 233.

147. Harpur, *Miracles of Jesus,* 15; Smith, *Bible Dictionary,* 83; Metzger and Murphy, *Oxford Annotated Bible,* 6, 48; Rousseau and Arav, *Jesus and His World,* 88.

148. McConkie, *Mortal Messiah,* 2:35; Ogden and Skinner, *Verse by Verse,* 145.

149. Berrett and Ogden, *Discovering the Bible,* 123; Ogden, *Where Jesus Walked,* 116.

150. Ward, *Jesus and His Times,* 229; Ogden, *Where Jesus Walked,* 116; Rousseau and Arav, *Jesus and His World,* 94–96.

151. McConkie, *Doctrinal Commentary,* 166; Ward, *Jesus and His Times,* 228; Talmage, *Jesus the Christ,* 185.

152. Talmage, *Jesus the Christ,* 205; Smith, *Bible Dictionary,* 387.

153. McConkie, *Mortal Messiah,* 2:45; Smith, *Bible Dictionary,* 212; Edersheim, *Jesus the Messiah,* 123; Talmage, *Jesus the Christ,* 186–87; *Life and Teachings,* 69.

154. McConkie, *Mortal Messiah,* 2:47; Rousseau and Arav, *Jesus and His World,* 296; Edersheim, *Times of Jesus,* 343; Harpur, *Miracles of Jesus,* 21.

155. *Life and Teachings,* 145; Ward, *Jesus and His Times,* 233.

156. McConkie, *Mortal Messiah,* 2:104; *Jesus and His Apostles,* 55; Talmage, *Jesus the Christ,* 203; Dummelow, *Bible Commentary,* 660.

157. Edersheim, *Sketches of Jewish Life,* 16; Dummelow, *Bible Commentary,* 661–62; Smith, *Bible Dictionary,* 138.

158. Dummelow, *Bible Commentary,* 662.

159. Dummelow, *Bible Commentary,* 662; McConkie, *Doctrinal Commentary,* 330.

160. Argyle, *According to Matthew,* 82.

161. McConkie, *Mortal Messiah,* 2:117; Rhymer, *Life of Jesus,* 66.

162. McConkie, *Mortal Messiah,* 2:118; Brown, *Aramaic Approach,* 156–58.

163. Lamsa, *Gospel Light,* 26; Ogden and Skinner, *Verse by Verse,* 178.

164. Ogden, *Where Jesus Walked,* 72; Lamsa, *Gospel Light,* 192; Gower, *New Manners,* 56.

165. Berrett and Ogden, *Discovering the Bible,* 134.

166. Metzger and Murphy, *Oxford Annotated Bible,* 53; Ogden, *Where Jesus Walked,* 132.

167. Talmage, *Jesus the Christ,* 218; McConkie, *Doctrinal Commentary,* 220; Ogden and Skinner, *Verse by Verse,* 187.

168. Lamsa, *Gospel Light,* 30; Dummelow, *Bible Commentary,* 642; McConkie, *Doctrinal Commentary,* 222; Galbraith, Ogden, and Skinner, *Jerusalem,* 169–70.

169. McConkie, *Doctrinal Commentary,* 232; Metzger and Murphy, *Oxford Annotated Bible,* 8; Dummelow, *Bible Commentary,* 644.

170. Lamsa, *Gospel Light,* 44; Dummelow, *Bible Commentary,* 645.

171. Dummelow, *Bible Commentary,* 645; Argyle, *According to Matthew,* 55.

172. Argyle, *According to Matthew,* 56; Rhymer, *Life of Jesus,* 70; Edersheim, *Times of Jesus,* 664; Lamsa, *Gospel Light,* 214.

173. Lamsa, *Gospel Light,* 47.

174. Dummelow, *Bible Commentary,* 649.

175. McConkie, *Mortal Messiah,* 2:249; Ogden, *Where Jesus Walked,* 127; Clark, *Lord of the Gospels,* 133.

176. Lamsa, *Gospel Light,* 55, 231.

177. Edersheim, *Jesus the Messiah,* 148; Dummelow, *Bible Commentary,* 653; Harpur, *Miracles of Jesus,* 27; Rousseau and Arav, *Jesus and His World,* 361.

178. Harpur, *Miracles of Jesus,* 27–28; Ludlow, *Companion,* 91; Edersheim, *Times of Jesus,* 378.

179. Edersheim, *Sketches of Jewish Life,* 154–56; Ward, *Jesus and His Times,* 117; Dummelow, *Bible Commentary,* 659; Connolly, *History of Jewish People,* 60–61.

180. Smith, *Bible Dictionary,* 413; Ward, *Jesus and His Times,* 230; Metzger and Murphy, *Oxford Annotated Bible,* 49.

181. Bennion, *Church of Jesus,* 6; Geographic, *Everyday Life,* 332.

182. Harpur, *Miracles of Jesus,* 17; Edersheim, *Jesus the Messiah,* 120.

183. Lamsa, *Gospel Light,* 62; Argyle, *According to Matthew,* 69.

184. Smith, *Bible Dictionary,* 421; Dummelow, *Bible Commentary,* 655; Harpur, *Miracles of Jesus,* 32; Talmage, *Jesus the Christ,* 287.

185. Berrett and Ogden, *Discovering the Bible,* 145; Lamsa, *Gospel Light,* 64.

186. Harpur, *Miracles of Jesus,* 36; McConkie, *Doctrinal Commentary,* 313.

187. McConkie, *Mortal Messiah,* 3:13, 19; Berrett and Ogden, *Discovering the Bible,* 119, 364.

188. Lamsa, *Gospel Light,* 169.

189. McConkie, *Mortal Messiah,* 3:199; Talmage, *Jesus the Christ,* 178; Smith, *Bible Dictionary,* 277.

190. Ward, *Jesus and His Times,* 158–59; Talmage, *Jesus the Christ,* 60.

191. Dummelow, *Bible Commentary,* 783; Lamsa, *Gospel Light,* 185.

192. Edersheim, *Sketches of Jewish Life,* 42; Ogden, *Where Jesus Walked,* 22; Bruce, *New Testament History,* 40; Tinsley, *According to Luke,* 45.

193. Talmage, *Jesus the Christ,* 181, 208; Smith, *Bible Dictionary,* 232; *Jesus and His Apostles,* 55.

194. Talmage, *Jesus the Christ,* 182; Bruce, *New Testament History,* 182.

195. McConkie, *Doctrinal Commentary,* 120; Tinsley, *According to Luke,* 45.

196. Albright and Mann, *Matthew,* 105–6.

197. Dummelow, *Bible Commentary,* 647; Bruce, *New Testament History,* 158; Metzger and Murphy, *Oxford Annotated Bible,* 50.

198. Edersheim, *Jesus the Messiah,* 130, 148; Dummelow, *Bible Commentary,* 657; Talmage, *Jesus the Christ,* 244; Metzger and Murphy, *Oxford Annotated Bible,* 86; Bornkamm, *Jesus of Nazareth,* 39.

199. Ogden, *Where Jesus Walked,* 124.

200. Ogden, *Where Jesus Walked,* 93; Talmage, *Jesus the Christ,* 184; Lamsa, *Gospel Light,* 236–37; Dummelow, *Bible Commentary,* 658.

201. *Life and Teachings,* 78.

202. Ogden, *Where Jesus Walked,* 103; Metzger and Murphy, *Oxford Annotated Bible,* 17; Dummelow, *Bible Commentary,* 667.

203. Edersheim, *Jesus the Messiah,* 186; Argyle, *According to Matthew,* 75; Harpur, *Miracles of Jesus,* 42.

204. Schauss, *Jewish Festivals,* 10; Heschel, *Sabbath,* 29; Madsen, *Radiant Life,* 72.

205. Pax, *Footsteps of Jesus,* 131, 135; Madsen, "'Wilt Thou Be Made Whole?' Medicine and Healing in the Time of Jesus," in *Lord of the Gospels,* 113;

Ogden, *Where Jesus Walked,* 140; Edersheim, *Jesus the Messiah,* 110; Rousseau and Arav, *Jesus and His World,* 155–56.

206. McConkie, *Mortal Messiah,* 2:70; Rhymer, *Life of Jesus,* 92; Talmage, *Jesus the Christ,* 195.

207. Ogden, *Where Jesus Walked,* 82.

208. Talmage, *Jesus the Christ,* 198.

209. Ogden, *Where Jesus Walked,* 4; Smith, *Bible Dictionary,* 329.

210. Metzger and Murphy, *Oxford Annotated Bible,* 17; Edersheim, *Temple,* 184; Talmage, *Jesus the Christ,* 201–2.

211. Edersheim, *Jesus the Messiah,* 254; Dummelow, *Bible Commentary,* 667.

212. Pax, *Footsteps of Jesus,* 97; Talmage, *Jesus the Christ,* 201; Rhymer, *Life of Jesus,* 85.

213. Godfrey, "The Surprise Factors in the Teachings of Jesus," in *Lord of the Gospels,* 56–57; Ford, *Parables of Jesus,* 143.

214. Matthews, *Behold the Messiah,* 167.

215. Edersheim, *Jesus the Messiah,* 170; Smith, *Bible Dictionary,* 367; McConkie, *Mortal Messiah,* 2:268.

216. Lamsa, *Gospel Light,* 177–78; Ogden, *Where Jesus Walked,* 132.

217. Metzger and Murphy, *Oxford Annotated Bible,* 14; Dummelow, *Bible Commentary,* 663.

218. Ogden, *Where Jesus Walked,* 79.

219. *Life and Teachings,* 120; Ogden, *Where Jesus Walked,* 83; Lamsa, *Gospel Light,* 94.

220. Edersheim, *Jesus the Messiah,* 172; Lamsa, *Gospel Light,* 94.

221. Ogden, *Where Jesus Walked,* 75; Ward, *Jesus and His Times,* 103.

222. *Life and Teachings,* 121; Ogden, *Where Jesus Walked,* 90–91; Lamsa, *Gospel Light,* 160; Edersheim, *Jesus the Messiah,* 174.

223. Lamsa, *Gospel Light,* 100; Smith, *Bible Dictionary,* 210.

224. McConkie, *Mortal Messiah,* 2:332–33; Dummelow, *Bible Commentary,* 675; Edersheim, *Times of Jesus,* 461.

225. Edersheim, *Jesus the Messiah,* 213; Dummelow, *Bible Commentary,* 675; Matthews, *Behold the Messiah,* 63.

226. Draper, "He Has Risen," in *Lord of the Gospels,* 54; Argyle, *According to Matthew,* 111; McConkie, *Mortal Messiah,* 2:335; Albright and Mann, *Matthew,* 175–76.

227. Pax, *Footsteps of Jesus,* 130.

228. Edersheim, *Jesus the Messiah,* 114; Talmage, *Jesus the Christ,* 310; *Life and Teachings,* 142; Harpur, *Miracles of Jesus,* 48; McConkie, *Mortal Messiah,* 2:341–42, 350, 368.

229. Dummelow, *Bible Commentary,* 677; Ogden and Skinner, *Verse by Verse,* 309.

230. Ogden, *Where Jesus Walked,* 5; McConkie, *Mortal Messiah,* 2:359.

231. *Israel,* 96; Bruce, *New Testament History,* 33; Berrett and Ogden, *Discovering the Bible,* 127; Ward, *Jesus and His Times,* 77; McConkie, *Mortal Messiah,* 2:362.

232. *Jesus and His Apostles,* 140–41; Talmage, *Jesus the Christ,* 324; Ogden, *Where Jesus Walked,* 24; Connolly, *Time of Jesus,* 62.

233. Geikie, *Words of Christ,* 520, as quoted in McConkie, *Mortal Messiah,* 2:382–83; Farrer, *Life of Christ,* 194–213.

234. Talmage, *Jesus the Christ,* 325.

235. Talmage, *Jesus the Christ,* 325; McConkie, *Mortal Messiah,* 2:400–1.

236. Geikie, *Words of Christ,* 524–46, as quoted in McConkie, *Mortal Messiah,* 2:400–1.

237. Pax, *Footsteps of Jesus,* 131.

238. McConkie, *Mortal Messiah,* 3:8; Ogden, *Where Jesus Walked,* 38.

239. McConkie, *Mortal Messiah,* 3:10.

240. McConkie, *Mortal Messiah,* 3:8; Jacobs, *Jewish Belief,* 11; Lane, *According to Mark,* 260–61.

241. Lamsa, *Gospel Light,* 188; Dummelow, *Bible Commentary,* 679; *Jesus and His Apostles,* 97; Harpur, *Miracles of Jesus,* 56.

242. Talmage, *Jesus the Christ,* 331; Dummelow, *Bible Commentary,* 728, 790.

243. Edersheim, *Jesus the Messiah,* 258.

244. Ogden, *Where Jesus Walked,* 58, 63–64.

245. Harpur, *Miracles of Jesus,* 66–67.

246. Ogden, *Where Jesus Walked,* 22; Berrett and Ogden, *Discovering the Bible,* 140; Ward, *Jesus and His Times,* 306; Ogden and Skinner, *Verse by Verse,* 329.

247. McConkie, *Doctrinal Commentary,* 382; McConkie, *Mortal Messiah,* 3:35.

248. Metzger and Murphy, *Oxford Annotated Bible,* 25; Talmage, *Jesus the Christ,* 337; Stern, *Jewish New Testament,* xxiii.

249. McConkie, *Doctrinal Commentary,* 391; McConkie, *Mortal Messiah,* 3:46–47; Ludlow, *Companion,* 232; Talmage, *Jesus the Christ,* 338; Ogden and Skinner, *Verse by Verse,* 333.

250. *Israel,* 95, 110; Ward, *Jesus and His Times,* 242; Berrett and Ogden, *Discovering the Bible,* 113, 143; Edersheim, *Times of Jesus,* 538; Rousseau and Arav, *Jesus and His World,* 212.

251. McConkie, *Mormon Doctrine,* 803; McConkie, *Doctrinal Commentary,* 403.

252. Smith, *Bible Dictionary,* 218; Metzger and Murphy, *Oxford Annotated Bible,* 26; Lamsa, *Gospel Light,* 103–4.

253. Edersheim, *Times of Jesus,* 549.

254. Ward, *Jesus and His Times,* 229; Ogden and Skinner, *Verse by Verse,* 351.

255. Dummelow, *Bible Commentary,* 686; Edersheim, *Jesus the Messiah,* 289; Talmage, *Jesus the Christ,* 442; Edersheim, *Temple,* 66.

256. Dummelow, *Bible Commentary,* 687.

257. McConkie, *Doctrinal Commentary,* 508; Dummelow, *Bible Commentary,* 758; Ogden, *Where Jesus Walked,* 99; Smith, *Bible Dictionary,* 153; McConkie, *Mortal Messiah,* 3:248; Godfrey, "The Surprise Factors in the Teachings of Jesus," in *Lord of the Gospels,* 58–59.

258. Rhymer, *Life of Jesus,* 96; Talmage, *Jesus the Christ,* 344, 390; McConkie, *Mortal Messiah,* 1:160, 3:122; Schauss, *Jewish Festivals,* 178.

259. McConkie, *Mortal Messiah,* 1:184; Edersheim, *Times of Jesus,* 563.

260. McConkie, *Mortal Messiah,* 3:134–35.

261. McConkie, *Mortal Messiah,* 1:177; Farrar, *Life of Christ,* 254–61.

262. Smith, *Bible Dictionary,* 91; Dummelow, *Bible Commentary,* 751; Edersheim, *Times of Jesus,* 567.

263. Pax, *Footsteps of Jesus,* 117; *Life and Teachings,* 255; Ogden, *Where Jesus Walked,* 24.

264. Ogden, *Where Jesus Walked,* 111; Smith, *Bible Dictionary,* 428; Dummelow, *Bible Commentary,* 666; Lamsa, *Gospel Light,* 85; Edersheim, *Jesus the Messiah,* 306.

265. Dummelow, *Bible Commentary,* 751.

266. Ward, *Jesus and His Times,* 117.

267. Edersheim, *Sketches of Jewish Life,* 69; Godfrey, "The Surprise Factors," in *Lord of the Gospels,* 62.

268. Edersheim, *Jesus the Messiah,* 307–8, 310; Schauss, *Jewish Festivals,* 189–90, 200.

269. Argyle, *According to Matthew,* 163.

270. Talmage, *Jesus the Christ,* 449; Metzger and Murphy, *Oxford Annotated Bible,* 108; McConkie, *Mortal Messiah,* 3:261.

271. Dummelow, *Bible Commentary,* 763.

272. Metzger and Murphy, *Oxford Annotated Bible,* 140; Edersheim, *Sketches of Jewish Life,* 149–50.

273. Berrett and Ogden, *Discovering the Bible,* 51, 53; Talmage, *Jesus the Christ,* 392.

274. *Life and Teachings,* 189; Talmage, *Jesus the Christ,* 392.

275. *Life and Teachings,* 189; Edersheim, *Times of Jesus,* 607.

276. Dummelow, *Bible Commentary,* 688; McConkie, *Doctrinal Commentary,* 548; Talmage, *Jesus the Christ,* 440.

277. Talmage, *Jesus the Christ,* 444; McConkie, *Mortal Messiah,* 3:301; Lamsa, *Gospel Light,* 112.

278. Merrill, "Behold, the Lamb of God," in *Lord of the Gospels,* 132; Talmage, *Jesus the Christ,* 451; McConkie, *Mortal Messiah,* 3:304; Lamsa, *Gospel Light,* 115.

279. Ogden, *Where Jesus Walked,* 93–94.

280. Lamsa, *Gospel Light,* 117–18; Smith, *Bible Dictionary,* 152.

281. Talmage, *Jesus the Christ,* 453; *Life and Teachings,* 205–6; *Jesus and His Apostles,* 118; McConkie, *Doctrinal Commentary,* 489; Rhymer, *Life of Jesus,* 99.

282. Edersheim, *Temple,* 318–19; Talmage, *Jesus the Christ,* 465; McConkie, *Doctrinal Commentary,* 489.

283. *Jesus and His Apostles,* 143.

284. Ogden, *Where Jesus Walked,* 6.

285. Smith, *Bible Dictionary,* 84; Ward, *Jesus and His Times,* 246.

286. Metzger and Murphy, *Oxford Annotated Bible,* 104; Talmage, *Jesus the Christ,* 419.

287. Berrett and Ogden, *Discovering the Bible,* 80; Ogden, *Where Jesus Walked,* 36; Pax, *Footsteps of Jesus,* 129; *Israel,* 54; Dummelow, *Bible Commentary,* 764.

288. Harpur, *Miracles of Jesus,* 81.

289. Talmage, *Jesus the Christ,* 471; Dummelow, *Bible Commentary,* 764; Ogden, *Where Jesus Walked,* 99.

290. Talmage, *Jesus the Christ,* 302; Jacobs, *Jewish Belief,* 235; Metzger and Murphy, *Oxford Annotated Bible,* 143; Edersheim, *Jesus the Messiah,* 428, 431; Dummelow, *Bible Commentary,* 793; Berrett and Ogden, *Discovering the Bible,* 78; Pax, *Footsteps of Jesus,* 148; Farrar, *Life of Christ,* 510.

291. Berrett and Ogden, *Discovering the Bible,* 94; Ward, *Jesus and His Times,* 246; Ogden and Skinner, *Verse by Verse,* 457.

292. Ogden, *Where Jesus Walked,* 32–33.

293. Lamsa, *Gospel Light,* 118; Talmage, *Jesus the Christ,* 478; Edersheim, *Sketches of Jewish Life,* 47.

294. *Life and Teachings,* 239; Merrill, "Behold, the Lamb of God," in *Lord of the Gospels,* 134; Ward, *Jesus and His Times,* 203; Ogden, *Where Jesus Walked,* 114–15, 138; Pax, *Footsteps of Jesus,* 150.

295. Ogden, *Where Jesus Walked,* 99; Smith, *Bible Dictionary,* 276.

296. Dummelow, *Bible Commentary,* 694; Talmage, *Jesus the Christ,* 486; McConkie, *Doctrinal Commentary,* 578.

297. Ward, *Jesus and His Times,* 250; Metzger and Murphy, *Oxford Annotated Bible,* 68; Farrar, *Life of Christ,* 331–39.

298. *Jesus and His Apostles,* 55.

299. McConkie, *Mortal Messiah,* 3:195, 345–46; Ogden, *Where Jesus Walked,* 57, 89; Talmage, *Jesus the Christ,* 487–88, 490, 502; Argyle, *According to Matthew,* 159.

300. Matt. 21:28–44; 22:2–14; 25:1–12.

301. Talmage, *Jesus the Christ,* 64, 505.

302. Talmage, *Jesus the Christ,* 368; Ogden, *Where Jesus Walked,* 130–31; Edersheim, *Sketches of Jewish Life,* 26.

303. Pax, *Footsteps of Jesus,* 97; Ward, *Jesus and His Times,* 213, 215; Connolly, *History of Jewish People,* 30; Senior, *Gospel,* 40.

304. Smith, *Bible Dictionary,* 301; Talmage, *Jesus the Christ,* 524; *Life and Teachings,* 254.

305. Ward, *Jesus and His Times,* 214; Edersheim, *Sketches of Jewish Life,* 241.

306. *Life and Teachings,* 207, 254; Talmage, *Jesus the Christ,* 60; Pax, *Footsteps of Jesus,* 102.

307. Talmage, *Jesus the Christ,* 392; Ward, *Jesus and His Times,* 133; Dummelow, *Bible Commentary,* 731.

308. Ogden, *Where Jesus Walked,* 73, 132; Dummelow, *Bible Commentary,* 731.

309. Ogden, *Where Jesus Walked,* 90.

310. Ward, *Jesus and His Times,* 117; Argyle, *According to Matthew,* 176.

311. Ogden, *Where Jesus Walked,* 112; Merrill, "Behold, the Lamb of God," in *Lord of the Gospels,* 137.

312. Ludlow, *Companion,* 178; McConkie, *Mortal Messiah,* 3:466; Edersheim, *Jesus the Messiah,* 516–17; Bailey, "A Message of Judgment from the Olivet Sermon," in *Lord of the Gospels,* 21–22; Ward, *Jesus and His Times,* 115; Talmage, *Jesus the Christ,* 535–36.

313. Ogden, *Where Jesus Walked,* 109; Lamsa, *Gospel Light,* 141; Gower, *New Manners,* 142.

314. McConkie, *Mortal Messiah,* 2:199; Godfrey, "The Surprise Factors in the Teachings of Jesus," in *Lord of the Gospels,* 60; Edersheim, *Jesus the Messiah,* 352; Bornkamm, *Jesus of Nazareth,* 80.

315. Godfrey, "The Surprise Factors in the Teachings of Jesus," in *Lord of the Gospels,* 60–61; Dummelow, *Bible Commentary,* 749; McConkie, *Mortal Messiah,* 2:200.

316. Smith, *Bible Dictionary,* 14; Ogden, *Where Jesus Walked,* 71, 133–34; Berrett and Ogden, *Discovering the Bible,* 327; Talmage, *Jesus the Christ,* 476; Ward, *Jesus and His Times,* 48.

317. McConkie, *Mortal Messiah,* 4:13–15; McConkie, *Doctrinal Commentary,* 702.

318. *Life and Teachings,* 55; McConkie, *Doctrinal Commentary,* 704.

319. Metzger and Murphy, *Oxford Annotated Bible,* 116; Ogden, *Where Jesus Walked,* 141.

320. Smith, *Bible Dictionary,* 401; McConkie, *Mortal Messiah,* 4:22; Edersheim, *Sketches of Jewish Life,* 47, 92; Pax, *Footsteps of Jesus,* 160; Schauss, *Jewish Festivals,* 48.

321. Rhymer, *Life of Jesus,* 144; McConkie, *Mortal Messiah,* 4:26–27, 31; Ogden, *Where Jesus Walked,* 143.

322. Metzger and Murphy, *Oxford Annotated Bible,* 67; Talmage, *Jesus the Christ,* 551; McConkie, *Mortal Messiah,* 4:32; Dummelow, *Bible Commentary,* 731; Edersheim, *Times of Jesus,* 808.

323. *Life and Teachings,* 280.

324. Dummelow, *Bible Commentary,* 797–98.

325. McConkie, *Mortal Messiah,* 4:53–55; Pax, *Footsteps of Jesus,* 161.

326. Hunter, *According to John,* 137; Rhymer, *Life of Jesus,* 81; *Life and Teachings,* 280; Smith, *Bible Dictionary,* 366; Ludlow, *Companion,* 415; Edersheim, *Temple,* 253.

327. McConkie, *Mortal Messiah,* 4:56, 68.

328. Dummelow, *Bible Commentary,* 766; Smith, *Bible Dictionary,* 76; Rhymer, *Life of Jesus,* 144.

329. Talmage, *Jesus the Christ,* 553; McConkie, *Mortal Messiah,* 4:40; Ogden, *Where Jesus Walked,* 53; Ward, *Jesus and His Times,* 251; Hunter, *According to John,* 134; Farrar, *Life of Christ,* 377–78.

330. Hunter, *According to John,* 145; Tinsley, *According to Luke,* 38.

331. McConkie, *Mortal Messiah,* 4:109, 111; McConkie, *Doctrinal Commentary,* 760; *Jesus and His Apostles,* 172.

332. Smith, *Bible Dictionary,* 268; Berrett and Ogden, *Discovering the Bible,* 38; Rousseau and Arav, *Jesus and His World,* 211; Galbraith, Ogden, and Skinner, *Jerusalem,* 165–67.

333. Ogden, *Where Jesus Walked,* 143; Berrett and Ogden, *Discovering the Bible,* 49; Gower, *New Manners,* 115; Galbraith, Ogden, and Skinner, *Jerusalem,* 201–23.

334. McConkie, *Mortal Messiah,* 4:107; Pax, *Footsteps of Jesus,* 161; Schauss, *Jewish Festivals,* 81; Edersheim, *Temple,* 142.

335. Smith, *Bible Dictionary,* 260.

336. McConkie, *Mortal Messiah,* 4:124, 127.

337. Smith, *Bible Dictionary,* 76; Brown, *Death of the Messiah,* 163–78.

338. McConkie, *Mortal Messiah,* 4:129–32; Edersheim, *Jesus the Messiah,* 574–76.

339. Ward, *Jesus and His Times,* 227; McConkie, *Mortal Messiah,* 4:130; Dummelow, *Bible Commentary,* 713.

340. Ogden, *Where Jesus Walked,* 144; Talmage, *Jesus the Christ,* 571; Edersheim, *Jesus the Messiah,* 571, 577; Edersheim, *Times of Jesus,* 849; Rousseau and Arav, *Jesus and His World,* 333.

341. McConkie, *Mortal Messiah,* 4:131.

342. Ward, *Jesus and His Times,* 254; McConkie, *Mortal Messiah,* 4:143, 146; Talmage, *Jesus the Christ,* 576; McConkie, *Doctrinal Commentary,* 784; Edersheim, *Times of Jesus,* 255; Dummelow, *Bible Commentary,* 694; Ludlow, *Companion,* 432; Edersheim, *Jesus the Messiah,* 578; Stern, *Jewish New Testament,* 146.

343. McConkie, *Doctrinal Commentary,* 788; McConkie, *Mortal Messiah,* 4:147; Talmage, *Jesus the Christ,* 576.

344. Talmage, *Jesus the Christ,* 66; Ward, *Jesus and His Times,* 211; Roberts, *Outlines,* 32; McConkie, *Mortal Messiah,* 4:164–66.

345. Bruce, *New Testament History,* 62–63, 67; Connolly, *History of Jewish People,* 29.

346. McConkie, *Doctrinal Commentary,* 788–91; Dummelow, *Bible Commentary,* 714; Ludlow, *Companion,* 190.

347. Ward, *Jesus and His Times,* 254; Pax, *Footsteps of Jesus,* 132; Talmage, *Jesus the Christ,* 179; McConkie, *Mortal Messiah,* 4:160; Lamsa, *Gospel Light,* 208.

348. McConkie, *Mortal Messiah,* 4:160–61; Brown, *Death of the Messiah,* 79.

349. Edersheim, *Sketches of Jewish Life,* 40; Hunter, *According to John,* 169.

350. Hunter, *According to John,* 169; Ogden, *Where Jesus Walked,* 113; Edersheim, *Times of Jesus,* 844; Argyle, *According to Matthew,* 201; Spong, *Liberating the Gospels,* 71; Brown, *Death of the Messiah,* 607.

351. Talmage, *Jesus the Christ,* 580, 583; Rhymer, *Life of Jesus,* 93; McConkie, *Doctrinal Commentary,* 788–91.

352. Talmage, *Jesus the Christ,* 581, 586; Dummelow, *Bible Commentary,* 714; Metzger and Murphy, *Oxford Annotated Bible,* 71; Edersheim, *Jesus the Messiah,* 586; Brown, *Death of the Messiah,* 517–19.

353. Talmage, *Jesus the Christ,* 596; Argyle, *According to Matthew,* 210; Edersheim, *Jesus the Messiah,* 595; McConkie, *Mortal Messiah,* 4:200–1; Berrett and Ogden, *Discovering the Bible,* 56; Rousseau and Arav, *Jesus and His World,* 145; Stern, *Jewish New Testament,* 40–41.

354. Ward, *Jesus and His Times,* 202; Talmage, *Jesus the Christ,* 586; *Life and Teachings,* 312–13; Connolly, *History of Jewish People,* 48.

355. Talmage, *Jesus the Christ,* 341; *Israel,* 78.

356. Ogden, *Where Jesus Walked,* 145; Berrett and Ogden, *Discovering the Bible,* 30; Lamsa, *Gospel Light,* 384; Danker, *Greek-English Lexicon,* 185–86.

357. McConkie, *Mortal Messiah,* 4:174–75; Talmage, *Jesus the Christ,* 587.

358. McConkie, *Mortal Messiah,* 4:177–80; Smith, *Bible Dictionary,* 111; Ogden, *Where Jesus Walked,* 127.

359. McConkie, *Mortal Messiah,* 4:182; Talmage, *Jesus the Christ,* 590; Schauss, *Jewish Festivals,* 83.

360. McConkie, *Mortal Messiah,* 4:185.

361. Talmage, *Jesus the Christ,* 592; Ogden, *Where Jesus Walked,* 52; McConkie, *Mortal Messiah,* 4:187–88; Smith, *Bible Dictionary,* 414.

362. Pax, *Footsteps of Jesus,* 192; Edersheim, *Jesus the Messiah,* 68; Ward, *Jesus and His Times,* 256; *Life and Teachings,* 313; Smith, *Bible Dictionary,* 11.

363. McConkie, *Mortal Messiah,* 4:192; Edersheim, *Times of Jesus,* 873; Ogden, *Where Jesus Walked,* 126; Gower, *New Manners,* 162.

364. Ogden, *Where Jesus Walked,* 103; Ludlow, *Companion,* 196; Argyle, *According to Matthew,* 214; Smith, *Bible Dictionary,* 386.

365. Pax, *Footsteps of Jesus,* 190; Talmage, *Jesus the Christ,* 593, 595, 601.

366. Ward, *Jesus and His Times,* 256; McConkie, *Mortal Messiah,* 4:184; Talmage, *Jesus the Christ,* 591; Ogden, *Where Jesus Walked,* 146; Smith, *Bible Dictionary,* 41; Bruce, *New Testament History,* 204.

367. McConkie, *Mortal Messiah,* 4:189.

368. Smith, *Bible Dictionary,* 302; Ward, *Jesus and His Times,* 256; Rousseau and Arav, *Jesus and His World,* 243; Galbraith, Ogden, and Skinner, *Jerusalem,* 156–57; Connolly, *Time of Jesus,* 52.

369. Ward, *Jesus and His Times,* 256.

370. *Israel,* 25.

371. Pax, *Footsteps of Jesus,* 196; Edersheim, *Jesus the Messiah,* 605; Edersheim, *Times of Jesus,* 881; Ward, *Jesus and His Times,* 259.

372. Edersheim, *Jesus the Messiah,* 601.

373. Ward, *Jesus and His Times,* 259; McConkie, *Doctrinal Commentary,* 814.

374. Talmage, *Jesus the Christ,* 606, 618; Ward, *Jesus and His Times,* 259.

375. Pax, *Footsteps of Jesus,* 196.

376. Ogden, *Where Jesus Walked,* 146.

377. Edersheim, *Jesus the Messiah,* 602; McConkie, *Mortal Messiah,* 4:206; Lane, *According to Mark,* 561–62.

378. Talmage, *Jesus the Christ,* 619; Pax, *Footsteps of Jesus,* 196; Ward, *Jesus and His Times,* 259; Rousseau and Arav, *Jesus and His World,* 75.

379. Hunter, *According to John,* 179; Talmage, *Jesus the Christ,* 607.

380. Ward, *Jesus and His Times,* 260.

381. Talmage, *Jesus the Christ,* 612; McConkie, *Mortal Messiah,* 4:211.

382. Pax, *Footsteps of Jesus,* 197; Edersheim, *Jesus the Messiah,* 188.

383. Rousseau and Arav, *Jesus and His World,* 326.

384. McConkie, *Mortal Messiah,* 4:218–19; Talmage, *Jesus the Christ,* 129.

385. Hunter, *According to John,* 178; Edersheim, *Times of Jesus,* 885, 887; Danker, *Greek-English Lexicon,* 761.

386. *Life and Teachings,* 40.

387. Smith, *Bible Dictionary,* 91.

388. Ogden, *Where Jesus Walked,* 91; Hunter, *According to John,* 179; Smith, *Bible Dictionary,* 154; Stern, *Jewish New Testament,* 69.

389. Dummelow, *Bible Commentary,* 718.

390. Edersheim, *Times of Jesus,* 890.

391. Talmage, *Jesus the Christ,* 616, 619.

392. Rhymer, *Life of Jesus,* 170; McConkie, *Mortal Messiah,* 4:238–39; Ward, *Jesus and His Times,* 117.

393. McConkie, *Mortal Messiah,* 4:238; Pax, *Footsteps of Jesus,* 205; Dummelow, *Bible Commentary,* 719; Ogden, *Where Jesus Walked,* 31.

394. Edersheim, *Jesus the Messiah,* 621; Jacobs, *Jewish Belief,* 235; Talmage, *Jesus the Christ,* 153; Ogden, *Where Jesus Walked,* 133; Edersheim, *Sketches of Jewish Life,* 155; Ward, *Jesus and His Times,* 116.

395. Dummelow, *Bible Commentary,* 748; Rousseau and Arav, *Jesus and His World,* 4, 167; Pax, *Footsteps of Jesus,* 208.

396. McConkie, *Doctrinal Commentary,* 838; Metzger and Murphy, *Oxford Annotated Bible,* 45.

397. Edersheim, *Sketches of Jewish Life,* 155; Ward, *Jesus and His Times,* 116, 240; McConkie, *Mortal Messiah,* 4:261; Lamsa, *Gospel Light,* 211; Jacobs, *Jewish Practice,* 13; Rhymer, *Life of Jesus,* 170.

398. Ogden, *Where Jesus Walked,* 128; *Jesus and His Apostles,* 192; Finegan, *Archeology,* 198.

399. McConkie, *Mortal Messiah,* 4:257; McConkie, *Doctrinal Commentary,* 843.

400. McConkie, *Mortal Messiah,* 4:265; Talmage, *Jesus the Christ,* 633.

401. Lamsa, *Gospel Light,* 160.

402. McConkie, *Mortal Messiah,* 4:296; Talmage, *Jesus the Christ,* 649; Ogden, *Where Jesus Walked,* 138.

BIBLIOGRAPHY

Ackroyd, R., A. R. C. Leaney, and J. W. Packer. *The Gospel According to Matthew.* London: Cambridge University Press, 1963.

Albright, W. F. and C. S. Mann. *Matthew: Introduction, Translation, and Notes.* A volume in *The Anchor Bible.* Garden City, New York: Doubleday, 1971.

Arndt, William F. and F. Wilbur Gingrich. *A Greek-English Lexicon of the New Testament and Other Early Christian Literature.* Chicago: University of Chicago Press, 1979.

Bammel, E. and C. Moule, eds. *Jesus and the Politics of His Day.* Cambridge, England: Cambridge University Press, 1988.

Barrett, C. K. *The New Testament Background.* San Francisco: Harper & Row, 1989.

Bennion, Lowell L. *The Church of Jesus Christ in Ancient Times.* Salt Lake City: Deseret Sunday School Union, 1963.

Berrett, LaMar C. and D. Kelly Ogden. *Discovering the World of the Bible.* Provo, Utah: Grandin Book, 1996.

Black, Matthew. *An Aramaic Approach to the Gospels and Acts.* Oxford: Clarendon Press, 1971.

Bornkamm, Gunther. *Jesus of Nazareth.* Minneapolis: Fortress Press, 1995.

Brown, Raymond E. *An Introduction to the New Testament.* New York: Doubleday, 1997.

————. *The Birth of the Messiah—A Commentary on the Infancy Narratives in the Gospels of Matthew and Luke.* New York: Doubleday, 1993.

————. *The Death of the Messiah: From Gethsemane to the Grave—A Commentary on the Passion Narratives in the Four Gospels.* New York: Doubleday, 1994.

Bruce, F. F. *New Testament History.* New York City: Doubleday-Galilee, 1980.

Cartidge, D. R. and D. L. Dungan, eds. *Documents for the Study of the Gospels.* Minneapolis: Fortress Press, 1994.

Charlesworth, J. H. *Jesus within Judaism.* New York: Doubleday, 1988.

Clark, J. Reuben, Jr. *Behold the Lamb of God.* Salt Lake City: Deseret Book, 1962.

————. *Our Lord of the Gospels.* Salt Lake City: Deseret Book, 1957.

Connolly, Peter. *A History of the Jewish People in the Time of Jesus from Herod the Great to Masada.* New York: Peter Bedrick Books, 1983.

————. *Living in the Time of Jesus of Nazareth.* Oxford: Oxford University Press, 1983.

Crossan, John D. *The Historical Jesus: The Life of a Mediterranean Jewish Peasant.* San Francisco: Harper, 1992.

Danker, Frederick William, ed. *A Greek-English Lexicon of the New Testament and Other Early Christian Literature.* Chicago: University of Chicago Press, 2000.

Dummelow, J. R., ed. *A Commentary on the Holy Bible.* New York City: Macmillan, 1964.

Edersheim, Alfred. *Jesus the Messiah: An Abridged Edition of the Life and Times of Jesus the Messiah.* Grand Rapids: Wm. B. Eerdmans Publishing, 1976.

————. *Sketches of Jewish Social Life.* Peabody, Massachusetts: Hendrickson Publishers, Inc., 1994.

——. *The Life and Times of Jesus the Messiah.* Peabody, Massachusetts: Hendrickson Publishers, Inc., 1995.

——. *The Temple: Its Ministry and Services as They Were at the Time of Christ.* Grand Rapids: Wm. B. Eerdmans Publishing Company, 1994.

Farrar, Frederic W. *The Life of Christ.* London and New York: Cassell and Company, 1890.

Feldman, L. H. and G. Hata. *Josephus, the Bible and History.* Detroit: Wayne State University Press, 1988.

Finegan, Jack. *The Archeology of the New Testament: The Life of Jesus and the Beginning of the Early Church.* Princeton, New Jersey: Princeton University Press, 1969.

Ford, Richard Q. *The Parables of Jesus: Recovering the Art of Listening.* Minneapolis: Fortress Press, 1997.

Frank, Harry Thomas. *Discovering the Biblical World.* New York: Harper & Row, 1975.

Galbraith, David B., D. Kelly Ogden, and Andrew C. Skinner. *Jerusalem, the Eternal City.* Salt Lake City: Deseret Book, 1996.

Geike, Cunningham. *The Life and Words of Christ.* New York: Columbian Publishing, 1891.

Goldstein, M. *Jesus in the Jewish Tradition.* New York: Macmillan, 1950.

Gower, Ralph. *The New Manners and Customs of Bible Times.* Chicago: Moody Press, 1987.

Harpur, James. *The Miracles of Jesus.* London: Reader's Digest, 1997.

Heschel, Abraham Joshua. *The Sabbath: Its Meaning for Modern Man.* New York City: Noonday Press, 1951.

Hite, Steven J. and Julie M. Hite, comps. *The New Testament: With the Joseph Smith Translation.* Orem, Utah: The Veritas Group, 1994.

Hunter, A. M. *The Gospel According to John. The Cambridge Bible Commentary: New English Bible.* R. Ackroyd, A. R. C. Leaney, J. W. Packer, eds. New York: Cambridge University Press, 1965.

Israel: Pictorial Guide. Herzlia, Israel: Palphot Ltd., n.d.

Jackson, Kent and Robert L. Millet, eds. *The Gospels. Vol 5. Studies in Scripture Series.* Salt Lake City: Deseret Book, 1986.

Jacobs, Louis. *The Book of Jewish Belief.* West Orange, New Jersey: Behrman House, 1984.

——. *The Book of Jewish Practice.* West Orange, New Jersey: Behrman House, 1987.

Jesus, the Son of Man. Copenhagen, Denmark: Scandinavia Publishing House, 1982.

Jospe, Raphael. "Sabbath, Sabbatical, and Jubilee: Jewish, Ethical Perspective," *The Jubilee Challenge, Utopia or Possibility?* Hans Ucko, ed. Geneva, Switzerland: WCC Publications, 1997.

Kee, Howard Clark. *The New Testament in Context: Sources and Documents.* Englewood Cliffs, New Jersey: Prentice-Hall, 1984.

Lamsa, George M. *Gospel Light: Comments on the Teachings of Jesus from Aramaic and Unchanged Eastern Customs.* Philadelphia: A. J. Holman Company, Bible Publishers, 1936.

Lane, William L. *The Gospel According to Mark: The English Text with Introduction, Exposition and Notes.* Grand Rapids, Michigan: William B. Eerdmans Publishing Company, 1974.

The Life and Teachings of Jesus. Prepared by the Church Education System. 2d. ed., rev. Salt Lake City: Corporation of the President of The Church of Jesus Christ of Latter-day Saints, 1974.

The Life and Teachings of Jesus and His Apostles. Prepared by the Church Education System. 2d. ed., rev. Salt Lake City: The Church of Jesus Christ of Latter-day Saints, 1979.

Ludlow, Daniel H. *A Companion to Your Study of the New Testament: The Four Gospels.* Salt Lake City: Deseret Book, 1982.

Madsen, Truman G. *The Radiant Life.* Salt Lake City: Bookcraft, 1994.

Malina, Bruce J. *The New Testament World: Insights from Cultural Anthropology.* Louisville, Kentucky: Westminster/John Knox Press, 1992.

Martin, James C. *The Life and World of Jesus the Messiah—The Gospels in Context.* Gaithersburg, Maryland: Preserving Bible Times, 2002.

Matthews, Robert J. *Behold the Messiah.* Salt Lake City: Bookcraft, 1994.

McConkie, Bruce R. *Doctrinal New Testament Commentary: The Gospels.* 2 vols. Salt Lake City: Bookcraft, 1988.

——. *Mormon Doctrine.* Salt Lake City: Bookcraft, 1979.

——. *The Mortal Messiah: From Bethlehem to Calvary.* 4 vols. Salt Lake City: Deseret Book, 1981.

——. *The Promised Messiah: The First Coming of Christ.* Salt Lake City: Deseret Book, 1978.

Metzger, Bruce M. *The Text of the New Testament: Its Transmission, Corruption, and Restoration.* New York: Oxford University Press, 1992.

Metzger, Bruce M. and Roland E. Murphy, eds. *The New Oxford Annotated Bible: Containing the Old and New Testaments.* New York City: Oxford University Press, 1991.

Murphy, Frederick J. *The Religious World of Jesus: An Introduction to Second Temple Palestinian Judaism.* Nashville: Abingdon Press, 1991.

National Geographic Society. *Everyday Life in Bible Times.* National Geographic Society, 1967.

The New Testament of the New Jerusalem Bible. New York City: Doubleday, 1986.

Ogden, D. Kelly. *Where Jesus Walked: The Land and Culture of New Testament Times.* Salt Lake City: Deseret Book, 1991.

Ogden, D. Kelly and Andrew C. Skinner. *Verse by Verse: The Four Gospels.* Salt Lake City: Deseret Book, 2006.

Pax, Wolfgang E. *In the Footsteps of Jesus.* Jerusalem: Nateev Publishing, 1970.

Pettingill, William L. and R. A. Torrey. *1001 Bible Questions Answered.* New York: Inspirational Press, 1997.

Rhymer, Joseph. *The Illustrated Life of Jesus Christ.* London: Bloomsbury Publishing Limited, 1991.

Roberts, B. H. *Outlines of Ecclesiastical History.* Salt Lake City: Deseret News, 1902.

Rousseau, John J. and Rami Arav. *Jesus and His World: An Archaeological and Cultural Dictionary.* Minneapolis: Augsburg Fortress Press, 1995.

Schauss, Hayyim. *The Jewish Festivals: A Guide to Their History and Observance.* New York City: Schocken Books, 1938.

Senior, Donald. *The Gospel of Matthew.* Nashville: Abingdon Press,1997.

Smith, Joseph, Jr. *Inspired Version, The Holy Scriptures Containing the Old and New Testaments, an Inspired Revision of the Authorized Version.* Independence, Missouri: Herald Publishing House, 1944.

Smith, William. *The New Smith's Bible Dictionary.* Reuel G. Lemmons, ed. Garden City, New York: Doubleday & Company, 1966.

Spong, John S. *Liberating the Gospels: Reading the Bible with Jewish Eyes.* New York: Harper Collins, 1996.

Stambaugh, John E. and David L. Balch. *The New Testament in Its Social Environment.* Philadelphia: Westminster Press, 1986.

Stern, David H. *Jewish New Testament: A Translation of the New Testament that Expresses Its Jewishness.* Jerusalem: Jewish New Testament Publications, 1995.

Talmage, James E. *Jesus the Christ.* Salt Lake City: Deseret Book, 1983.

Tinsley, E. J. *The Gospel According to Luke. The Cambridge Bible Commentary: New English Bible.* R. Ackroyd, A. R. C. Leaney, J. W. Packer, eds. New York: Cambridge University Press, 1965.

Van Orden, Bruce A. and Brent L. Top. *The Lord of the Gospels: The 1990 Sperry Symposium on the New Testament.* Salt Lake City: Deseret Book, 1991.

Wagenknecht, Edward. *The Story of Jesus in the World's Literature.* New York: Creative Age Press, 1946.

Ward, Kaari, ed. *Jesus and His Times.* Pleasantville, New York: Reader's Digest, 1990.

West, Franklin L. *Jesus: His Life and Teachings.* Salt Lake City: Deseret Book, 1953.

Page 51: *Bethany* © Producer. Courtesy of wikimedia commons; for more information, visit www.commons. wikimedia.org.

Page 53: *To Fulfill All Righteousness* © Simon Dewey. Courtesy of Altus Fine Art. For print information, visit www.altusfineart.com.

Page 54: *Denying Satan* by Carl Heinrich Bloch. Courtesy of Det National-historiske Museum på Frederiks-borg, Hllerød.

Page 56: *Bethany* by דניאל צבי: Courtesy of wikimedia commons; for more information, visit www.commons. wikimedia.org.

Page 60: *Christ Healing* by Carl Heinrich Bloch. Courtesy of Det National-historiske Museum på Frederiks-borg, Hllerød.

Page 62: *Fig Tree* © Acousticdad. Courtesy of wikimedia commons; for more information, visit www.commons. wikimedia.org.

Page 64: *Turning Water to Wine* by Carl Heinrich Bloch. Courtesy of Det Nationalhistoriske Museum på Frederiksborg, Hllerød.

Page 66: *Capernaum Synagogue* © David Shankbone. Courtesy of wikimedia commons; for more information, visit www.commons. wikimedia.org.

Page 70: *Jerusalem from Mt. Olives* © Wayne McLean. Courtesy of wikimedia commons; for more information, visit www.commons. wikimedia.org.

Page 71: *The Buyers and Sellers Driven Out of the Temple* by Gustave Doré, *The Doré Bible Illustrations,* Dover Publications, 1974.

Page 72: *Jesus Talks with Nicodemus* by Julius Schnorr von Carolsfeld, *Treasury of Bible Illustrations Old and New Testaments,* Dover Publications, 1999.

Page 73: *John the Baptist Preaching in the Wilderness* by Gustave Doré, *The Doré Bible Illustrations,* Dover Publications, 1974.

Page 78: *The Rebuilding of the Temple* by Gustave Doré, *The Doré Bible Illustrations,* Dover Publications, 1974.

Page 79: *Au Sable Chasm—Jacob's Well* by Seneca Ray Stoddard. Courtesy of wikimedia commons; for more information, visit www.commons. wikimedia.org.

Page 80: *Woman at the Well* © Simon Dewey. Courtesy of Altus Fine Art. For print information, visit www.altusfineart.com.

Page 81: *Christ Healing the Sick at Bethesda* by Carl Heinrich Bloch. Courtesy of Brigham Young University Museum of Art. All Rights Reserved.

Page 83: *Jehovah Creates the Earth* © Walter Rane. For more information, visit www.walterrane.com

Page 84: *Torah and Jad* © Merlin. Courtesy of wikimedia commons; for more information, visit www.commons. wikimedia.org.

Page 86: *Eliyahu Hanavi Synagogue. Nabi Daniel, Downtown Alexandria* © Moshirah. Courtesy of wikimedia commons; for more information, visit www.commons.wikimedia.org.

Page 89: *Light and Truth* © Simon Dewey. Courtesy of Altus Fine Art. For print information, visit www. altusfineart.com.

Page 91: *Jesus Healing the Man Possessed with a Devil* by Gustave Doré, *The Doré Bible Illustrations,* Dover Publications, 1974.

Page 92: *Sea of Galilee Boat 1898.* Courtesy of wikimedia commons; for more information, visit www.commons. wikimedia.org.

Page 93: *Fishers of Men* © Simon Dewey. Courtesy of Altus Fine Art. For print information, visit www. altusfineart.com.

Page 95: *Jesus Preaching at the Sea of Galilee* by Gustave Doré, *The Doré Bible Illustrations,* Dover Publications, 1974.

Page 96: *These Twelve Jesus Sent Forth* © Walter Rane. For more information, visit www.walterrane.com

Page 98: *White-Crowned Sparrow* © Wolfgang Wander. Courtesy of wikimedia commons; for more information, visit www.commons.wikimedia.org.

Page 100: *The Sermon on the Mount* by Gustave Doré, *The Doré Bible Illustrations,* Dover Publications, 1974.

Page 101: *Bushel Ibex Louvre* © Marie-Lan Nguyen. Courtesy of wikimedia commons; for more information, visit www.commons.wikimedia.org.

Page 103: *The Pharisee and the Publican* by Julius Schnorr von Carolsfeld, *Treasury of Bible Illustrations Old and New Testaments,* Dover Publications, 1999.

Page 106: *Christ in the Synagogue* by Gustave Doré, *The Doré Bible Illustrations,* Dover Publications, 1974.

Page 109: *The Raising of the Widow's Son* by Julius Schnorr von Carolsfeld, *Treasury of Bible Illustrations Old and New Testaments,* Dover Publications, 1999.

Page 111: *Peace, Be Still* © Simon Dewey. Courtesy of Altus Fine Art. For print information, visit www.altusfineart.com.

Page 114: *Christ Heals the Sick* by Julius Schnorr von Carolsfeld, *Treasury of Bible Illustrations Old and New Testaments,* Dover Publications, 1999.

Page 118: *Old Wineskin* © Oscar Calero. Courtesy of istockphoto.com

Page 120: *Touch of Faith* © Simon Dewey. Courtesy of Altus Fine Art. For print information, visit www.altusfineart.com.

Page 122: *Lion's Gate and Bethesda, Illustration for La Terre-Sainte et les Lieux Illustrés par les Apôtres by Adrien Egron 1837 engraved* by Emile Rouargue. Courtesy of wikimedia commons; for more information, visit www.commons.wikimedia.org.

Page 123: *The Disciples Plucking Corn on the Sabbath* by Gustave Doré, *The Doré Bible Illustrations,* Dover Publications, 1974.

Page 124: *Wheat* © David Monniaux. Courtesy of wikimedia commons; for more information, visit www.commons.wikimedia.org.

Page 127: *Parable Sower* by Alexander Bida. Courtesy of wikimedia commons; for more information, visit www.commons.wikimedia.org.

Page 129: *Sickle33* © Chmee2. Courtesy of wikimedia commons; for more information, visit www.commons.wikimedia.org.

Page 129: *Illustration_Lolium_Temulentum* by Prof. Dr. Otto Wilhelm Thomé. Courtesy of wikimedia commons; for more information, visit www.commons.wikimedia.org.

Page 131: *Sourdough Miche & Boule* © Chris R. Sims. Courtesy of wikimedia commons; for more information, visit www.commons.wikimedia.org.

Page 133: *The Daughter of Herod Receiving the Head of John the Baptist* by Gustave Doré, *The Doré Bible Illustrations,* Dover Publications, 1974.

Page 135: *Lord, Save Me* © Simon Dewey. Courtesy of Altus Fine Art. For print information, visit www.altusfineart.com.

Page 138: *The Basin* © Daniel Ventura. Courtesy of wikimedia commons; for more information, visit www.

commons.wikimedia.org.

Page 139: *Tyre, Lebanon—Main Colonnaded Street in Al Mina Excavation Area* © Heretiq. Courtesy of wikimedia commons; for more information, visit www.commons.wikimedia.org.

Page 142: *He Anointed the Eyes of the Blind Man* © Walter Rane. For more information, visit www.walter-rane.com

Page 143: *Mt. Hermon from Manara* by Beivushtang. Courtesy of wikimedia commons; for more information, visit www.commons.wikimedia.org.

Page 145: *The Transfiguration* by Carl Heinrich Bloch. Courtesy of Det Nationalhistoriske Museum på Frederiksborg, Hllerød.

Page 147: *Mustard Seeds* © David Turner. Courtesy of wikimedia commons; for more information, visit www.commons.wikimedia.org.

Page 148: *Christ with Children* by Carl Heinrich Bloch. Courtesy of Det Nationalhistoriske Museum på Frederiksborg, Hllerød.

Page 152: *Pool of Siloam—Jerusalem* by Abraham. Courtesy of wikimedia commons; for more information, visit www.commons.wikimedia.org.

Page 155: *He Had Compassion* © Walter Rane. For more information, visit www.walterrane.com

Page 156: *Sukkah on Top of Another Sukkah in "Neot Kedomim," Israels* © Ori229. Courtesy of wikimedia commons; for more information, visit www.commons.wikimedia.org.

Page 158: *Sheepfold* © Steven Walling. Courtesy of wikimedia commons; for more information, visit www.commons.wikimedia.org.

Page 161: *Eger Vineyard* © Elin. Courtesy of wikimedia commons; for more information, visit www.commons.wikimedia.org.

Page 163: *The Scape Goat* © William Holman Hunt. Courtesy of wikimedia commons; for more information, visit www.commons.wikimedia.org.

Page 165: *Jericho* by Effi Schweizer. Courtesy of wikimedia commons; for more information, visit www.commons.wikimedia.org.

Page 167: *The Raising of Lazarus* by Carl Heinrich Bloch. Courtesy of Det Nationalhistoriske Museum på Frederiksborg, Hllerød.

Page 170: *Wild Ass Khur* © Sballal. Courtesy of wikimedia commons; for more information, visit www.commons.wikimedia.org.

Page 171: *Entry of Jesus into Jerusalem* by Gustave Doré, *The Doré Bible Illustrations,* Dover Publications, 1974.

Page 173: *Some Figs* by Carlosar. Courtesy of wikimedia commons; for more information, visit www.commons.wikimedia.org.

Page 174: *Augustus & Agrippa* © CNG coins. Courtesy of wikimedia commons; for more information, visit www.commons.wikimedia.org.

Page 175: *Half Shekel* © CNG coins. Courtesy of wikimedia commons; for more information, visit www.commons.wikimedia.org.

Page 176: *Tefillin* by Trapisondista. Courtesy of wikimedia commons; for more information, visit www.commons.wikimedia.org.

Page 178: *Do Not Even Think About It!* © Klearchos Kapoutsis. Courtesy of wikimedia commons; for more information, visit www.commons.wikimedia.org.

Page 179: *Lucerne Ebraiche Con Menorah* © Daniel Ventura. Courtesy of wikimedia commons; for more information, visit www.commons.wikimedia.org.

Page 180: *Sheep and Goats* by the United States Federal Government. Courtesy of wikimedia commons;

for more information, visit www.commons.wikimedia.org.

Page 183: *4SederFoods* © Jonathunder. Courtesy of wikimedia commons; for more information, visit www.commons.wikimedia.org.

Page 185: *And It Was Night* © Benjamin McPherson.

Page 188: *Jesus Washes the Disciples' Feet* by Julius Schnorr von Carolsfeld, *Treasury of Bible Illustrations Old and New Testaments,* Dover Publications, 1999.

Page 190: *Olive Trees in the Garden of Gethsemane* © Chad Rosenthal. Courtesy of wikimedia commons; for more information, visit www.commons.wikimedia.org.

Page 191: *Mount of Olives* © James Emery. Courtesy of wikimedia commons; for more information, visit www.commons.wikimedia.org.

Page 193: *The Agony in the Garden* by Gustave Doré, *The Doré Bible Illustrations,* Dover Publications, 1974.

Page 195: *Christ Is Captured* by Julius Schnorr von Carolsfeld, *Treasury of Bible Illustrations Old and New Testaments,* Dover Publications, 1999.

Page 198: *The Trial of Christ* by Julius Schnorr von Carolsfeld, *Treasury of Bible Illustrations Old and New Testaments,* Dover Publications, 1999.

Page 200: *Peter's Betrayal* by Carl Heinrich Bloch. Courtesy of Det Nationalhistoriske Museum på Frederiksborg, Hllerød.

Page 202: *The Demise of Judas* by Julius Schnorr von Carolsfeld, *Treasury of Bible Illustrations Old and New Testaments,* Dover Publications, 1999.

Page 206: *Jesus before Pilate, The New Testament: A Pictorial Archive* from *Nineteenth-Century Sources,* Dover Publications.

Page 209: *Ecce Homo!* by Antonio Ciseri. Courtesy of wikimedia commons; for more information, visit www.commons.wikimedia.org.

Page 212: *Christ Bearing His Cross* by Julius Schnorr von Carolsfeld, *Treasury of Bible Illustrations Old and New Testaments,* Dover Publications, 1999.

Page 214: *Jesus Dies on the Cross* by Julius Schnorr von Carolsfeld, *Treasury of Bible Illustrations Old and New Testaments,* Dover Publications, 1999.

Page 217: *Jesus Dies on the Cross* by James Tissot.

Page 219: *It Is Finished* © Liz Lemon Swindle. Used with permission from Foundation Arts. For print information, go to www.foundationarts.com, or call 1-800-366-2781.

Page 221: *Grey Day Golgotha* © J. Kirk Richards. For print information, go to www.jkirkrichards.com.

Page 224: *Discipleship* © Liz Lemon Swindle. Used with permission from Foundation Arts. For print information, go to www.foundationarts.com, or call 1-800-366-2781.

Page 225: *Garden Tomb* © Garth R. Oborn. For print information, go to www.anneoborn.com/garth.

Page 227: Mary at the Tomb by James Tissot.

Page 228: *Why Weepest Thou?* © Liz Lemon Swindle. Used with permission from Foundation Arts. For print information, go to www.foundationarts.com, or call 1-800-366-2781.

Page 229: *Jesus* © Liz Lemon Swindle. Used with permission from Foundation Arts. For print information, go to www.foundationarts.com, or call 1-800-366-2781.